D1074919

Polishing the Diamond: A History of the
University of Maryland Eastern Shore

Polishing the Diamond
A History of the
University of Maryland
Eastern Shore

by

Dr. William P. Hytche
President Emeritus
University of Maryland
Eastern Shore

FOUR-G Publishers, Inc.

2002

ISBN 1-885066-68-6

Hytche, William P.
     Polishing the Diamond: A history of the University of Maryland Eastern Shore, by William P. Hytche. FOUR-G Publishers, 2001.

     308 pages, tables, photos, CD

All inquiries should be addressed to:

Office of Development
Alumni House
University of Maryland Eastern Shore
Princess Anne, MD
TEL: 410-651-7773

e-mail: alumni@mail.umes.edu

Published by:
FOUR-G Publishers, Inc.
3934 Allen Drive
Jackson, MS 39212
TEL: 601-371-1309, FAX: 601-371-1374

Cover design by Mary Wismar-Davis
Printed in the United States

CONTENTS

From Maryland State College to the
University of Maryland Eastern Shore

The Progressive Years of the
University of Maryland Eastern Shore

EPILOGUE: An Interview with President Dolores Margaret Richard Spikes (1997-2001) 226

Appendices

DEDICATION

(Figure 1)
Dr. W. Augustus Low

Dr. W. Augustus Low, a former professor of history at Maryland State College (now University of Maryland Eastern Shore), was a major contributor to this history. The first four chapters are based on a manuscript he had begun many years ago. Just before Dr. Low left the University in the early sixties, he came to my office with an armful of papers and said, "Please don't throw these away because you may have to finish this one day." I laughed because I was a mathematician and had no ambitions as either a historian or a writer. However as the years went by, I felt he had worked too hard on this project and it was too important to be left undone. Now it is done; and in addition to dedicating this work to the memory of Dr. Low, I dedicate it to his family—particularly his children. Finally, I dedicate it to all of the readers who may benefit from the information provided herein.

Dr. Low was born in 1917 at Greenville, Mississippi and educated in the public schools of St. Louis, Missouri. He received his B.A. degree at Lincoln University in Missouri, and his M.A. and Ph.D. degrees at the University of Iowa. Prior to his coming to Maryland, he taught in the public schools of St. Louis, Missouri; at the Agricultural and Technical College of Greensboro, North Carolina; and at Florida A & M College in Tallahassee, Florida. Low was the author of several historical works; and upon his arrival in Princess Anne, he immediately found interest in the early history of the school.

The University of Maryland Eastern Shore has done its best to support this project; and while this book tells much of the story, at least three more books could be written about the history of this fine institution.

PREFACE

Historically Black Colleges and Universities (HBCU's) have been among the most powerful social, educational and economic-change agents in this country. They literally created an African-American middle class during the time when African Americans could not pursue education, for the most part, except at these institutions. Their graduates became the preponderance of professionals (to include doctors, lawyers, judges, etc.) in this country. It is no wonder then that in the eyes of the alumni of HBCU's and to the students attending them, these universities are icons of freedom, of hope, and of an opportunity for African Americans to open doors where none had existed before.

Yet in spite of the superhuman, altruistic, and tremendous contributions of HBCU's, there are those today who ask, "Why do we still need them?" They dare ask this question when facts relative to poverty; to insufficient education; to lack of representation in many professional fields such as engineering, mathematics, and physics still exist. The gaps have not been closed. The historical mission and the nurturing atmosphere of these institutions are still necessary to give added value to any of the opportunities that African Americans may achieve, largely for the poor, in this country.

The University of Maryland Eastern Shore (UMES) is one of these institutions. It is a historically-black institution rooted in the black church and founded by slaves and ex-slaves who knew the value of education to freedom and to economic independence. UMES has a glorious history, but it is also a history marked with prejudice, marked with trials and tribulations, and marked with the lack of resources and opportunities necessary for much of this life.

A 1980 publication called "The Post Land-Grant University," commissioned by the University of Maryland, has a separate chapter devoted to UMES. So gloomful were the writers that they predicted that this institution would never grow beyond two thousand students; intimated in deed that it had little or no future; and in essence, to the African-American reader, toyed with the idea that this University would never become anything worthwhile. Today, the writers of that report would be astounded to see a growing institution with over three thousand students. Had the State had the foresight to see the potential for growth once the campus was made to look like more than somebody's backyard, had they had that foresight and provided the housing and classroom buildings necessary it is no doubt that UMES would today be housing about five thousand students.

Fortunately there were some in Maryland, white and black, who believed in the American dream. William P. Hytche was foremost among those dreamers. Others saw, believed his sincerity, and joined him. Together with a few local townspeople, with a board inspired largely by its few African-American members, and with a legislature inspired by the Legislative Black Caucus and a few other Assembly members of well-meaning, Dr. Hytche transformed this campus into one of the most beautiful in the nation. But a new classroom building was slow to come and as of this writing it still has not been built, though construction is expected to begin perhaps this coming spring. When that happens; when additional housing is provided; and when more importantly, reputable programs at the doctoral and professional level as well as more at the undergraduate levels are added; we will see UMES become a premier institution amongst all — including non-HBCU institutions.

This history by Dr. Hytche recounts the struggles and the successes and recognizes those who gave so much of themselves to create opportunities for young people to learn. It describes his own frustrations, his own moments of glee, his life's work in a university that will long be remembered for its successful contributions — for the manner in which it has made a way out of no way. Those who believe in opportunity, those who believe in equality for mankind, those who believe that all persons deserve a chance, these people will find this book irresistible and hard to put down once they start reading it. The UMES community owes Dr. William P. Hytche much indebtedness in recording the history of UMES. It is a lesson that ought to be taught to all young people — black or white, older ones as well — about survival, courage, hope, faith, and understanding.

Dr. Dolores R. Spikes, President, 1997-2001
University of Maryland Eastern Shore

PREFACE

This publication is primarily a study of a university that began as a small African-American school located on the historic Eastern Shore in the small town of Princess Anne, Maryland. The circumstances underlying its existence overshadow the obscurity and size of the school while they reveal many of the significant aspects found in the history of the education of the American Negro in general. The origin, founding, and development of the University along with the forces that are now keeping it vibrant are therefore related mosaics in the larger pattern of the position of the Negro in his emancipation from chattel slavery to questionable citizenship.

Although the school exists in the remote locale of the lower Eastern Shore, a distinct geographical and cultural region of the State, the symbolism of the school's existence—its name or reputation—has found its way into larger circles where it has become a rationale for the prevailing social and political issues that have transcended geographical boundaries. Among the first issues were the rights of Negroes to an education and the responsibility of a democratic government towards its citizens regardless of race, color, and creed. Related issues were thus directly related to the fiery trials and tribulations encountered by the University year after year just to keep its doors open. The hardest of these trials and tribulations to overcome were the earliest struggles of racial injustice, low enrollment, and inadequate funding.

The story of the school is unique. Few schools have encountered as many real or theoretical stages of development as chronicled in the chapters of this historical narrative. Founded largely as a result of the cooperation between a Negro and a white Methodist minister, the school has passed successively, if not always successfully, through many phases since it first opened in an old Colonial building called Olney. Because the founding and the growth of the school were conditioned by the atmosphere of the Civil War and of Reconstruction, the school was regarded first as a preparatory school; then as an academy, a junior college, and a four-year college; and finally as a full-fledged doctoral-degree granting university.

In the beginning, the affairs of the school were controlled by the Methodist Episcopal Church, then by the church and State jointly, and finally solely by the State. The beginning of the school's transformation can be traced back to 1891 when the school was designated as the only Negro institution within the State to receive federal funds. The designation was made in order to qualify the State for receipt of land-grant funds under the Second Morrill Act of 1890. Already existing as a branch of Morgan College, the school likewise became a branch of the Maryland Agricultural College, a predecessor of the University of Maryland. Although the arrangement benefited the contracting parties, the school itself was left to make it the best way it could. As a result, the situation proved unsatisfactory to federal authorities who realized that land-grant funds, a chief source of support for the school, were being used badly by a complacent, bifurcated administration. After some delay, the school was purchased outright by the State and was placed completely under the control of the University of Maryland, which besides having problems of internal administration, was fighting to obtain enough support from the State to become a "great university." When the school was acquired by the State, it was a college in name only with almost as many faculty members as students.

Nevertheless, along with a school in Bowie, Maryland, it was the only institution that the State operated for the higher education of Negroes. In the State, where Negroes were highly inarticulate in politics even though they were a sizable demographic minority, recourse to the courts was made to bridge the wide gap between the theory and practice of equality in education. Some action was taken by the State as evidenced in the appointment of several commissions to study the problem—an easy step in procrastination. Although various recommendations were made, including out-of-state scholarships for Negroes and more state aid for Negro schools, the various commissions made no recommendations for the unqualified admission of Negroes to all state-supported institutions. Hardship, perseverance, and men and women of vision steadied the school until a tremendous increase of state support brought forth a new name, a projected reorganization, and a great deal of controversy that cut across educational, racial, and political issues. What has finally evolved into one of the top historically black institutions of higher learning for all races began with the old Reconstruction rights of Negroes to participate as citizens within the framework of American democracy. Thus, this is the story of the slow and painful metamorphosis of the Delaware Conference Academy into the University of Maryland Eastern Shore.

Unfortunately, the greatest difficulty encountered in the preparation of this study has been the woeful lack of materials that either never existed or were never preserved. Practically no records existed from 1886 to the early 1900s at the school. Even the collection of its catalogues was incomplete. Consequently, much of the smaller picture of life at the University remains obscured because of the lack of historical materials.

INTRODUCTION

There was a new freedom for the former slaves in the late 1800s. Along with the freedom, however, came violence, hardship, bloody labor riots, and the brutal acts of the Ku Klux Klan. Americans of this generation, particularly those of the South, felt keenly the scars left by the Civil War (1861-65). Almost immediately following the war, a series of Congressional measures called "Reconstruction Acts" were passed generally providing that the seceded Southern states were to be occupied militarily and administered as Congress saw fit. Shortly thereafter in 1868, the Fourteenth Amendment to the Constitution was passed as a legal guarantee that no state should abridge the privileges of its citizens. In 1870, the Fifteenth Amendment assured the right to vote without regard to race, color, or previous condition of servitude. Then one year later in 1871, the Ku Klux Klan Act was passed that was designed to ensure the Negro of the full benefits set forth in the Thirteenth, Fourteenth, and Fifteenth amendments. In addition, Congress passed other legislation to guarantee the civil rights granted to the Negro.

Nevertheless, efforts to establish the Negro as an articulate, political force to replace the vacuum left by the destruction of slavery were only temporarily successful at best because the majority of Southern Whites were conditioned to the traditional belief of white superiority and its manifold implications. Thus, they sometimes reacted violently and emotionally toward the new status of the Negro who sought more political freedom and economic security.

Like most former slave states, Maryland, a border state, was confronted with problems surrounding the collapse of slavery. Comparatively, Maryland's problems seemed to have been less severe than those in the states of the Cotton Kingdom. Maryland had its slave areas or black belts, but the number of slaves in the State during the first half of the nineteenth century never exceeded 30 percent of the total population. Slaves were concentrated mainly on the Eastern

Shore and on the southern part of the State's Western Shore. In fact, nearly half of the Negroes in Maryland were free at the outbreak of the Civil War. Perhaps these demographic factors help to explain the relatively greater freedom, mobility, and self-reliance that the Maryland Negroes enjoyed in comparison with Negroes in the Lower South as well as the relatively limited amount of freedom, mobility, and self-reliance that the Maryland Negroes enjoyed in comparison with Negroes in the North. Reconstruction measures passed by Congress, therefore, did not go unchallenged in Maryland.

On November 1, 1864, a new constitution went into effect abolishing slavery in the state of Maryland and providing an oath of allegiance to be taken by certain officials. Slaveholding interests opposed the new constitution, and the loyalty oath was contested strongly on the Eastern Shore. Finally, the loyalty oath was abolished by the Constitution of 1867, and the State remained sharply divided by the question of slavery and secession. Despite the tension, however, Maryland did not secede. Moreover, the question of Negro suffrage created controversy over the Negroes' new legal status — their status as new citizens, and their right to share the privileges of democracy. Whereas there were no outrages or serious mob violence by the Klan, such as occurred in some localities of the Lower South, there were many legal contests. Needless to say, Negro rights were often questioned, and legal decisions often showed that these rights were acknowledged in principle but in practice were neither always respected nor enforced.

Perhaps the greatest heritage that Reconstruction passed on to Negroes was the implicit right to an education as free men. Much of the story of Negro education can be traced in the history of Negro schools, for education has been one of the fundamental social urges of Negroes with their schools reflecting this aim. The story of the University of Maryland Eastern Shore is no exception in that it is related to the larger, complex struggle of the Negro within the State or the nation at large. Like many other Negro schools, this school in Maryland grew out of the forces of Reconstruction. Therefore, its subsequent development and existence were contingent upon the interpretation and application of these forces and the success of the aid offered it by acts of Congress.

Established by an act of March 3, 1865, as an outgrowth of the Department of Negro Affairs, The Freedmen's Bureau was perhaps the greatest investment that Congress made in the reconstruction of the South. Food, clothing, and fuel were to be distributed to destitute refugees and freedmen. In addition, forty acres of land from confiscated or abandoned lands of the insurrectionary states were to be distributed to loyal refugees and freedmen.[1] Many were disappointed, however, when the forty acres and the mule never materialized.

On the whole, the Bureau achieved its purpose in providing immediate relief for displaced persons, especially freedmen. Even more successful was its work in Negro education. Negroes were given employment in army camps; and special refugee camps were set up to provide for the hungry, the destitute, and the sick. Chaplains were usually detailed to look after Negroes. In its four and one-half years of existence, the Bureau issued more than 15 million rations and spent about 5 million dollars on schools.

Eventually, the Bureau aided in the establishment of public education for Negroes in all of the United States. It was generally recognized by the federal government that education was one of the chronic needs of the freedmen and that freedmen should at least be literate if they were to meet the responsibilities inherent in their freedom. To no small extent, the broad bases for the public education of the Negro, higher and lower, are traceable to the work of the Freedmen's Bureau in cooperation with private and religious philanthropies. Though the problem of abandoned lands or refugees was less acute in Maryland, the protection of the Negroes and their rights, the establishment of Negro schools, and cooperation with benevolent associations were problems.

The Bureau was especially aware of the problem of protecting the Negroes and their rights in the state of Maryland but sometimes encountered difficulties not the least of which was the unpopularity of its officials who were required to make reports on violence against the Negroes, their person, property, or schools. Thus, there were many troubling cases. Among the most prevalent practices that confronted the Bureau was that of Negroes being forcefully bound as apprentices to former slaveholders. Often with the approval of local courts, teenage youngsters of former slaves would be held in forced labor. Officials of the Bureau received written reports from the various county courts showing that there had been at least 2,281 bound apprentices since emancipation.

There are letters in the records of the Bureau that indicate the seriousness of the practice. Reverend Samuel Sawyer, a former army chaplain, wrote to the Bureau in October 1865 stating that Julia Handy of Annapolis was being annoyed by her old master, a Colonel John Walton, who had bound three of her children. The children had run away, and the mother was arrested and jailed as a means of reprisal. During the same month (October 30, 1865), a Negro, William Tilghman of Burnetsville, Somerset County, wrote a letter explaining that his son was bound by former slaveholder Edward Howard. Although his spelling was unorthodox, Tilghman pleaded as best he could for his son's release.

The Bureau's support of Negro schools was the greatest practical aspect of its program in the state of Maryland. Materials, equipment, and funds were given for schools; and encouragement and cooperation were given to Negro groups and to the Baltimore Association for the Moral and Educational Improvement of the Colored Race (The Association), which prior to 1869 was the chief agency in the State for operating and coordinating a program of Negro education.

In addition to the Bureau's work, religious and private philanthropies were very influential in providing relief and educational facilities for freedmen. Several organizations came into existence either during or immediately after the Civil War. Several of these groups were consolidated as the U.S. Commission for Relief of National Freedmen with headquarters in Washington, D.C. By 1865, this consolidated body was replaced by the American Freedmen's Aid Union which, after two more changes of name, was discontinued in 1869. Other organizations for freedmen's aid were the African Civilization Society, the Baltimore Association for the Moral and Educational Improvement of the Colored Race, and the Delaware Association for the Moral and Educational Improvement of the Colored Race. In addition, churches came to the aid of the freedmen, putting forth an effort that was comprehensive, decisive, valuable, and permanent in the history of Negro education.

The period following the close of the Civil War, therefore, saw the establishment of large educational foundations that were financed mainly by wealthy Northerners, the captains of industry or the barons of wealth, who had made or were making fortunes out of the nation's economic revolution. Philanthropy was regarded as a civic and national responsibility, a moral duty of the rich to share their wealth with the illiterates and the unfortunate. Invariably, Negro education was materially aided in such categories as building construction, endowment, scholarships, teacher training, and industrial education. In both principle and practice, perhaps for the sake of expediency, the great philanthropies avoided the question of all Negro rights except the right of the Negroes to an education.

Conservative in outlook and character, Northern philanthropy was acceptable to Southern Whites who, for the most part, were selected to administer the funds. Consequently, concerning the education of the Negro, the race will be forever indebted to the great philanthropies. The Peabody Foundation was the earliest of them. Established in 1882, the John F. Slater Fund made twelve grants to Negro schools that were located chiefly in Virginia, North Carolina, South Carolina, Georgia, and Alabama.[2] Shaw, Hampton, and Tuskegee were Negro schools that shared its first benefits. There was also the Rosenwald Fund, which financed the construction of school buildings and the expense of scholarships. Likewise, there was the Anna T. Jeanes Foundation whose endowment came from a kind, reticent, seventy-pound Quaker woman of Philadelphia. She began the fund in 1907 with more than a million dollars to assist in the establishment of rural schools for the great class of Negroes to whom the small rural and community schools were alone available.

At first, the benefits of the great philanthropies, like the services of the Freedmen's Bureau, went mainly to the Lower South, bypassing Maryland. The great foundations that came after the turn of the century, however, gave somewhat more generously to Maryland and the Border States.[3] On the other hand, the state of Maryland as well as the states of the Lower South gave only scant governmental support or encouragement to Negro education—or to public education in general. So, in the explosive atmosphere of Reconstruction, public education in Maryland and the South existed mainly on the law books. Accordingly in 1866, the year following the close of the Civil War, the state of Maryland gave no material support for the education of its freedmen. From the point of organization of moral temper, the State was not disposed to undertake seriously the problem of Negro education. Furthermore in 1866, the first annual report of the State's superintendent of schools recommended that the State should provide separate schools for Negroes in "every district where 30 or more pupils will regularly attend."[4] Consequently, provisions for Negro education in the State were left almost wholly to the counties and Baltimore City.

The extent of the support of public education was reflected in the condition of Negro schools. The amount paid to colored schools for the entire State, excluding Baltimore, was $4,580.31 in 1870.[5] That amounted to about twelve cents per student for the year. About twenty dollars was added to this amount the following year. Somerset County, which would be the future home of the University of Maryland Eastern Shore, spent $86.77 on colored schools for the year 1870-1871.[6] Fourteen years later, in 1884, the amount of money spent by the counties was $102,047 while Somerset County spent $5,200.

For the first few decades after the Civil War, most of the Negro public schools in the State were crude, frame shacks. In many instances, classes were conducted in churches equally as crude in construction as well as design. Only about half of the pupils of "school age" attended any schools at all, and only about one-half of those enrolled attended regularly. In addition, the length of the school term varied from about four to six months. The three "R's" — reading, writing, and arithmetic — were the basic subjects in which instruction was given generally by teachers who were driven and who taught as many students as their one-room building could hold.

Eventually, there were increases in enrollment, attendance, teacher salaries, and the length of the school term; but public Negro education in Maryland remained primarily elementary in scope, curriculum, and organization until World War I. In fact, Negro high schools did not appear in the State until after World War I.[7] There were only seventy-five Negro children in public schools above the seventh grade in all the counties of Maryland as late as 1916.[8] Negro county schools were far more impoverished than those in Baltimore. The chief aid for the establishment of post-World War I schools for Negroes in Maryland came from churches, charitable organizations, and interested individuals, including the indigent Negroes themselves.

The Whites of Maryland and the Lower South were not particularly disposed to accept the idea of public education for either Whites or Negroes. The Southern tradition in education was intimately interwoven with beliefs in educating only Southern gentlemen. Therefore, many Southerners scoffed at the idea of education for the masses, and thought that the education of the Negro would lead ultimately to race degeneracy and the disruption of white supremacy. One Virginian, writing under the name of "Civis," after stating his argument clearly against all public schools, turned against the "hideous doctrine of Negro equality" through education.

> I oppose it because its policy is cruelty in the extreme to the Negro himself. It instills into his mind that he is competent to share in the higher walks of life, prompts him to despise those menial pursuits to which his race has been doomed, and invites him to enter into competition with the white man for those tempting prizes that can be won only by a quicker and profundity sagacity, by a greater energy and self-denial, and a higher order of administrative talent than the Negro has ever displayed.[9]

Indeed, the fear of equality plagued the minds of white Southerners who frequently rationalized that the Negro's right to vote or to attend school would be tantamount to the mongrelization of the white race. Sometimes resentment flared into violence, fanned by the harsh arrogance of racists who were steeped in the sociology and sanctity of white supremacy and of Southern womanhood. Negro schools were often the target of such resentment.

Opposition to Negro schools was given full and free expression in the interior of Alabama, Louisiana, Kentucky, Maryland, Mississippi, Tennessee, and Texas.[10] In some communities, Negroes were not permitted to attend schools, and teachers were not allowed to teach. Schoolhouses, including churches, were sometimes burned. Some teachers, many of whom were Northern Whites, suffered intimidation, insult, scorn, and ostracism; a few were killed.[11] Everywhere the rights of Negroes to an education during the period of Reconstruction were circumscribed by their former status as slaves. In the state of Maryland, opposition and resentment appeared to be strongest in areas of the old "black belts" of slavery, namely, the Eastern Shore and Southern Maryland. Indeed, in its position on emancipation, education, and "Negroism," Somerset County was akin to counties in the deepest part of the South.

A Negro church, housing the first Negro school in Somerset County, was burned several months after the close of the Civil War. Despite the fact that some encouragement was given by the Association, practically nothing was done for Negro schools in Somerset County, particularly the one in Princess Anne. It is likely that Negroes, who were called upon by the Association and the Bureau to make contributions, were restrained by fear of reprisals from Whites. Consequently, the Association closed the first school in Princess Anne in June 1868 and questioned the wisdom of erecting another to take its place.

Although the rights of the recently freed Negroes were being fiercely debated, opposition became less violent and virulent as the years passed. Gradually, the idea of educating the Negro began to receive some local sympathy and support. By the turn of the century, many communities accepted the presence of Negro schools as long as they were segregated; unequally supported; controlled by Whites with Negro teachers; or devoted to such special fields as elementary, industrial, or religious education. Certainly, this was true in the state of Maryland.

Although the vast majority of Negro schools, public and private, gave only elementary instruction then through the eighth grade, a great number of organizations began to provide better buildings and a higher type and quality of instruction out of which the Negro college eventually evolved. Still, much of the instruction remained at the elementary level and carried a religious stamp. Some of the earliest Negro schools were discontinued or changed their names while some were absorbed by the states or lived as landmarks in the history of the higher education of the Negro, publicly- or privately-supported.

To understand through the eyes of the author the struggle of Negroes in establishing an institution of higher education on the Eastern Shore of Maryland, it is necessary to examine this struggle as part of their larger struggle to emerge from slavery to freedom. When Negroes were reduced to slavery in Maryland and the rest of the United States, they were denied all education except that which was designed to fit them for servitude. Therefore, the Negroes' struggle to free themselves from slavery naturally included the struggle to obtain the right to a free education. Led by inspired, determined Negro leaders, educators, church members, and workers as well as aided by sympathetic Whites and philanthropists, Negroes faced their fears and frustrations. They held on to their concerns and hopes as they fought to build schools for themselves against opposition from forces determined to trap them in perpetual subservience.

Negroes combated such forces as white supremacy, discrimination, envy, rivalry, resentment, and underfunding to obtain full rights as free citizens, including a higher education. From this historical background of the Negroes' quest for higher educational opportunities emerged today's University of Maryland Eastern Shore, which developed from humble beginnings and a stormy existence. Its story begins with the founding of the Centenary Biblical Institute by the Methodist Episcopal Church in 1869.

ENDNOTES

1   U.S. Statutes, Vol., XIII, p. 507.
2   Ullin W. Leavell, Philanthropy in Negro Education (Nashville, TN), 1930, p. 64.
3   Leavell, op.cit., p. 174.
4   Annual Report, State Board of Education, 1866, p. 64. Hereafter cited as Report (Supt.).
5   Report (Supt.), 1870, p. 6.
6   Ibid.
7   High school subjects were added to the old Baltimore Normal School (later Bowie) for Negroes (founded in 1867) as early as 1883, but grammar subjects were not dropped until 1896. At this time the City recognized the school as a high school. This school became known as the Frederick Douglass High School, and it remained the only Negro high school in the State until 1918.
8   Report (Supt.), 1920, p. 148.
9   Bennet Puryear, The Public School in its Relation to the Negro (Richmond), 1877, p.17.
10   Pierce, op. cit., p. 80, cites House Ex. Doc., 38th Cong., no. 70, p. 179.
11   Annual Report, Methodist Episcopal Church, 7th, p.15. Hereafter cited as Report (M.E.).

ACKNOWLEDGMENTS

Converting an author's words into a finished book requires the efforts and assistance of an endless list of individuals. In preparing this study, I am grateful to many, including a large number of dedicated and talented people, whose help has been most valuable.

First, my sincere thanks are extended to the U.S. Office of Education as well as to the libraries, archives, colleges, courthouses, and several private homes that were helpful in providing the source materials for this book. Included are the New York Public Library, the Enoch Pratt Library, the Library of Congress, the National Archives, Morgan State University, the University of Maryland, the University of Maryland Eastern Shore, Hampton University, the Somerset County Courthouse, and the many persons who aided in the collection of data by responding to questionnaires, interviews, requests, and letters.

Specifically, I wish to acknowledge many who were helpful in the early years of this process, some of whom have passed on. They include Dr. John Lash, a faculty member who read the first manuscript years ago and made valuable suggestions; Mrs. Ann R. Anderson, librarian, who borrowed many volumes not available in the school's collection; Dr. Hermon F. Wilson, a physician of San Francisco, California and a son of one of the founders; Major Walter R. Brown, Secretary of Hampton Institute; Drs. Edward and Harold Trigg, sons of one of the principals; the Reverend John H. Nutter; the Reverend W. E. Stanley; Mr. Julius A. Oliver; and Miss Lida L. Brown.

In addition, thanks are extended to former students, alumni, librarians, officials in various governmental organizations, friends, staff, and faculty who have made worthy contributions. Proving invaluable as resources, critics, and good friends were Dr. Dennis Anderson Bethea, Mrs. Emma Boyer, Mrs. Lilly Waters Bunday, Mr. and Mrs. James I. Dennis, Mr. Stephen H. Dix, Dr. Lillian Singleton Dove, Mrs. Crystal Bird Fauset, the Reverend David H. Hargis, Mr. Joseph

Hayman, Mr. William Hayman, Mr. T. Waldo Kiah, Mrs. Daisy Bailey Jones, Mr. Horatio Jones, Mr. Joseph P. Joynes, Mrs. Bessie Maddox Lane, Mrs. Anna H. Maddox, Mrs. Lyda G. Miles, Mrs. Selena Gertrude Nutter, Mrs. Roxie P. Pinkett, Miss Lillian J. Sterling, Mr. Edward N. Wilson, Mrs. Hattie D. White, Mr. McKinley Wright, Mr. James Taylor, Mrs. Anne Taylor, Ms. Brenda Warwick, Mr. Charles Gregg, Dr. Diann R. Showell-Cherry, Dean Jessie C. Smith, Mr. Joseph Hayman, Mr. Keith Bingham, Dr. Kermit Cottman, Ms. Mary Stewart, Mr. Roma Jones, Mr. Theodore Adams, Mr. Thomas Wiles, Dr. Bryant Mitchell, Mr. Allen Vital, Mr. Harold Rush, the Reverend Charlotte Nichols, Dr. H. DeWayne Whittington, Mr. James M. Glovier, and Mr. Marshall Cropper, Mr. and Mrs. Daniel L. Ridout, Mrs. Charlotte Reid-Rolley, Dr. Mortimer Neufville, Dr. Samuel L. Donald, Mr. Kaye D. Pinhey, and Dr. Anugrah Shaw.

At FOUR-G Publishers, Inc., I have had the good fortune to work with Dr. George C. Grant who has remained available and faithful in helping me to maintain my perspective through his helpful suggestions. I have immense gratitude for his contribution.

With appreciation, I acknowledge the many helpful observations and comments from my reviewers and proofreaders, Dean Jessie C. Smith, Ms. Elizabeth C. Vaughn, Dr. Rex Vaughn, Dr. Jodellano Statom and my dedicated assistant, Mrs. Suzanne Waters Street, who has been my strong right hand throughout this project.

More than to anyone else, I give special thanks to my wife, Deloris, who constantly gave me encouragement in bringing this project to completion. To her, I am deeply indebted.

(Figure 1.5)
May 2000 History Meeting participants.
Left to Right, seated: Dr. Kermit Cottman, Reverend
Charlotte Nichols, Dr. Diann Showell-Cherry, Dr. William P.
Hytche, Mr. Roma Jones, Mrs. Anne Taylor,
Mr. Joseph Hayman.
(2nd Row): Mr. Jim Glovier, Mrs. Suzanne Waters Street,
Mrs. Mary Stewart, Dr. H. DeWayne Whittington, Ms.
Brenda Warwick, Mr. Charles Gregg, Dean Jessie Cottman
Smith, Mr. Allen Vital.
(3rd Row): Mr. Theodore Adams, Mr. Keith Bingham, Dr.
Bryant Mitchell, Mr. Marshall Cropper, Mr. Thomas Wiles,
Mr. Harold Rush, and Mr. James Taylor.

CHAPTER ONE

METHODISM AND THE CENTENARY BIBLICAL INSTITUTE — 1866-1890 —

The Freedmen's Aid Society

Like many religious and philanthropic organizations, the Methodist Episcopal Church responded quickly and diligently to the plight of the freed Negro. On March 8, 1866, Bishop Davis W. Clark, one of the prominent leaders of the church, called for an organization to give aid to the freedmen. Accordingly, on one warm afternoon in August of the same year, ministers and laymen met at the Trinity Methodist Episcopal Church in Cincinnati, Ohio. The meeting lasted for two days and resulted in the formation of the Freedmen's Aid

(Figure 1.1)
Centenary Biblical Institute

Society of the Methodist Episcopal Church. Bishop Clark, who initiated the movement, was elected as the Society's first president. John M. Walden, another well-known figure in Methodism and a former antislavery journalist and legislator, became the first corresponding secretary, a position that became very important in the later life of the Society. A school was soon named in each man's honor—Walden (later known as Meharry Medical College) in Nashville, Tennessee and Clark in Atlanta, Georgia.

Thus, in a city that served as a station in the Underground Railroad of slavery days and as the home of the author of Uncle Tom's Cabin, another

1

milestone was passed on the stony road of the Negro's transition from slavery to freedom. Although the Society was not incorporated by the legislature of Ohio until 1870, work began within three months after the Society's formation.

The Society recognized early where its task lay. It well knew that education was essential for the Negro; that the need for the enlightenment of the Negro was chronic and should be alleviated; that courage was necessary in the tense atmosphere of Reconstruction in order for the education of the Negro to succeed; and that the Negro was capable of and should not be denied the right to an education, including higher education. The Society, which was not beyond providing clothing and bedding for freedmen immediately after the close of the War, was primarily concerned with the spiritual welfare of the Negro and thus began its impressive work in the education of Negroes.

Indeed, the work of the Methodists was impressive. Within a few years after the War, the Methodist Episcopal Church, the largest of Methodist denominations, worked through its Society to help to introduce a common school system in the South and the establishment of schools for Negroes. By 1869 three years after its Freedmen's Aid Society began, the Church had raised about $165,000, which was an incredible amount of money for the times. In addition, it had set up sixty schools of higher learning in the South, which embraced the states of Alabama, Kentucky, Louisiana, Mississippi, North Carolina, South Carolina, Tennessee, and Virginia.[1] Methodist schools already established included Central Tennessee College, Clark University (Georgia), Huntsville College (Alabama), Claflin College (South Carolina), and Shaw University (North Carolina). At this time, however, the Methodists had not actually set up a school of higher learning in the state of Maryland.

The Founding of the Centenary Biblical Institute

As a pioneer in the field of Negro education, the Freedman's Aid Society encouraged the establishment of only one school in Maryland. This school was the Centenary Biblical Institute, the parent body of two institutions of higher learning in the State. It was easily the first successful institution operated expressly for the higher education of Negroes in Maryland, and its very name suggests the influence of Methodism.

Several months after the organization of the Freedmen's Aid Society, a group of interested persons, including Bishop Levi Scott and Bishop Edward

R. Ames, both of the Baltimore Conference, decided to begin a school for freedmen from Baltimore. Levi Scott was a native of Delaware, having been born in Odessa in 1802. The son of a Methodist minister who died in 1803, Scott began his career in the ministry as a young man of twenty-three. He was elected to the bishopric in 1852 and later served as a missionary in Africa. He died in 1882 near the place of his birth. In several ways, the life of Edward R. Ames parallels that of Scott. Ames was born about the same time (1806) in Ohio. He began work in the church as a young man, served as corresponding secretary of the Missionary Society, and also became a bishop in 1852.

The idea to begin the school was set in motion on Christmas Day 1866 when, at an informal gathering, Scott and Ames appointed a board of trustees. The following trustees were appointed: Thomas Kelso, William Harden, William Daniel, William B. Hill, John Lanahan, Henry W. Drakely, Hugh L. Bond, James H. Brown, Charles A. Reid, Isaac P. Cook, Robert Turner, Samuel Hindes, and Francis A. Crook. Knowing that the General Conference had already called for the observation of the centenary of the church, the board decided that the establishment of a school for freedmen would be a fitting and worthwhile observance. Instruction would be theological, and ministers would be taught the Bible. Thus the word "Biblical" was added to "Centenary," and the school took its name among the dozens of institutes operating or being established at the time as seminaries for ministers.

An appropriation of $5,000 from the Missionary Society of the church, collected from centenary funds for the education of Negro preachers, was given to the treasury of the newly appointed board of trustees. Nearly one year after the meeting on Christmas Day, the name of the proposed school was chartered by the Superior Court of Baltimore on November 27, 1867. The charter required that the assent of any two bishops was necessary to make changes in the course of the study of and the tenure of instructors, and vacancies on the board of trustees were to be filled by the presiding bishop of the next session of the Baltimore Conference. Thus, from the very beginning, it was understood that the Baltimore Conference, a white Methodist group, would have the responsibility for the control of the Institute.

The Institute existed mainly in name only for the first two years after the charter was granted. James H. Brown and William Harden, local ministers of the Baltimore Conference and two of the first trustees, gave limited instruction beginning in the year of 1867. Little is known about their work. It is known, however, that two classes were under their charge "to each of which they lectured once a week."[2] Irregular classes were held in churches, and some instruction was given in the three "R's." However, even by standards of the best private Negro schools in the Lower South, it would be an exaggeration to say that a Methodist school for Negroes was in operation in Maryland before 1872.

Building Expansion

It was not until five years after its charter was granted that the Institute moved into its own building and began to assume the appearance of a regulated and well-organized enterprise showing promise of growth. Under the appeal of Richard S. Rust, the new corresponding secretary of the Freedmen's Aid Society, and with the unanimous endorsement of the Baltimore Conference, the trustees purchased a building near downtown Baltimore at 44 Saratoga Street in May 1872. School was formally opened in this building on October 9 of that year.

J. Emory Round, a thirty-seven year old white minister, was appointed to take charge of the school on September 6, 1872.[3] He was the only regular teacher until 1877, the year of the first graduating class. First enrolled were eight or possibly nine students: Nathaniel Carrol, Tilghman Jackson, Perry H. Matthews, Alfred R. Shockley, Benjamin W. Brown, Thomas O. Carrol, Charles Smith, and A.W. Lowber.

During the first academic year, 1872-73, the rolls showed a total enrollment of approximately 30 students. Nearly two-thirds of this group were married local preachers or "exhorters" of the gospel, well advanced in years. In fact, all except one of the persons listed were "ministers" or "candidates" for the ministry.[4] During the second academic year, the rolls showed a total enrollment of 40 persons; and in the third year, a total of 56. The total enrollment for the next twelve years more than quadrupled, reaching a total of 263 during the school year 1886-87.[5]

As time progressed the enrollment steadily increased, but the number of students attending classes regularly was considerably less. Listed according to the level of instruction, as shown by a report to the Delaware Conference, the enrollment for the year 1885 was made up of 36 students "who recite at night only," nine who were given "special studies on Saturdays," and 18 in the

"Model School" connected with the Normal Department.[6] Obviously, if one of these categories were excluded by a report on regular enrollment, the total enrollment would be less. It is thought that reports on enrollment generally included all students who kept their names on the rolls.

Most of the enrollees at the Institute came from Baltimore; only a few came from the counties. No doubt the policy of liberally granting scholarships was an inducement to enrollees from Baltimore, but many students who came from places other than Baltimore encountered a serious problem of housing. Baltimore was a teeming city, a commercial market for the South with no wide margin of surplus dwellings (particularly for Negroes who lived chiefly in squalid, blighted and dense ghetto populations).

To the out-of-town student who came to the Institute, Baltimore, one of the largest cities in the nation, was a fascinating experience. In spite of its size, the city bore much of the flavor of rural life or the market place. Horse-drawn carriages, including the trolleys, were a common sight along thoroughfares that were often paved with cobblestones. The clomping of horses' hooves, the jingle of harnesses, and the rumble of wheels added to the noise of this bustling metropolis. The din was often pierced by the solicitous staccato of hucksters of vegetables or peddlers of crabs, oysters, and fish. Without the benefit of public playgrounds, children added their cries to the din, returning homeward to their haven at nightfall, fearful of the city's poorly lit streets and alleys.

Financial Support

During the first fifteen years, the Society maintained one hundred teachers in the field and gave instruction to an estimated 750,000 pupils. It was unlike anything previously experienced in Negro education in Maryland. More than $1 million had been spent between 1866 and 1882,[7] and a bulk of the funds went to Negroes. For example, the General Conference for the years 1879-83 appropriated eight times more money for Negro schools than for white schools—a total of nearly $400,000 for Negroes compared to $50,000 for whites.[8]

In support of the Conference, throughout the nation Methodist churches made contributions to the Society. It was one of the main agencies of the church to receive funds set aside for benevolent purposes. The minutes of the various regional conferences, following a classification approved by the General

Conference in 1872, listed the Society separately and distinctly under the general heading of "Benevolent Collections," along with such subheadings as "Missions," "Board of Church Extension," and "Education." Here was the inescapable indication that the church gave special attention to funds for Freedmen's Aid. The name of the Society was officially changed to the "Freedmen's Aid and Southern Education Society" in 1888. The name was amended again in 1892 and 1904. Nevertheless, a great deal of benevolent collections continued to be given to the Negro.

The constitution of the Society simply emphasized the need for contributions, donations, and legacies. Any person who contributed $20 was made an honorary member; $100, an honorary manager; and $500, a patron.[9] Following the lead of the General Conference, the various regional conferences adopted similar constitutions. The constitution of the Delaware Conference made a person an honorary member of its Freedmen's Aid Society for $1 annually, a member for life for $10, and a patron for $25. [10]

Indeed, the need for funds was constantly stressed in the literature or at meetings of the Society. The funds were solicited to maintain schools, to improve or to purchase real estate, to pay the salaries of teachers, and to set up endowments. A printed form stating, "Persons disposed to make bequests to the Society by will are requested to observe the following form," constantly appeared in *The Annual Report*, which was the official publication of the Society. The corresponding secretary, therefore, was kept busy and well earned the salary of $4,000 annually.

Despite every effort, within twenty years after its founding, the Society was in debt and had a difficult time maintaining the system it had created. In short, income was inadequate to meet the growing demands of the program. Thus, at its twenty-first annual meeting, the Society resolved to ask the General Conference for a special donation of $75,000, and maintenance rather than expansion became accepted policy. This policy was especially ironic because it went into effect at the same time that Methodists in Maryland were considering the establishment of their second school, the future University of Maryland Eastern Shore.

In the same year (1885-86), funds of the Society were being carefully distributed among the first schools founded by Methodists with no appropriation for real estate or buildings in Maryland. This action, however, was nondiscriminatory. Instead, it was an effort on the part of the Society to make secure and to improve, as far as practicable, a few of the older schools in the Lower South where population and social pressures were heaviest. Nevertheless, the enrollment of the Institute had increased rapidly and the school's building near downtown Baltimore was severely overcrowded. To remedy this condition, the trustees set out to obtain a larger and more suitable building. One of the trustees at the time, John F. Goucher, offered to donate $5,000 in cash for the erection of a new building if an additional $6,500 would be raised by the remaining trustees.[11] Goucher went so far as to purchase a 90 ft. x 140 ft. lot on the northwest corner of Fulton and Edmondson Avenues and to promise it as a site for the proposed building.

Goucher was a prominent citizen of Baltimore and in the affairs of the Institute. His great interest and support of education in the State has been greatly rewarded with a place of high recognition in the history of higher education. Born in Waynesburg, Green County, Pennsylvania, on June 7, 1845, he graduated from Dickinson College in 1868. As a young man, he became interested in both the ministry and matrimony. On Christmas Eve 1877, Goucher married Mary Cecelia Fisher, the daughter of a wealthy, well-established family of Pikesville. Her wealth became the basis of later philanthropies for the establishment of a woman's college in Baltimore named Goucher College in 1910 and for the support of Methodist missionary schools in the Far East, especially the Anglo-Japanese Methodist College in Tokyo, Japan.

Goucher's gifts in 1879 were not the last he would give to the Institute. He "generously contributed" $1,500 to the school again in 1884. In 1885, he subscribed $5,000 to a campaign for the Institute's endowment. Records state that Goucher gave additional smaller sums to the trustees, including the down payment to purchase the first structure to house a branch of the Institute, the future University of Maryland Eastern Shore. Indeed, Goucher gave his time, talents, and prestige to further the work of the Institute while he served for many years as a member and president of the board of trustees. It is one of the odd quirks of history that the Institute was not named in his honor at the time it was rechartered as Morgan College in 1890. It is, furthermore, an ironical oversight that no building or remembrance has been erected to his memory by any institution of higher learning for Negroes in the State or that the official school bulletin of Morgan State College scarcely mentions his name.

The trustees gladly accepted Goucher's offer to donate the $5,000 in

7

cash. The $6,500 that Goucher stipulated as a condition of his offer was raised within three years. Negro churches of Baltimore gave money; on one occasion, the John Wesley Church gave $200. Moreover, Thomas Kelso (1784-1878), president of the trustees, left the school a legacy of $1,500. In addition to these sums, the Freedmen's Aid Society of the church gave $5,990.55. By June of 1880, the trustees had collected $16,000 on the building program.

The Institute's new building was dedicated on Wednesday, June 16, 1880. It was a big occasion for those interested in the education of Negroes in Maryland. With clear skies, a moderate temperature, and a pleasant wind blowing from the Chesapeake Bay, the cornerstone was laid at about four o'clock in the afternoon. Bishop Levi Scott, now a venerable man of seventy-eight years, was the respected principal participant in this ceremony, which was witnessed by several hundred persons, the majority of whom were Negroes. Among those present were ministers of the three patronizing Methodist conferences: Baltimore, Delaware, and Washington. J. Emory Round, the principal of the Institute, and Goucher, its benefactor, were among the ministers who came to witness this landmark in the local history of the education of the Negro. A collection amounting to about $200 was obtained from the audience and "good" music was rendered by the choir of Baltimore's Sharp Street Church, where thirteen years earlier the first classes were held. With an eye toward future history, some catalogues and appropriate documents were placed within a receptacle of the cornerstone, which was to be closed on the following Monday.

It is likely that the building was completed in November as planned. It was constructed of a light-colored stone and, including equipment, cost approximately $30,000. The new building was proudly displayed on an engraving in *The Annual Report* of the Society for 1881. The Society's able secretary, Richard S. Rust, regarded it as the best Methodist theological school for Negroes.

In the numerous advertisements found in official publications of the school, the word "commodious" was used persistently to describe the building. Whereas the building was commodious at the time of its completion, it would soon become overcrowded, and in subsequent years its luster would become dark and dingy.

The support of the Institute came from collections of the Freedmen's

Aid Society of the Baltimore, Delaware, and Washington Conferences and from subscriptions or legacies of individuals who knew of the school from first-hand information derived from living in Baltimore. No organized philanthropy, outside of the Methodist Church or of support from the State, came to the aid of the Institute.

The Society agreed early in the process that the Institute and its teachers' salaries would be the primary responsibility of the Baltimore, Delaware and Washington Conferences. The Society expected these three conferences to honor the pledge by taking the lead in this glorious enterprise. The Delaware and Washington Conferences embraced the bulk of the Negro churches of the Methodist Episcopal denomination along the eastern region of the nation, containing districts in the states of New Jersey, Pennsylvania, Delaware, Maryland, and Virginia. With the Baltimore Conference consisting of white members and being less embracing, its clergymen were generally appointed as trustees.

Because of perennial financial problems, the heads of the Institute usually were available when the conferences met in session. Invariably, they would either address the conferences or discuss with members the financial needs of the Institute. W. Maslin Frysinger, the second head of the school (1882-88), busied himself with the collection of monies. His pleas to the conferences were eloquent and persistent. He began a tradition which the fourth head, John Oakley Spencer, carried on untiringly. Frysinger wrote a passionate plea in one of his reports for all to give, even the poor widow with her "two mites, which, perhaps, she has saved out of the earnings of her toil and it will be counted more in the Master's sight than the most royal gift. " Frysinger further sought to meet the request of the Society through the establishment of an endowment for the Institute. He was empowered by the trustees to solicit $5,000 from the Delaware Conference and much larger sums from the Baltimore and Washington Conferences. By 1886 he was able to report that $27,000 had been pledged, and $10,000 had been collected and "safely invested" toward the endowment.

The usual funds from Freedmen's Aid and contributions for the endowment trickled in from the various districts of the conferences. It appears upon examination of returns that the various churches, particularly Negro congregations with limited means, actively supported the cause of keeping the doors of the Institute opened. In Maryland districts, both east and west of the

9

Chesapeake Bay, there was a conscientious and prideful effort among Negroes of Methodist churches to raise monies for the Institute.

The vast efforts put forth by Methodists, both locally and nationally, could not prevent the shadow of debt from creeping across the records of various schools. The Centenary Biblical Institute was no exception. Like the Society, the Institute went into debt and remained there for the greater part of its existence as a privately supported institution. From financial records of income, expenditures, and other available sources, it may be gathered that collections from Freedmen's Aid hardly came to $5,000 annually before 1900. Consequently in 1904, the outstanding debt of the school (known then as Morgan College) was $6,200; by 1923, the debt was increased to approximately $80,000. Campaigns to raise monies in order to lift the debt were carried on perennially, but they never yielded enough income to meet the demands of the school's program.

With the passing of the nineteenth century, the period of inspired and intense effort to support Negro schools — economically and morally through philanthropy and churches — was beginning to fade away in Maryland and in the South. The infectious energy generated under the stimulus of Reconstruction began to wane. To many persons, the challenge to educate the freedmen no longer held the newness or offered the attraction and excitement of former years. Thus, the plight of the former slaves and their children began to recede to the back of the minds of Americans. People instead became absorbed by other currents in American life and were removed in time and temper from the "rights" of freedmen manifested a generation earlier. At the time that the Institute in Baltimore was attempting to expand, to establish branches, and to support itself, Methodist support was on the decline. The day of government and state aid had not yet arrived.

Academic Program

Before 1880 when the Institute moved into its new building on Baltimore's Fulton and Edmondson Avenues, the academic side of its program was fairly well clarified and defined. The primary purpose of the school was to train young men for the ministry, and a classification of theological or seminary was accordingly designated in official reports. The atmosphere and discipline that surrounded academic life were, therefore, religious in nature.

Yet, the number of students enrolled for theology became relatively less and less as the total enrollment increased. Thus to encourage enrollment in the ministry, prospective theological students were offered free tuition, room, and books while other students were charged approximately $1 or $2 per month for tuition, $1 per week for board, and $1 per week for laundry. Previously, approximately $25 would take care of the expenses of a theological student for an entire year.

Another purpose of the Institute was to provide young men with the fundamentals of reading, writing, and arithmetic so they would be qualified to pursue the higher studies required of a student of the ministry. In keeping with this purpose, the school maintained a Preparatory Department that gave instruction in the lower subjects. Coming in 1880 chiefly from areas where well over half of the Negro population was illiterate, most of the students who enrolled at the Institute were sorely deficient in the basics of reading and writing. The Preparatory Department then was not only the largest in size, but it was one of the most important phases in the educational programs of the school.

In conjunction with the Preparatory Department, there was a Normal Department for the purpose of training prospective teachers. This phase of the program was set up to keep the school in step with the nationwide interest in teacher training and to prepare the youth to face the pitiful scarcity of Negro teachers. Women were employed as instructors in the Normal Department, a fact that coincided with the right to an education and by inference, the right to teach. It is not definitely known, however, when girls were admitted for instruction. It is thought that they were first enrolled by way of the Normal Department, possibly through the branch set up specifically for normal study in Baltimore in 1886. Furthermore, no sharp line of demarcation ever existed between preparatory and normal studies.

A glance at the five teachers on the staff in 1884, when the total enrollment stood at 184, shows that there were two teachers in the Theological Department and three in the Preparatory Department. J. Emory Round, the former principal and senior professor, and Professor T.B. Snowden taught theology. In the Preparatory Department, Mrs. Mary Caden was listed as head, assisted by Benjamin O. Bird and Miss Lizzie Dennis. In the following year, there was a "Model School " of 18 pupils in the Normal Department in which Mrs. I. Diffenderfer, a volunteer white citizen of Baltimore, gave special instruction. It seems to have been a policy that, as the occasion arose, services of volunteer white instructors were accepted. In addition to the services of Diffenderfer, Professor Burns of the local Easton and Burnett College gave instruction in bookkeeping. Furthermore, besides the head of the school, white instructors were kept on the regular staff for many years.

About the same time that the Normal Department was getting under way, the trustees were attempting to make arrangements for instruction in industrial subjects. A report in 1887 stated that the Institute was beginning "industrial work as rapidly as the means permitted." Another report in the following year mentioned a school of industry with two teachers and 30 students. The nature of this school of industry is not known. It is likely that this undertaking was only a token gesture in keeping with the contemporary trend of providing industrial training, particularly for Negroes. While minute details of the Institute's program are not known, enough evidence is available to conclude that during the middle of the 1880s, noticeable changes took place. Plans were ambitious, and pains from growth were obvious. It is not surprising, then, that the new commodious building at the corner of Fulton and Edmondson, like the old building on Saratoga Street, became overcrowded.

There were about 226 students enrolled for the school year 1885-86, too many to permit much elbowroom in the school's only building. Consequently, at the beginning of that term, 60 applicants for admission were turned away. The trustees decided that in order to relieve this state of affairs, it would be helpful to reopen the old building formerly in use on Saratoga Street. Furthermore, the possibility of opening another school was not overlooked as shown in one statement by Frysinger who said, "To accommodate the lower grades of our institution, we need a Preparatory School in the Washington Conference and another in the Delaware Conference, and these are among the possibilities of the near future." Frysinger made this statement in a report to the Delaware Conference, which met at the Bainbridge Church in Philadelphia on May 6-11, 1886. No mention was made in official records of exactly where the branch schools were to be set up or how funds for their support were to be secured. No records were handed down telling how the trustees with their limited resources would be able to support the schools, which were said to be "a possibility of the near future." The official reports of the Washington and Delaware Conferences and the Society were silent about the establishment of the proposed branches.

The Institute Becomes Morgan College

The important fact, however, is that the branches were established. An announcement by the Society in 1888 classified the Institute as collegiate, conducting instruction in three different schools: two in Baltimore and one in Princess Anne, Maryland. Frysinger was listed as having the position of president and professor of practical theology while Round was listed as head of the Normal Departments, professor of practical theology, and professor of exegetical theology. Benjamin O. Bird was principal of one of the newly-opened schools, the Delaware Conference Academy in Princess Anne, and John H. Nutter was principal of the Baltimore City Academy. Altogether, there were about a dozen members on the staff during the years 1886-88.

With the establishment of its 2 branches, which were intended to promote studies at the elementary level, the Institute was enabled to give consideration to the higher subjects demanded by prevalent standards of a collegiate curriculum for teachers and ministers. Students who graduated from the Institute were exposed to a study of the classics and the Bible. The catalogue of the school, first published in 1873, outlined the subjects required in the collegiate departments, namely normal and theological. By the 1880s, the course of study was developed to last for four years, embracing a study of the classics, English, science, and the Bible. For the freshman year, catalogues listed such subjects as Greek for students of theology, mathematics, English, Latin, and science. Virgil, Livy, and Horace were taught in courses in Latin while Herodotus and Homer were included in courses in Greek. Algebra, trigonometry, surveying, physiology, and zoology were freshman subjects in mathematics and science. The remaining three collegiate years followed suit. Thus, like many other collegiate schools of the period, the curriculum was highly formal and classical. Eventually, the predominant philosophy of liberal arts was transmitted to the branch in Princess Anne.

Within a few years, the Institute's branch in Baltimore, variously known as the Centenary Normal School or the Baltimore City Academy, passed out of the control of the trustees when the City began to show more interest in the public education of Negroes. To take the place of this defunct branch, the trustees gave encouragement and support to a school in Lynchburg, Virginia, known as the Virginia Collegiate and Industrial Institute or Morgan Annex. The other branch in Princess Anne, though not solely founded by the trustees as shown later, survived the many vicissitudes of Negro education in Maryland. Eventually it became collegiate itself, bearing such names in its subsequent history as the Delaware Conference Academy, the Industrial Branch of Morgan College, the Eastern Branch of the Maryland Agricultural College, the Eastern Branch of the Maryland State College of Agriculture, Princess Anne Academy, Princess Anne College, Maryland State College, and finally the University of Maryland Eastern Shore. Whatever it has been called, this branch of the Institute became a focal point of problems common to the education of the Negro at state and national levels. In addition, an exploration of its history reveals the unique place that this branch in Princess Anne, a modus- operandi for public aid, occupies in the history of education in Maryland. Furthermore, its history reveals how the Eastern Shore of Maryland, which is a distinct cultural and geographical region of the State, profoundly influenced the land-grant destiny of the school.

ENDNOTES

CHAPTER 1

[1] Report (M.E.), 3rd, pp. 8-9.

[2] Report (M.E.), 8th, p.37.

[3] Round was born in Westwind, Herkimer County, New York, on November 25, 1835, and died in Baltimore on June 18, 1892. His salary began at $1500 annually.

[4] Report (M.E.), 8th, R.D. Williams, op.cit.

[5] Report (M.E.), 8th, p. 39.

[6] Compiled from the Report (M.E.) and the Minutes.

[7] Richard S. Rust, The Freedmen's Aid and Southern Education Society and Its Work (Cincinnati), 1989, p. 5. White and Negro Methodist groups spent 3.3 million dollars on educational work between 1868-1915.

[8] Lewis M. Haywood, The Colored Man in the Methodist Episcopal Church (Cincinnati), 1890, p. 220.

[9] Report (M.E.), 6th.

[10] Minutes of the Session, Delaware Conference, 1884. Hereafter cited as Minutes.

[11] Minutes, 1885, p. 33.

CHAPTER TWO

THE SHORE AND SOMERSET

Characteristics of the Eastern Shore

In addition to being distinct culturally, the Eastern Shore is a distinct geographical region of the state of Maryland. Flat, low, and narrow, it lies along the Atlantic Seaboard and is separated from the mainland by the Chesapeake Bay. When reproduced on maps, it gives the appearance of being a crudely shaped geologic fist beginning at Wilmington, Delaware, with an extended forefinger pointing near Norfolk, Virginia. Because it embraces portions of three states, namely Delaware, Maryland, and Virginia, the Eastern Shore is frequently abbreviated as the Delmarva Peninsula. Traditionally, however, this peninsula is known simply as the Eastern Shore, a.k.a. the "Shore". The Shore is composed of nine counties in Maryland: Cecil, Kent, Talbot, Dorchester, Wicomico, Somerset, Worcester, Caroline, and Queen Anne's; two counties in Virginia: Accomac and Northampton; and most of Delaware's three counties: Kent, Dorchester and New Castle. Kent County is located partly in Delaware and partly in Maryland.

The Bay side of the Shore is cut by more than a dozen rivers whose waters, generally beginning as small streams, drift lazily toward the Bay through wide estuaries often flanked by marshy lands and flats. Rivers have left many "necks" and "points" as they empty into the Bay. Mostly, the rivers bear Indian names such as Pocomoke, Manokin, Wicomico, Nanticoke, and Choptank, reminiscent of days before the Europeans settled the Shore. Indeed, the geography of the Shore's waters has profoundly influenced the ecology of the region. Shoremen have only to travel a few miles before navigable water is found in rivers, creeks, sounds, and bays. Because of the poor natural drainage of the region, backyards, farms, and roads were often blemished

15

with puddles of sluggish water. The northern portion, however, is much better drained than the southern section; for as one travels northward, the land increases in elevation and becomes gently rolling in such counties as Cecil, Queen Anne's, and Talbot. Dorchester County begins the flat, monotonous plain movement to the ocean.

The earliest communities, generally small in size, grew chiefly on or near the rivers, which were the arteries for the social and economic life of the region. Pocomoke City and Snow Hill thrived on the Pocomoke River, Cambridge and Denton on the Choptank River, Salisbury on the Wicomico River, Chestertown on the Chester River, and Princess Anne on the Manokin River.

The Shore also has a distinct historical and socioeconomic background. Before the coming of railroads and paved highways, the Shore was almost completely waterbound. Consequently, a great number of merchant ships with passengers and freight plied the Bay. Then after the coming of railroads, the development extended primarily north and south with the main terminals at Wilmington, Delaware, and Cape Charles, Virginia. Outlets to the Western Shore, however, were more practical and convenient by water than by rail.

Traditionally, Shoremen were mainly farmers or fishermen. Their wealth was dependent upon the produce of the land or of the waters. Since the Shore could boast of no great industrial, commercial, or financial center, the counties on the Shore that depended upon landed wealth were among the poorest of the State. In contrast, on the Western Shore, Baltimore, the economic capital of the State, was the hub of economic life and activity—of banking, industry, and insurance — while Annapolis was the political capital of Maryland.

Farmers on the Shore were largely absorbed in the cultivation of tobacco until the nineteenth century when its production became unprofitable. With slave labor as a powerful factor, tobacco was grown in all counties on the Shore until the midcentury. For example, eight million pounds were produced in Queen Anne's alone in 1849.[1] Yet in 1889, less than fifty years later, the entire Shore reported a yield of only fifty pounds. Then, with the coming of railroads, markets along the eastern seaboard became more readily accessible to the rest of the world. Diversified farm produce and poultry were shipped over the roads, strengthening an economy that was dislocated by the historic collapse of the tobacco industry.

In addition, the waters of the Shore offered both a pleasurable pastime and a profitable livelihood in fishing. The Bay and rivers abounded with either oysters, crabs, or a dozen varieties of fish, thus offering a lively trade that left its impression upon the character of the people of Crisfield and Deal Island in Somerset County. For example, much of the main street of Crisfield, along which a railroad track extended, is said to have been built up with oyster shells; and a small neck on Tilghman's Island was built up with shells in order to house a portion of Tilghman's fishery. Familiar sights on the Shore included fishermen dressed in boots and raincoats, seashells along wharves and piers, and white sails of schooners and sloops on bays, rivers, or harbors.[2]

At the beginning of the nineteenth century, the population of the Eastern Shore consisted of about 100,000 persons, about one-third of whom were Negroes. At the end of the next hundred years, the population was only about twice this number; and the number of Negroes was declining. Their number declined from about 58,000 in 1890 to about 50,000 in 1930. During this period, Somerset County's Negro population alone declined from 9,500 to 8,000. Many Negroes were migrating to Baltimore, increasing the city's Negro population.

Strangely enough, the people of the Shore were strongly influenced by the historic forces of Methodism as well as of slavery. Revivals and camp meetings were common occurrences each summer before and after the slave period among Negroes and Whites alike. The influences of slavery were deep-rooted and strong and left the Negro divided on such matters as equality before the law, ownership of property, or educational attainment despite the vigorous and extensive discipline of Methodism. In fact, Methodism eventually gave the Negro his only source of leadership in civic affairs. Indeed, some of the outstanding figures who defied the slave system were natives of the Shore, namely Harriet Tubman of Bucktown in Dorchester County and Frederick Douglass of Tuckahoe in Talbot County.

Mainlanders often accused both White and Negro Shoremen alike of being backward and unprogressive culturally and economically, in education and in business. Not entirely without justification, this criticism often drew resentment that evolved into political conflict or sectionalism. It is no coincidence, for example, that the State maintained two official state treasurers until 1851 and two official land offices until 1841—one for the mainland and one for the Shore. But in any forthright political contest, where state politics caused geographical and sectional lines, the Shore was likely to muster less show of strength than the mainland. Also, with few exceptions, Maryland's governors have come from the mainland since the Civil War. Moreover, the unwritten gentleman's agreement that stated that one U.S. senator must come from the Shore was discarded after the War.

Geographically, the Shore's isolation permitted its people to go their own way, to become self-reliant, and to be proud of their ability to get along without too much outside interference. Politically, however, this isolation was often a handicap to the Shore; and historically, the isolation was an ever-present reality extending into the recesses of the Shore's institutional life, including that of the Negro schools.

The Town of Princess Anne

Of all the towns on the Shore in 1886, Somerset County's Princess Anne was one of the oldest. Provincial but proud, the citizens of this quaint village showed little interest in changing their way of life, which was more akin to the eighteenth century than to the nineteenth century. Many of the citizens of the community, Negro and White alike, were openly satisfied with their way of life, which they remembered and admired as having been good enough for their ancestors, thus good enough for them. Consequently, newcomers or new ideas were regarded with a curious and cautious skepticism while traditional hospitality was reserved for old friends and families.

There was a strong regard for class and family in Princess Anne, and genealogy held a high place in class stratification inasmuch as many of the residents tended to revere names strongly reminiscent of the history of the town and county. Such names were Waters, Dennis, Dashiell, Maddox, and Nutter. Family ties were pervasive and intricate, and there was a remarkable willingness and unity among the leading citizens to preserve and to perpetuate the even tenor of life. Resentment was likely to result when an outsider made unfavorable criticism, when an old resident scoffed at the mores, or when new ideas threatened to disturb the old pattern of living. Streets were unpaved but dignified by the presence of old buildings and older trees. Those well-known, old buildings imparted a sense of history and importance to the citizens of the town, which had been a county seat since 1733. On the north bank of the Manokin River in Princess Anne, there was the Manokin Presbyterian Church, rebuilt in 1765. Teackle Mansion, originally built in 1801, stood further away on the south bank. It was a symbol of mystery, intrigue, and gossip inspired by a provocative novel, The Entailed Hat, written by George Alfred Townshend in 1884. There was also the Washington Hotel, originally erected as a colonial structure in 1744.

From the point of community service, there were other important buildings, including several churches, among which were an Episcopal church for Whites and the newly dedicated Metropolitan Methodist Church for Negroes. The railroad was extended from Salisbury through Princess Anne shortly after the close of the Civil War through the enterprising efforts of John W. Crisfield, a lawyer and president of the Eastern Shore Railroad Company. In addition to a railroad station, Princess Anne had a bank and a county courthouse, which was rebuilt in 1904 after a fire.[3]

Property Acquisition and History of "Olney"

Approximately one-half mile east of the courthouse on an unpaved county road was yet another old building well known to the citizens of Princess Anne. It was called "Olney" and had been occupied or owned by some of the leading townspeople since its completion in 1798 by Ezekiel Haynie, a physician and surgeon who served in the Continental Army.[4] It is highly probable that the word "Olney," an English place and proper name, was used to suggest the family's English origin. It could be that the family came from the town Olney in England (located near Northampton), or some of Haynie's relatives may have been known by that name.

The role of Olney in 1886 caused some consternation among old citizens of the town. For the first time in the history of the Eastern Shore, an old landmark passed into the hands of Negroes for purposes of higher education, that is, for education higher than that given in the local county schools. This was a new experience for an old community that, in addition to the slave tradition, remembered the days of Reconstruction when the town received its first ill-fated Negro school. The pattern of Negro and White relations in the town was strongly influenced by the slave tradition wherein benign paternalism was the reward for "good Negroes" and, conversely, reprimand was the penalty for Negroes who did not "know their place." Consequently, it is not surprising that the transfer of Olney to Negroes, aided by "outsiders," was looked upon with some misgivings and resentment. Surprisingly, there is no record of violence or hostility against the transfer of this historic landmark. Instead, it became a fascinating page in the history of Princess Anne and Somerset County.

The land about Olney was situated at the watershed of the Manokin River. As early as 1620, Europeans entered this river to trade with Indians called "Manokins," who lived in the vicinity of its head streams.[5] The river was an avenue of approach to the area until soil erosion prevented its use. It appears, however, that the area was not appreciably settled by Europeans until after the Restoration of Charles II in 1660. One of the earliest settlers to receive land "rights" on the Manokin was William Waters, who was granted a title to 1,280 acres on September 5, 1663. His progeny and those of his slaves as well increased as the years passed, and in time the name of Waters, among Negroes and Whites alike, became one of the most widely known names in Somerset. Throughout the years, the school in Princess Anne has generally kept a Waters on its rolls.

Other settlers who came up the Manokin and settled near its head streams during the generation after Waters were John Hobbs, Abraham Heath, William Powell, Thomas Wilson, and George Manlove.[6] Manlove obtained patents for a section of land near the Manokin called "Manlove's Discovery," later known as "Beechwood" in 1668. "Beechwood" bordered upon land that later became known as "Deep Still" and "Spittle," the site of the future Olney, which would eventually evolve into the University of Maryland Eastern Shore. Evidently, the Manloves and Waters intermarried, for "Beechwood" remained the ancestral home of the Waters family for more than two hundred years.[7]

It is interesting to observe that one of the earliest settlers of the area was a free Negro, Anthony Johnson, who came from the Eastern Shore of Virginia to Somerset about 1662. The Johnsons lived for a time in the Manokin area. Later they moved to a branch on the Wicomico River, passing on several hundred acres of land to their descendants.[8] They were probably the first free Negroes in Somerset County or the Eastern Shore—perhaps the first documented in the state of Maryland. The land on the Wicomico was called "Anthony's Vineyard," or "Tony's Vineyard." It is probably much of the same land in Wicomico County near Salisbury known as the community of "Tony Tank."

The land records of Somerset County have been remarkably preserved and show how the land about the head streams of the Manokin River eventually passed into the hands of the school. For example, the families of the earliest settlers, Heath and Hobbs, were still living in the area over one hundred years after their settlement—and doubtlessly, some of the descendants are still living in Wicomico and Somerset counties if one is to judge by the listings of telephone directories. Specifically on March 1, 1785, one Abraham Heath deeded to Josiah Hobbs several tracts of land amounting to $412.10. Some of the tracts were referred to in the deed as Hath's (or perhaps Heath's) Chance, Done's Nest Egg, Hap Hazard, Wilson's First, Heath's Gift, and Hogg's (or perhaps Hobb's) Ridge.[9] On October 7 of this same year, Josiah Hobbs sold two tracts of land, containing 114 acres to Ezekiel Haynie for the sum of $256.

Haynie was a physician from Snow Hill who served in the Continental Army and was also a founder of the Medical and Chiurgical [sic] (i.e. Chirugical) Faculty of Maryland. It is likely that Haynie's purchase comprised some of the tracts that Hobbs had purchased from Heath in March.[10] However, the system of transfer and description of land titles in colonial Maryland often left a margin for error. Sometimes the same land was described by several different names; and thus, the specific tracts of the Heath property that Haynie acquired from Hobbs couldn't be clearly defined. Nevertheless, the land that Ezekiel Haynie acquired lay at the head streams of the Manokin. One tract on Manloves Branch containing 92 acres is described in the deed as "Deep Still," perhaps because of its relatively lower elevation. Haynie's other tract known as "Spittle" lay on the east side of the Manokin one mile from a wading place that led to Beechwood.[11] "Deep Still" and "Spittle" eventually became the first farm and campus of the school.

Within three years after Haynie signed the deed, a home of late eighteenth-century colonial design was built upon the land. Whether it was Haynie or a member of the family who first called the home "Olney" is a matter of conjecture. Moreover, the cost of construction is unknown. It may be surmised however that Haynie, who subscribed to the habits and manner of the lesser eighteenth-century colonial aristocracy, commanded a substantial income in order to build a home of Olney's size and elegance—a brick structure of about eighteen rooms. Haynie died in the year following the completion of his home in 1799 at the age of thirty-nine.[12]

Haynie left three children and a wife, Betsy Bayly. Dying intestate, his estate descended equally to the three children, Richard Hampden, Henrietta,

21

and Charlotte. Richard, the only male heir, later sold his share to his brother-in-law, William Done, who was married to Charlotte. Charlotte and William had three children: John, William, and Henrietta. It is likely that the Dones lived at the ancestral farmstead known as "Done's Nest Egg," located less than a mile northeast of Olney. John Done, in 1744, constructed the original WashingtonHotel. The original "Done's Nest Egg," became the property of Dr. Eldon G. Marksman, who was not only licensed to practice medicine in Somerset County in 1926 but also served until 1947 as the school's physician. At a ceremony held in September 1950, testimonials were given by some of the leading citizens on behalf of Dr. Marksman's service to the community. The Republican candidate for governor, Theodore R. McKeldin, who won the election that November, gave one of the testimonials. At this ceremony, "Eldon Hall," a new office building, was dedicated on the land once known as "Nest Egg," and now referred to as "Eldon Hall Farm."

Charlotte's husband, William Done, like her father, died intestate and his three children inherited the Done interest in the Olney estate. Henrietta Done (1813-75), the daughter of William and Charlotte and the granddaughter of Ezekiel Haynie, married into a family of Joneses. Her daughter, likewise named Henrietta (1840-95), in turn married into a family of Stewarts. Thus the two-thirds share that the Dones held in the old Haynie property was legally possessed by several heirs: the descendants of the Joneses and the Stewarts from the maternal line and of the Dones from the paternal line.

The other child of Ezekiel Haynie, Henrietta, never married. Her one-third interest in the estate of her father was disposed of in her will made January 20, 1950.[13] She willed her share to the children of her niece and namesake, Henrietta Haynie Jones. Henrietta Haynie lived in Olney until she died. Her will was made in Princess Anne, but no tombstone marker has been found to indicate her place and date of death. The will was recorded under her name, but schedules of the census for 1840 and 1850 filed in the National Archives showed no name of Henrietta Haynie, which may mean that she was listed under the family name of relatives who may have been living with her in Olney. She came to love the place, made improvements upon it, and affectionately called it Olney. She lived fairly comfortably there for more than a half century. The number of slaves that her father left with the estate was unknown. However, it was known that Henrietta willed some fifteen slaves to her nephews. Some of the slaves mentioned in her will included "my servant boy John;" "my

22

servants Littleton, William, Tom, Caroline and her children; and Lizzy along with her son John Thomas." Additionally, with a passing note of gratitude for a slave's loyalty, she willed to her nephew, William Done (Charlotte's child), "my faithful servant Sarah, desiring that he will make her comfortable as long as she lives." [14]

It is highly probable that some of the descendents of these slaves, bearing the name of their parents' masters—Jones, Done, and Stewart—attended classes in the same building, Olney, where once Henrietta Haynie was served. Tradition says that recalcitrant slaves were manacled in a dungeon in the basement, which was probably true. However, it is utterly fantastic to believe along with tradition that an underground passage was used to convey slaves to and from the wharves in town to the basement of Olney. No doubt tradition has mingled stories of enchantment with the history of Olney.

Henrietta's ownership of about fifteen slaves during the 1850s placed her in the class of a moderate slaveholder. Prices of slaves during the 1850s were among the highest in American history. At this time, a field hand in Maryland would bring more than $1,200; domestic servants would command less. Thus, a conservative estimate of Henrietta's wealth in slaves would be about $14,000-$16,000. Tax records for this period are not available for Somerset, but the entire Olney estate during the 1850s was probably worth about $30,000, including slaves. Henrietta's library, probably housed in one of the large rooms downstairs, contained such works as Johnson's <u>Dictionary,</u> Hume's <u>History of England,</u> Gibbon's <u>Decline and Fall of the Roman Empire</u> and Pope's <u>Works.</u>

Upon Henrietta's death, the original land of Deep Still, Spittle, and the Olney home passed into the hands of the descendants of her sister Charlotte. These descendants—the Joneses, Stewarts, and Dones—each had conflicting claims to the estate. The disposition of the claims was so involved that a settlement in court was found necessary. Consequently, the matter was brought into the Chancery Court of Somerset before Judge Thomas A. Spence in the winter of 1867. Deciding that the estate should not be decided among the several claimants, the Court appointed a trustee, Isaac D. Jones, to dispose of the property at public sale.[15]

Isaac D. Jones, a local politician and Attorney General of the State, sold the entire estate to his friend, James U. Dennis, on June 25, 1867, for the sum of $9,000, which included a down payment of only $200. Dennis was likewise a local politician, a former radical secessionist, and a proslavery delegate at the Constitutional Convention of 1864. Within a few years Dennis, in turn, disposed of the property, in pieces, at a profit. His first sale was made on October 8, 1869 to Louis W. Morris (1823-78), a physician who maintained an office in the town of Princess Anne.[16] Exactly one month later, Dennis made an additional sale to Buelah C. Hirst for the sum of $6,500.[17] The sale to Buelah Hirst contained only sixteen acres, but it included the Olney home. Five years later in 1874, Dennis sold the remainder of the old Haynie property consisting of approximately 100 acres to Morris for the sum of $2,500.

Buelah Hirst, who now owned the Olney home and 16 acres of the old Haynie property, married T. Lyle Dickey on November 8, 1869, but in the following year the newlyweds moved to LaSalle County, Illinois. While in Illinois, they sold Olney and its 16 acres for $6,000 to Aaron D. Woodruff, a physician in Princess Anne.[18] By the early 1880s, Woodruff had died perhaps in Philadelphia, which was his place of residence for several years.[19] In his will, Woodruff appointed his friend, Richard C. Dale, a resident of Princess Anne, as the executor of his estate. It was then Dale who sold the Woodruff property of Olney and its 16 acres to John A. B. Wilson in Philadelphia on June 12, 1886, for the sum of $2,000.[20] This sum was paid in full by February 4, 1892, releasing the mortgage held by Dale. Within twenty years, the value of Olney and its 16 acres depreciated enormously. Buelah Hirst bought it for $6,500 in 1869, but Wilson contracted for less than one-third of this amount in 1886. Neglect was certainly one of the reasons for this depreciation.

As years passed, the school acquired more land adjacent to the original campus of 1886. Clara E. Morris (1835-1905), the widow of Louis W. Morris, sold the large portion of land to the school on January 3, 1890. It consisted of approximately 103 acres of the old Haynie tracts. Either the Morris family made substantial improvements upon the property, or they made a handsome profit from the sale. The latter was more likely. In 1874, Morris paid $2,500 for the 100 odd acres, reselling the property and improvements for $7,500 in 1890. Excluding the greater purchasing power of the dollar in 1874 in contrast to 1890, the monetary gain of $5,000 would far exceed the value of improvements mentioned in the deed of sale. As far as can be ascertained, the improvements made on the property consisted mainly of a two-story frame house of about six rooms and a small barn. The frame house stayed in use as a dwelling on the College farm for years.

The principal of the school, a former farm boy himself, was on hand at the time the sale was made but later revealed in an official report that he did not think too highly of the improvements spoken of in the deed. No doubt he was aware of the fact that the Morrises were overpricing the property, but he was also aware of the difficulties that Negroes encountered in the acquisition of land in Somerset. Therefore, considering the need of the school, he showed a strong interest in obtaining additional land, as shown in an excerpt from the deed: "They said B.O. Bird joins in the conveyance because he contracted to purchase the above described real estate from other grantors, but never paid the purchase money for the same and hereby consent to the said sale and this grant to the said Morgan College."[21]

The next acquisition of land came in 1916. The school acquired two tracts of the old Broughton estate by payment of two mortgages. Assignments were made to Morgan College on November 5, 1910 for $300 and $200 for land in East Princess Anne Election District, "being a part of what is known as the Broughton Home Place, and being a part of all that land which was conveyed by deed to the said Francis H. Dryden by Joshua W. Miles and wife" in June of 1906 for the sum of $4,000.[22] The two tracts consisted of 78 acres although the acreage is not shown in a description of titles. The total charge of the school, therefore, amounted to approximately 197 acres in 1916.

The school acquired no additional land during the next thirty years. It was not until March 8, 1946 that the school acquired an additional 100 acres from George W. Powell and his wife, both of Princess Anne, for the sum of $30,000 with 22 percent interest on the unpaid balance.[23] Powell and his wife signed the contract of sale in Somerset, and Harry C. Byrd, president of the University of Maryland, signed for the school before a notary in Prince Georges County. For many years, this land was known as "Egypt," but it may well have been some of the land once owned by the Heaths and Hobbs during the eighteenth century. Its relative elevation indicates that it may have been the colonial tract known as "Hobb's Ridge." The last tract of land was acquired in the following year on November 8, 1947, from William C. Hart.[24] No price is given in the deed, but there were 8.9 acres, formerly a part of "Beechwood." The acreage in 1947 now amounted to approximately 308.

Since 1886 when the school acquired its first land, the titles of ownership have reflected the various periods of history through which the school has passed. The school has always existed legally as part of another body, and therefore the titles of its properties have always been listed under the names of its legal parents, including the Centenary Biblical Institute, Morgan College, and the University of Maryland. The State first acquired a title to land on the campus in 1925, becoming part owner with Morgan College. Morgan College agreed to convey "in fee all that lot of land in East Princess Anne Election District, in Somerset County, in the state of Maryland, containing four hundred and sixty-two one thousandths of an acre...for the sum of five dollars and other good and valuable considerations."[25]

Through the University of Maryland, the state then acquired about 1/2 acre of land on the campus between Olney and the county road. The procurement of this half-acre was indeed a "good and valuable consideration" over and above the legal expression of a landed deed. The land was purchased expressly to provide a site upon which the State erected a building, further committing the State as a reluctant owner in an educational enterprise for Negroes under private control of Methodists. Then in 1936, Methodist control and ownership were legally ended when the State bought the school in Princess Anne for the sum of $100,000 for the use of the University of Maryland.[26]

ENDNOTES

CHAPTER 2

[1] <u>Maryland, Its Resources, Industries and Institutions</u> (Baltimore), 1893, p. 170.

[2] For an excellent account of the picturesque life that developed along the rivers, see Hulbert Footner, <u>Rivers of the Eastern Shore</u> (New York), 1944.

[3] See Charles J. Truitt, <u>Historic Salisbury Maryland</u> (New York), 1932, p. 73.

[4] Doris Maslin Cohn, "The Haynie Letters," <u>Maryland Historical Magazine</u>, vol 26, June, 1941, p.2. The author (a native of Princess Anne) is a great-great-great-granddaughter of Ezekiel Haynie, whose father, Richard, was a native of England.

[5] Clayton Torrence, <u>Old Somerset on the Eastern Shore of Maryland</u> (Richmond), 1935, p.7.

[6] A list of the settlers for Somerset is found in Torrence, <u>op. cit.</u>, pp. 464-467.

[7] Earle Swepson, <u>Maryland's Colonial Eastern Shore</u> (Baltimore), 1916, p. 422.

[8] Torrence, op cit., pp. 75-77.

[9] Land Records of Somerset County, Liber K, pp. 145, 146. Hereafter only the Liber reference is given.

[10] Two brothers, Wilson and William Heath, antecedents of Abraham Heath, were owners of the two tracts in 1765. See Liber D, pp. 11, 21.

[11] Liber K, p. 145, 146.

[12] Cohn, <u>op. cit.</u>, p.202.

[13] Liber J.P., vol. 5, p. 167-8.

[14] Liber J.P., vol. 5, p. 167-8.

[15] See Chancery Docket, L.W. 1866-1867, p. 14. The case is recorded in Chancery Records, Liber L.W., vol. 4, p. 672.

[16] Liber 11, p. 659.

[17] Liber 11, p. 622-3.

[18] Liber 12, p. 473-474.

[19] Liber S.C.L., vol. 5, p. 463.

[20] Liber H.F.L., vol. 4, pp. 287, 290.

21 Liber H.F.L., vol. 8, pp. 586-7.

[22] Liber S.F.D., vol. 46, p. 290; Liber O.T.B., vol. 43, p. 455; Liber S.F.D., vol. 55, pp. 426-426.

[23] Liber 135, p. 431. The Powell family bought the land from William T. Allen and wife of Wicomico County on December 5, 1908. Liber S.T.D., vol. 50, p. 2.

[24] Liber 141, p. 526. Plans were being made for the erection of a Negro high school on this site in the summer of 1950.

[25] Liber W.J.S., vol. 92, p. 63.

[26] Liber J.M.T., vol. 110, p. 323.

CHAPTER THREE

THE FOUNDING OF AN ACADEMY

(Figure 3.1)
Olney - the first building on the campus of the University of
Maryland Eastern Shore, then known as the Delaware Conference
Academy. The sketch appeared in Bernard C. Steiner's,
History of Education in Maryland, 1894.

Introduction

The land at the head streams of the Manokin, originally settled by the Waters, Manloves, Hobbs, and Heaths was subsequently owned by the Haynie family, James U. Dennis, Louis W. Morris, Beulah Hirst, Aaron D. Woodruff, and finally John A. B. Wilson. It was Wilson who sold the property to the Centenary Biblical Institute. Olney and sixteen acres, part of the original land known as "Deep Still," became the first campus of the University of Maryland Eastern Shore, then a branch of the Centenary Biblical Institute.

The school in Olney was predominantly a Methodist enterprise, because Methodists recognized the need for the education of the Negro when public

28

education in the State was still in its infancy. Specifically, the opening of Olney for purposes of Negro education may be traced to the influences of the Centenary Biblical Institute, the Delaware Conference of the Methodist Episcopal Church, and the individual efforts of Joseph R. Waters and John A. B. Wilson, both Methodist ministers on the Shore.

The Centenary Biblical Institute

Considering the matter of relieving heavy enrollment at the Centenary Biblical Institute by establishing a school in the jurisdiction of the Delaware Conference, the trustees agreed that the proposed school would be called the "Delaware Conference Academy" at a meeting of the board on June 9, 1886. This date is significant because it shows that the trustees were thinking of a new school but had no idea of where the school would be located. Ironically three days after this date, Wilson contracted to buy Olney for his own private purposes. Nothing is found in the records to indicate a decision of the trustees to establish a "Delaware Conference Academy, but the trustees gave the school in Olney its first name along with financial support."[1]

The Delaware Conference

Alert to the possibility of establishing a school within the jurisdiction of the Delaware Conference and growing in membership since its beginning in 1864, the Conference regarded the education of the Negro as one of its principal objectives. It supported the cause of education, primarily through the Institute, to the limits of its financial resources.

Several committees of the Conference served as steering agencies for educational policies and for the procurement of funds and as a liaison between the Conference and the Institute. One such agency was the Educational Society, whose chief concern was the procurement of money for Freedmen's Aid.[2] Another agency was the Standing Committee on Education, one of the several regular committees on which members were rotated at each conference. Its functions were not clearly defined; its services were token. Other agencies on education were the Freedmen's Aid Committee, the Endowment Committee, and the Committee on Female College. Shortly after the school opened in Olney, the Conference set up a committee on the Delaware Conference Academy, which later became the Advisory Board of Princess Anne Academy.

The minutes, usually carefully written and published, were silent on any initial move or effort by the Delaware Conference to set up a school in Princess Anne. The only reference ever made for the establishment of a school anywhere in the Conference is found in a committee report printed in the minutes of 1886. The report was made at the Conference held on May 6-11 at the Bainbridge Street Church in Philadelphia. Along with the struggle of women for equal rights in education on a nationwide level, the Committee on Female College, appointed by Bishop Foster to consider the necessity of founding an institution and to look for a site on which to build, indicated that Princess Anne, Maryland rather than Pocomoke City, Maryland was considered as a proposed site. [3]

Later at a committee meeting in Dover, Delaware, Princess Anne was dropped from consideration, but Pocomoke City was still a possibility because of the strong inducements of aid proffered by the citizens of that section of the state of Maryland. The committee felt that such an institution should be located in or near some of the large centers of population or in some place easily accessible. To understand the urgency in this task, one must take into consideration that originally the Centenary Biblical Institute was founded solely for the education of young men as preachers and teachers and not for females. Therefore, the contemplated female college existed only in name and on paper. The idea of setting up such a school in Princess Anne was abandoned by the committee that actually ceased to exist when women were permitted to attend the Institute. The discussion of the female college at the Conference, however, left false echoes and hearsay that the school in Olney first began as a school for girls.

As an official body, the Delaware Conference did nothing to direct the course of events that led to the opening of the school that first bore its name. John H. Nutter, who "attended the Conference every year without being absent or tardy for sixty-one years," recalled that the question of setting up the school in Princess Anne did not originate with the Delaware Conference.[4] On the other hand, there is no doubt that the Conference promoted and supported the school after its opening in Olney. Certainly, one of the members of the Conference, Joseph R. Waters, acting on his own initiative, put forth an effort to found a school in Princess Anne.

Joseph R. Waters

It has been stated that Joseph R. Waters, a Negro, was the founder of the school first held in Olney and that his idea was responsible for the beginning of the school.[5] There is much to be said for this point of view, for in the light of history, Waters stands out as one of the first figures in the early days of the school and as one whose interest in Negro education bordered on the margin of passion. Yet it is difficult to conclude, upon examination of available evidence, that Waters was solely responsible for the idea and promotion of the school. He and John A. B. Wilson may be regarded as co-founders.

Joseph Robert Waters was a product of the Eastern Shore. He was born in Fairmount, Maryland, not more than fifteen miles from the site of Olney, on May 8, 1856. Little is known about his early life, but tradition has indicated that he was somewhat self-made and that his early education was obtained almost wholly from a white tutor, perhaps Judge Thomas A. Spence of Snow Hill, Maryland.[6] As a youth, Waters no doubt attended such schools as the area provided for Negroes and experienced the hardships that confronted most Negro children who grew up in the atmosphere of Civil War and Reconstruction.

(Figure 3.2)
Joseph R. Waters

He became a member of the Delaware Conference at the age of twenty-two and served actively and conscientiously with the Conference for sixty-three years. For an additional four years of his life, though inactive, his name appeared on the Conference roster.[7] Additionally, it has been reported that Waters missed only one roll call at the Conference in sixty-six years. Waters served twenty years as a minister, two appointments as district superintendent, and two appointments as field secretary of the Conference Claimants Fund.[8] Moreover, his name appeared frequently on various committees of the Conference. He and A. R. Shockley, another prominent member of the Conference, together with

J. H. Scott and T. B. Chamberlain, laymen, made up a committee to examine and to visit the Institute in 1886.[9] It is highly probable that his work on these committees revealed to him more clearly the need of a school to relieve the overcrowded conditions of the Institute in Baltimore.

Four months before the Academy in Olney was opened, Waters was appointed by the Conference as minister to Princess Anne to take charge of this "vigorous station" that ranked high in the appointments of the Salisbury District. Negro Methodists of Princess Anne were making plans to build a new brick church, costing about $4,500,[10] and the appointment of Waters to this charge was an indication of the confidence that the Conference placed in him. He came to the charge in Princess Anne in 1886, and was on hand in the summer to influence the opening of the Academy for Negroes.

The cornerstone of the new church was laid on September 19, 1886, a few days after the Academy opened. It was laid under the supervision of Waters, who two years earlier was instrumental in purchasing the site. Ironically, that very site was the former location of the County jail and of a slave auction block that was located less than one-half mile from the site of Olney.[11]

(Figure 3.21)
Metropolitan United Methodist Church

From the earliest days, there were close ties between the church and the Academy. Both frequently cooperated in directing the social and cultural life of the community. In subsequent years, graduation exercises of the Academy were held at the church; and conversely, student attendance was mandatory for church services.

Apparently Joseph R. Waters, described as being

32

robust in physical stature, a well-proportioned man about six-feet-three-inches in height, and very much alert, was a remarkable man. Self-educated and strong in moral character, he was eager to help Negro youth receive an education. Forceful and vigorous as a speaker, he enjoyed robust health most of his long life, never having a permanent tooth extracted until he passed the age of seventy. Even at ninety, he could shave himself with an old-fashioned straight razor, which he carried as an heirloom.

He visited the school on numerous occasions after its opening and never seemed to tire of relating its founding. No doubt the role he himself played grew larger and larger in his mind as the years passed. On his last visit to the school in October 1944, he attended a Founders' Day observance. Richard Thomas, a faculty member present at the event, said that he opened the door of Reverend Waters's car and escorted him to a room in the old Practice House (Olney). The next day Waters returned to speak in the gymnasium of Kiah Hall. According to Thomas, Waters was cautioned by his doctors to speak for only ten minutes; but with his heart in his subject and his love for the school, his powerful baritone voice was heard by his listeners for at least a half-hour.

Joseph Waters spent his last days with relatives at Lawnside, New Jersey, where he died on July 29, 1946. He was buried in Fairmount, the village of his birth. For many years, a picture of his likeness was displayed on the walls of the school's library until somehow the picture was lost. It was the only likeness or remembrance that the school ever displayed of Waters, who ironically remembered the school throughout his long life.

John Alfred Banum Wilson

John Alfred Banum Wilson was eight years older than Waters. He was born on the Eastern Shore in Milton, Delaware, on September 14, 1848. Wilson attended

(Figure 3.3)
John Alfred Banum Wilson

school in Milton, but as a boy of twelve withdrew to go to sea with his father, John P. Wilson, a captain of sea-going vessels. At the age of nineteen, he had learned enough about seamanship from his father to hold the rank of first mate.[12] While at sea, Wilson educated himself from a small library that he carried in a sea chest, studying Greek and Latin in his cabin in order to fill the wide gaps in his formal education.[13] He became a member of the Wilmington, Delaware Conference in 1871, the same year of his marriage to Mary Jefferson. During his life, he distinguished himself as an outstanding lecturer, minister, and temperance worker. Besides being a cofounder of the school, he was likewise a cofounder of the town of Parksley, Virginia.[14]

At the age of eighteen, John Wilson was converted to Methodism, and at twenty he became a circuit minister in Sussex County, Delaware. Later, he served on the Eastern Shore of Maryland and became a presiding elder of the Salisbury District in 1882 and of the Dover District in 1886. From 1892 to 1896, he was minister of the Eighteenth Street Church in New York City. From there, he served the First Church in Los Angeles for two years, then to the Howard Street Church in San Francisco, and finally to Grass Valley, California where he died on April 30, 1906.[15]

Like Joseph Waters, Wilson was largely a self-made man intensely interested in the work of Methodism. At the forefront of the reform movements of his day, Wilson championed the cause of prohibition and the rights of women and Negroes at a time when it was both unpopular and unsafe to support these reforms. For years he was a most prominent figure, the storm center of religious, philanthropic, and temperance work on the peninsula of Delaware, Maryland, and Virginia.[16] Perhaps he influenced one of his sons, Clarence True (1872-1939), to begin a distinguished career in temperance work.[17] Another son, Hermon, became a physician. One writer gives the following tribute to Wilson:

> Dr. Wilson is endowed with an iron frame, a clear head, a warm loving heart and an earnest purpose. As a preacher he is clear, logical, thoughtful, intensely earnest, magnetic, and at times wonderfully eloquent. In character, unsullied; in spirit, charitable; in manners, suave; in courage, indomitable; in resolution, firm; in labors, abundant; never saying go, but come; himself always lifting the heavier end and doing the lion's share; sensitive by nature to any slight or any injustice done himself

or others; always defending himself; a man of such personality that no one will fail to be conscious of his presence, and those who are aggressive will rejoice in it and as naturally cluster around him as iron filings will cling to a magnet. In short, Dr. Wilson is a born leader and is so recognized by his friends and opposed by his foes. It may be further added that he is the soul of honor. He is open, free and confiding - at times, too much so for his own good. He is the friend of the oppressed everywhere, white or colored. He is a firm believer in the temperance cause and has often spoken in no uncertain language upon this great question. It was through his efforts that the Delaware Conference Academy, a colored institution, was founded at Princess Anne, Maryland; and in honor of him, the Delaware Conference has placed his life-size portrait upon the walls of that institution.[18]

John Wilson seemed to have been an uncompromising prohibitionist, an early organizer of the Prohibition Party in Delaware and Maryland, and an antisaloon campaigner. On one occasion while campaigning against saloons in 1874 near his native home in Leipsic, Delaware, he was attacked while in the company of an officer as they entered a bar room. Wilson was struck across the head with a ten-pound weight and bore the marks of the attack throughout his life.

At other times, Wilson was assailed. A few weeks after a meeting of Maryland's Prohibition Society, the Baltimore Sun (March 17, 1892) reported an article from Wilmington entitled *PENINSULA METHODISTS: Presiding Elder Wilson's Case at Grace Church*. The writer of this article reports that the Conference was unique in the history of Methodism inasmuch as Wilson's case clearly divided the Conference sharply into two factions, either for or against Wilson. One and one-half columns were reported on the Conference with about half of this space given to Wilson's case. The opposing faction accused him of corrupt administration and political hypocrisy. Friends said that Wilson's enemies were unduly jealous of his success and feared reprisals from Republicans; they cited Wilson's impressive and unprecedented record of church construction, membership, and collections. Wilson was completely exonerated of charges of corruption by a vote of sixty-one to fifty-seven, as the Conference voted tensely and silently.[19] No doubt Wilson's enemies, disliking his politics or success, had attacked but failed to damage his reputation. Though it is not definitely known, the close exoneration was a Pyrrhic victory for Wilson, who shortly afterwards went to New York and later to the Pacific Coast, never returning to the Shore he knew and loved so well.

Wilson was a progressive in the matter of Negro-white relations. Many Negroes of the Shore held him in high esteem; whereas on the other hand, many Whites deplored his friendly disposition toward Negroes. John H. Nutter recalled that Wilson was a "Christian man and a friend of the Colored people."[20] Hermon F. Wilson, John Wilson's son, recalled that his family was practically ostracized by Whites of Princess Anne because of his father's friendly relations with Negroes, for the friendship of Whites with Negroes was forbidden by the codes of white superiority. During this time when the social code placed a strong taboo upon shaking hands or eating with Negroes as well as upon referring to Negroes with ordinary titles of courtesy such as "Mr." or "Mrs.," Wilson was capable of ignoring such deep-seated prejudices.[21]

Furthermore his relations with Joseph Waters were cordial, a fact that was influenced by mutual interest in Methodism, prohibition, and education. It is not definitely known, but it is probable that Waters and Wilson first met in the early 1880s when John Wilson was presiding elder of the Salisbury District (1882-86). Certainly, they saw a great deal of each other during the summer of 1886 when both were in Princess Anne. By July, Waters and Wilson were in agreement that a school for Negroes should be set up in Princess Anne or in the vicinity. Perhaps it was Waters who first mentioned the question of a site to Wilson.[22]

At first, their efforts to find a suitable site and building were of little avail. It is thought that one of the places considered was the old site of the Washington Academy, located approximately 1 ½ miles south of Princess Anne on the road to Pocomoke City. It was decided that the old building there was so dilapidated that an attempt at restoration would be impractical.[23] Washington Academy had been a white school and was called the School on Back Creek from 1767 to 1795. Martin Luther, a signer of the Declaration of Independence, taught there. After a fire in 1795, the school was moved into a large brick building in 1800 near Jones Creek and renamed Washington Academy in honor of the nation's first president. The academy was abandoned after the Civil War, but the brick structure remained standing, unsuitable for habitation. Both men knew that the trustees of the Institute would be reluctant to risk funds in reconstructing a project of this sort. In 1891, Washington Academy's bricks were used in the construction of a public school in Princess Anne. In 1939, some of the same bricks were used again in the construction of the Washington High School. Eventually Waters and Wilson agreed that Olney, recently purchased by the Wilsons with the idea that it would become a permanent home for the family, should become the home of the proposed school. They concluded correctly that the trustees would endorse and support the establishment of the Delaware Conference Academy in Olney.

It is not likely that the Wilsons ever lived in Olney. Furthermore, the Wilsons had some misgivings as to the risk of their investment. In the first place, Wilson was appointed presiding elder of the Dover District, further to the north, in the same year that he and his wife contracted to buy Olney. In the second place there was some doubt that Olney, a comparatively large dwelling, could be maintained and purchased on the small salary paid to ministers of that day. In the third place, John Wilson's attitude toward Negroes and Negro education was such that he needed few reasons or suggestions, even with Waters' persuasion, to dispose of Olney for purposes of Negro education. Wilson knew the pattern of race relations in Princess Anne and vicinity, having himself seen how aloof Whites treated his family. Wilson knew that unless he disposed of the property, the mores of the community would have prevented or delayed the sale of Olney to Negroes. Indeed, few Whites of the community sanctioned Wilson's sale of Olney and "kicked up quite a stir" when they learned of the transaction.[24] There is no evidence to show, however, that there were organized efforts to prevent the sale or occupancy, perhaps only gossip and grumblings. Certainly, the sale did not add to Wilson's popularity among Whites.

Once the decision to sell Olney was made, the trustees of the Institute were notified. Accordingly, John F. Goucher, avid financial supporter of Negro education, and W. Maslin Frysinger, head of the Centenary Biblical Institute in Baltimore, joined Waters and Wilson in Princess Anne and examined the property.[25] On August 24, 1886, Wilson and his wife formally deeded Olney and sixteen acres to the Centenary Biblical Institute on terms similar to those that Richard C. Dale had granted to the Wilsons on June 12.[26] Goucher personally paid Wilson $500, the amount Wilson had actually invested when he agreed to buy the property from Dale. Goucher did not ask the trustees to reimburse him for this amount. It was simply one of the many donations that he generously made for the cause of Negro education.[27]

A Missed Opportunity

John Henry Nutter was offered the position as principal of the school to be held in Olney. At the time, Nutter was serving as a Methodist minister in the hamlet of Royal Oak, Maryland and was unaware that there was to be a Negro school in Princess Anne. His Presiding Elder, Walter J. Parker, assured him that the Institute was opening a new school in Princess Anne in addition to reopening the old building on Saratoga Street in Baltimore. Nutter could choose either school, and he selected the school in Baltimore. Unfortunately, he was failing in health and for this reason was thinking of resigning from the ministry. Nutter thought that the industrial work of the proposed school in Princess Anne would further impair his health. His decision, made without benefit of the hindsight of history, precluded his being the first head of the school that became the University of Maryland Eastern Shore. Still Nutter's life illuminated the story of the education of the Negro in Maryland.

Born near the village of Allen in Somerset County in 1857, he was a product of the Eastern Shore. His mother, Sally Jane Nutter, was a free woman; but his father, Sampson Cotterman, was a slave. Nutter was taught to read by his mother before he began his formal education. Therefore, when he first attended school as a boy of twelve, he was better qualified than most of his schoolmates. Later, Nutter recalled hesitantly that the school was a "government" school. Certainly, his early education reflects something of the nature of Negro education in Somerset County during Reconstruction.

The "government" school was held in a frame church located a "piece" out of Princess Anne. In fact, Nutter walked to and from school, a round trip of about eight or ten miles. Often puddles of water settled on the dirt road after a rain. When the road was iced over in winter, Nutter recalled that he would break the ice and wade through, shuddering from the freezing cold. Upon reaching the other side of a puddle, he would remove his boots, pour out the water, wring out his cotton stockings, and continue to school. He would then arrive at a school that was crowded, cold, and filled with smoke. "I don't know," he often said, "I guess I'm feeling some of the effects of it now."

Nutter's "fessors" had a "head" and a "foot" to the class, frequently lining up the students beside a wall for reading and spelling "matches." After having become the head of his classes in the lower grades, Nutter once

38

competed for honors in the highest class. A girl held the position for some time, but on one occasion she failed to spell a word correctly. When Nutter spelled the word, the teacher told him to take his place at the head of the class. Nutter was reluctant, being too shy to pass ahead of the girl. As the teacher insisted, however, he unwillingly gave in and, like Whittier's schoolboy, felt sorry for the girl whom he had outspelled.

Nutter became a teacher in the Mt. Vernon District of Somerset County at the age of seventeen, an age concealed from the local school superintendent who probably would not have employed a youngster in his teens. A few years later, Nutter went to the Institute in Baltimore where he and a classmate were the only two graduates of J. Emory Round's first class of 1877. Upon graduation, he went into the ministry, devoting most of his long life to the cause of Methodism. At one time, he was minister at the Metropolitan Church in Princess Anne, his "most critical experience," and presiding elder of the Salisbury District. On numerous occasions he addressed students and faculty either at the Church or on the campus. As a leader in the Delaware Conference, he was proud of the Academy and remembered it warmly.

Although he was reared in the atmosphere of Reconstruction, he grew to maturity and old age at peace with the times in which he lived. Before his death in the summer of 1949, he enjoyed excellent physical and mental health. His speech was clear, his voice was strong and steady, his full set of natural teeth was well-preserved, and his walk was unassisted. He could quote the Bible at length and converse intelligently about the latest topics in the morning newspaper. At his home in Pocomoke, 509 Bonneville Avenue, a tribute was hanging on the walls at the time of his death.

In Honor of
JOHN HENRY NUTTER '77

The Oldest and Best Beloved Alumnus
In whose acclaim the loftiest voices vie;
The proud, we are, to make his praise our cry.
Alumni Association of Morgan State College
May 30, 1942 [28]

The Centenary Biblical Institute Become Morgan College

Surviving under new names, the original Centenary Biblical Institute became Morgan College. With two branches, a growing enrollment, an ambitious curriculum, and a conscientious leadership, the trustees of the Institute sought to gain legal recognition of the school's new collegiate standing. Accordingly, they applied to the Assembly of Maryland to amend the old charter of 1867. The bill to amend originated in the House of Delegates and was reported favorably from the Committee on Corporations on Friday, March 13, 1890, becoming law on April 3. The name of the Institute was then legally changed to Morgan College in honor of Lyttleton F. Morgan, president of the board of trustees, who previously made substantial donations to the school.

The powers granted to the newly created Morgan College were identical to those of the newly incorporated Women's College of Baltimore at the same session of the Assembly. Goucher, who sponsored the establishment of Women's College, was largely responsible for the action on reincorporation. The old charter did not recognize the school as a college. The amended charter gave recognition along with powers to grant degrees:

> To admit students to the said College who shall merit the distinction of the degree of doctor of laws or of bachelor or master of arts; to grant to students in such college such certificate of proficiency and attainments in any special study as the said college may see proper to confer, and to grant the honorary degrees of doctor of laws, master of arts or such other degrees.[29]

This law was the first of its kind in the history of Maryland in regard to the collegiate education of the Negro. The charter was again amended in 1900, giving the school the power to maintain auxiliary schools and to acquire property. Thus, the branches that were established in 1886 were legally but tardily recognized. Provisions were likewise made in the new charter of 1900 for the rotation of members of the Board of Trustees. The Institute's new "collegiate" status is shown in the following duplicated advertisement of 1906.

The Institute's change of name or powers, however, was not accompanied by any great change in the method of administration, the nature and scope of the curriculum, the geographical background of students, or problems of the budget. For many years after the incorporation of 1890, the

40

MORGAN COLLEGE
Conducts
Collegiate, Biblical, Normal and Academic courses in Baltimore.
Rev. C.E. YOUNG, M.A., Dean,
Normal, Academic, Industrial courses at Princess Anne, MD.
FRANK TRIGG, M.A., Principal
Normal, Academic and Industrial courses in Lynchburg, VA.
REV. GEORGE E. STEPHENS, Principal

These courses are thorough and practical. Specialists are provided for the technical courses. Twenty-three teachers are employed in the various departments. It is a safe school in which to place young men and women.

Fifty industrial scholarships are distributed at the end of each school year among the students of Princess Anne Academy who have been faithful in attendance and in all duties, promptly met their bills, and have been satisfactory in conduct during the year. The amount of each scholarship is the same as the tuition paid.

For information, address the head of each school.
Send remittance to:
Hon. ALCAEUS HOOPER, Treasurer, 10 South Street, Baltimore, Md.
J.O. Spencer, President. [30]

influence of Methodism—its discipline, support, endowment, and leadership —was the greatest single factor in the history of Morgan College and in the higher education of the Negro in Maryland. No question in regard to control of the parent body, Morgan College, arose as long as Methodists were privately but laboriously supporting the school. The advent of federal aid through the school's branch in Princess Anne under the Morrill Act of 1890, however, brought into focus, chiefly after the turn of the century, the question of control of an institution publicly-supported, privately-owned, yet founded and administered by Methodists. Further, the coming of public and federal aid to Morgan College, through its branch in Princess Anne, posed another question in regard to the responsibilities of the State toward a class of its citizens. An exploration of these questions reveals much of the subsequent story of the higher education of the Negro in Maryland.

ENDNOTES

CHAPTER 3

[1] See Minutes, 1885, p. 35.

[2] Minutes, 1884, p. 30.

[3] Minutes, 1886, pp. 37-38.

[4] Nutter, Interview, op. cit.

[5] Daniel L. Ridout, "His Idea Started a College," The Central Christian Advocate, March 29, 1945. An interview with Lilly Waters Bunday, a daughter of Waters, on March 15, 1949, Philadelphia, likewise, supported this view.

[6] Lilly Waters Bunday, Interview, op. cit.

[7] For the circuits he served, see Minutes, 1948, p. 624.

[8] Ridout, op. cit.

[9] Minutes, 1885, p. 27.

[10] Ibid., p. 26.

[11] See "A Brief History of the Metropolitan Methodist Church," a program of the 62nd anniversary, September 26 - October 3, 1948, compiled and written by Horatio Jones, an instructor at the school since 1944.

[12] Perhaps he was a mate at the age of seventeen. See Standard Encyclopedia of the Alcohol Problem (Westerville, Ohio), 1930, vol. 6, pp. 2860-1, which contains a short biographical sketch.

[13] Letter from one of his sons, Hermon F. Wilson, San Francisco, California, dated April 13, 1949.

[14] Clark, op cit., vol. 2, p. 615.

[15] The dates for Wilson's birth and death are those given by his son. The dates given by the Standard Encyclopedia of the Alcohol Problem are September 30, 1848 and April 30, 1905.

[16] Pamphlet loaned by Hermon F. Wilson announcing his father as a lecturer for 1895-1896.

[17] Clarence True Wilson became internationally known as the founder of the Methodist Church Temperance Board. He died on February 16, 1939 at the Good Samaritan Hospital in Portland, Oregon. See the Salisbury Times, February 17, 1939.

[18] A writer in the Dover Index (Delaware) as quoted in pamphlet cited above.

[19] Sun, March 19, 1892.

[20] Nutter, Interview, op. cit.

[21] Dover Index, March 31, 1892, quoted in pamphlet, op. cit.

[22] Ridout, op. cit.

[23] Interview, Lilly Waters Bunday, op. cit. See Maryland: A Guide to the Old Line State (New York), 1940, p. 561.

[24] Interview with James I. Dennis, one of the first students, Princess Anne, October 9, 1948.

[25] Letter, Hermon F. Wilson, op. cit.

[26] Liber H.F.L., vol. 4, p. 309. The complete deed is given in Appendix C.

[27] The Trustees acknowledged Goucher's donation at their next meeting on February 4, 1887. See the Minutes of Proceedings for this date.

[28] From the records of Dr. W. Augustus Low, past historian, University of Maryland Eastern Shore.

[29] From the records of Dr. W. Augustus Low, past historian, University of Maryland Eastern Shore.

[30] From the records of Dr. W. Augustus Low, past historian, University of Maryland Eastern Shore.

CHAPTER FOUR

EARLY YEARS
1886-1936

(Figure 4.1)
Early years at the University of Maryland Eastern Shore.
Olney is at the center of the picture

Benjamin Oliver Bird (1886-1897)

Born on August 11, 1853[1] not far from Harper's Ferry in Loudoun County, Virginia, Benjamin Oliver Bird, an alumnus of the Centenary Biblical Institute, became the first head of the Academy in Princess Anne at thirty-three years old. From boyhood, he could recall the excitement of John Brown's Raid *(*1859*)* and the activities of Union and Confederate armies that followed several years later. His father, Samuel Bird, died when Benjamin was a child; and his mother, Annie, remarried and moved near Gettysburg, Pennsylvania.

Bird attended school only briefly—if at all—during his boyhood. For lack of schools rather than for lack of ability, he was fourteen years old before he learned the alphabet.[2] Having himself learned to read and to write, as a young man he taught others in Rockingham County, Virginia. It was probably

44

(Figure 4.2)
Benjamin Oliver Bird

while here that he decided to further his education at the Centenary Biblical Institute, which he entered in 1877, the year of Nutter's graduation. He was awarded a certificate in normal studies the following year. J. Emory Round took more than a passing interest in Bird, who was then a young man of twenty-four, intelligent, conscientious, and eager to learn. He encouraged Bird to take further courses in theology. When the regular teaching staff was increased, Bird was rewarded with a teaching position in the lower grades, which later grew into the Preparatory Department. Then on September 29, 1880, he married the former Portia E. Lovett, who was a former student at Storer College located at Harper's Ferry, West Virginia. Nine children were born from their marriage, and several became students at the Academy while their father was principal.

Bird left Baltimore for Princess Anne in the summer of 1886. It is likely that he purchased second-class tickets from the Maryland Steamboat Company on Light Street; and with his wife and two children, Irma and Oliver, he boarded the steamer Enoch Pratt on one afternoon at approximately five o'clock.[3] The steamer carried him and his family to Deal Island, where they transferred to a local river steamer that sailed up the Manokin to the wharf in Princess Anne, located near a section called "Bowling Hill." When the Birds arrived the next morning, tired and sooty from their overnight trip, no citizens were on hand to extend a welcome and hospitality. A barefooted Negro lad of fourteen named Joseph Hayman was at the docks and courteously greeted the "professor" and his family. He escorted them to the home of the Dennis family, where they were temporarily lodged.[4] Joseph Hayman, at such a tender age, could not have known that his life would be greatly influenced by the man, Bird. It would be an influence that would change lives in his family and in many others for generations.

Bird's first visit to Olney must have been disheartening, for Olney was a far cry from the commodious Institute he left behind in Baltimore. Once an elegant colonial structure, Olney was then deserted and had been used as a granary.[5] Trees, weeds, and tall grass were all around the building; inside the walls were beginning to crumble. There were several large cedars older than Olney left standing that gave some dignity to the site. Consequently, one of the first problems that faced Bird was to refurbish Olney in order to accommodate his family and the new students of the Academy. He began the task by renovating one room for himself and family. Soon students arrived, and Bird promptly put them to work either renovating the building or clearing the land.[6]

On September 13, 1886, the Academy opened in Olney with an enrollment of approximately nine students that before the year ended grew to 37 enrollees of whom at least 13 were girls. All except one of the students, a resident of New Jersey, came principally from Maryland's Eastern Shore. In fact, Somerset County supplied the vast majority of the students, who bore several of the area's oldest family names — Waters, Dennis, Gale, Maddox, and Tilghman. In Olney, eight boys and two girls were housed.[7] Extant records show neither the opening date nor the names of the first enrollees. An announcement on page 25 of the July 1925 edition of the <u>Morgan College Bulletin</u> states that there was an enrollment of 70 students. According to Hampton T. Johnson, one of the first students and a Methodist minister residing in Elkton, Maryland, in December 1948, the resident students were P. B. Worrick, J. P. Long, W. J. Holland, H.T. Johnson, A. D. Scot, A. L. Martin, W. E. Waters, O.W. Bird, Minnie G. Lovett, and Cora A. Waters. Nonresident students were Emily J. King, Mamie E. King, N. D. King, Daniel King, Mamie E. Gale, I. B. J. Dennis, Susie Dennis, George Mamer, William Johnson, Fred Maddox, Marie Maddox, Julia Bolden, Amie Whitelock, Martha Deal, George Morris, Henry Morris, John Morris, James Anderson, Sarah Anderson, Edward Tilghman, Annie Tilghman, Angeline Collins, Thomas Dennis, Nathanael Nutter, James I. Dennis, and Henry J. Gale.

During the first year Bird, assisted by his wife and Jacob C. Dunn, carried on courageously despite the inadequate income, unpaid salaries, and lack of enthusiasm among many people about the venture at Olney.[8] The exact nature of the instructional work is unknown because no early records of the Academy are in existence. Nevertheless, it may be gathered from interviews with some of the first students that Bird taught such subjects as mathematics, physiology, geometry, and algebra; his wife taught geography, history, and elocution or public speaking; and the last of the dynamic trio, Dunn, taught grammar and rhetoric. It is highly likely that a great deal of the instruction was of a religious nature.

Little is known about Dunn. It is known, however, that he taught intermittently at the Academy for about ten years.[9] He was generally well dressed and inclined to be somewhat flamboyant as a speaker. When he left the Academy, he devoted his time primarily to the ministry, becoming a statistical secretary of the Delaware Conference of the Methodist Episcopal Church to which he was admitted in 1895. His father was Daniel R. Dunn, a native of Queen Anne's County, Maryland and likewise a minister of the Delaware Conference. His mother was the former Harriet E. Heath, who married Daniel on January 3, 1865. Jacob died in 1915 at Orange, New Jersey, two years before his father.[10] He had lived for a time at 98 Hickory Street in Orange, New Jersey.

Academics

Instruction at the Academy was carried on at a level higher than that of the local county schools, a fact that one of the teachers in Somerset County, Emily J. King, considered when she enrolled in the first class. Yet, by contemporary standards, the Academy was basically an elementary institution during the early years of Bird's administration. During Bird's term of office, however, the patterns of Academy life, in both the curriculum and the administration, were solidly laid. The curriculum was eventually patterned after that of the Institute in Baltimore, consisting of three divisions: academic (i.e., theological), normal, and preparatory. In addition, instruction in so-called industrial subjects was offered during Bird's tenure. Thus, the course of study embraced the liberal arts as well as teacher training and industrial education. Diplomas were granted for the completion of instruction in the first two categories only, but students were required to take part in some phase of practical or manual work for several hours of each school week. Usually, one and one-half hours daily and a half-day on Saturdays were assigned to work in the trades.[11] After the turn of the century, the number of hours per day for industrial work was increased to two or three.

The greatest emphasis in instructional work was placed upon the liberal arts, a policy in vogue at the Institute and at most Negro schools of the period. This policy was strongly manifested throughout the entire history of the school.

During the first five years, the length of the course varied from one to three years, consisting of a "first class," "a middle class," and "a third class." By the time of Bird's death, the length of the course was increased. In addition to the preparatory work (one year), a normal course of two years and an academic course of one year were added.

Bird's administration coincided with a national stimulus to educate the Negro in mechanic arts and industrial education. It is not surprising, then, that the industrial program of the Academy was artificially grafted onto a curriculum that was fundamentally intended as preparation for the liberal arts. Funds for the industrial education of the Negro could be more readily obtained when other approaches were closed. Hampton and Tuskegee Institutes were the great symbols, and the former sent its graduates to the Academy to spread the idea. Yet though industrial education came to the Academy during Bird's term, it began as a stepchild of the curriculum.

The instruction was varied. Boys were taught shoemaking, carpentry, blacksmithing, tailoring and agriculture while girls were taught dressmaking, cooking, and sewing. Bird reported in 1891 that there were six students in blacksmithing, five in bricklaying, five in carpentry, nine in shoemaking, and seven in tailoring.[12] Additionally, reports show that Joseph N. Gibbons taught blacksmithing; George E. Lloyd, bricklaying; Charles H. Hayman, carpentry; John W. Gillett, shoemaking; and William B. Jones, tailoring. Reporting on the campus on designated days, instructors in the trades during the early years were generally local residents with more practical than formal training.[13]

During Bird's term, the number of students increased rapidly, and nearly approached the highest level for any year before 1947. The total enrollment for 1891 consisted of 85 students, 54 of whom were males ranging from the ages of eight to 33. Of this number, 42 were regular boarders on the campus;[14] and as in subsequent years, the vast majority of the students came from the Eastern Shore of Maryland. Two years later in 1893, there was an enrollment of 101 students of whom 55 were males: 76 from Maryland, nine from Delaware, six from Pennsylvania, 4 from New Jersey, two from New York, two from Virginia, and two from Bermuda.

These students were enrolled in three departments, namely the Classical (i.e. academic), Normal, and Preparatory Departments. In the Classical Department, six students were enrolled, including Uriel L. Blake and John Hodges of Wilmington, Delaware; David J. Hall of Fairmount; John Hubbard

48

and Walter J. Moore of Princess Anne; and Eleanor C. Pinkett of Salisbury. The nine students in the senior class of the Normal Department coming from families of Maryland's Eastern Shore were David H. Hargis of Crisfield, Joseph Hayman of Princess Anne, William Haywood of Snow Hill, George Hollis of Centreville, Edwin Jones of Mt. Vernon, Leah V. Lee of Royal Oak, Sarah E. Murphy of Still Pond (Kent County), Robert G. Waters of Port Deposit, and Martha V. Wright of Quantico. There were 23 students in the middle class of the Normal Department, including the well-known families of Dennis, Horsey, and Waters. Moreover, the first class of the Normal Department contained 34 students from the families of Ballard, Cottman, Dennis, Morris, Waters, and Joynes. For the year 1893, enrolled in the Preparatory Department were 28 students; and the seven who were related to the principal were Howard J. Bird and May S. Bird of Gettysburgh; Lorenzo Bird of Pittsburgh, Pennsylvania; and Oliver Bird, Irma Bird, Newton Bird, and Portia Bird of Princess Anne.

Graduation came during the last of May or the first of June, and the occasion was called Anniversary Day or Commencement Day. The first exercises, in reality an acknowledgment of attendance for the year, were held on June 3, 1887, nine months after the Academy was opened.[15] No copy of the program of the first exercises exists, and it is doubtful that one was ever made. In subsequent years, however, departments granted certificates, and programs were printed. It was not until 1891 that certificates were given to the graduates of the Normal Department to denote an equivalent of graduation from the higher studies of the Academy. F. J. Wagner, the president of Morgan who succeeded Frysinger, was the principal speaker at this occasion.[16]

During the early years, commencement was generally an affair that lasted for several hours. Addresses, orations, and declamations were the usual time-consuming essentials of the program with the addition of the leisurely awarding of various prizes. The eight graduates for 1892 were Washington I. Bean, Daniel J. Hall, Phillip B. Worrick, Uriel S. Blake, Charles E. Hodges, William E. Grant, Adam L. Martin, and Wilmore E. Waters, several of whom were among the first enrollees. In 1893, there were seven graduates, who were David H. Hargis, Sarah E. Murphy, Edwin Jones, John L. Parker, Leah V. Lee, Robert G. Waters, and Martha V. Wright.

Several of the graduates found teaching positions in Somerset County paying about two hundred dollars per year. During the commencement of 1893, David H. Hargis won a ten-dollar prize for giving the best oration in

English;[17] Sarah E. Murphy won the second prize of five dollars. Likewise, Estella L. Stansberry and Ella F. Horsey won prizes for the best declamations. Additional prizes were awarded for scholarship and deportment, and Martha V. Wright won $2.50 for excellence in household duties.[18]

Campus Life

In addition to an extensive academic program, students were occupied with other activities that reflected many attitudes peculiar to life in America at the turn of the century. Of course, student life and recreation were strongly disciplined by Methodism. Excluding Sundays, baseball was played by boys only on an open field to the east of the campus. There were also croquet and tennis. Athletic drills, required of both boys and girls, were generally held at one o'clock in the afternoon. Band, musical, or literary programs were generally held on Saturday nights. In fact a source of pride for both students and faculty was the band, being frequently called upon to give performance at special occasions.

Going to church and chapel were required rituals. Separated by sex, students formed a line on the campus and marched to the Metropolitan Church, which reserved a section for people from the Academy. Students and "professors" were in good attendance every Sunday causing the minister to perform at his optimal level.[19] Chapel was held several times weekly on the first floor of the boys' dormitory, which was located a few yards to the north of Olney. Those who attended the church or chapel invariably heard lectures or addresses by various ministers of the Delaware Conference or by the trustees and presidents of Morgan College. Occasionally, nationally known Negro figures, including Booker T. Washington, W. E. B. DuBois, and Madame C. J. Walker visited the Academy.

Financial Support

The Academy faced financial difficulties from the earliest days. It is thought that the first few months were particularly trying because funds from the Institute, including Bird's salary, were delayed. This immediate difficulty was soon overcome, and the Academy's chief source of income for the next five years came from the Institute and from student fees. After 1891, federal land-grant funds became the chief source of income, but control of expenditures was divided between institutions in Baltimore, College Park, and Princess Anne. The Academy did not completely overcome this three-way control until the 1930s. Never having its own board of control, the Academy's finances were handled by parties whose interests were not wholly centered in the affairs of the Academy in Princess Anne. More than any other head of the Academy, however, Bird exercised a high degree of independent action in regard to the control of finances, being given a high degree of autonomy by the trustees who appointed him. This was not the case with men who followed him. It was mainly because as the Academy acquired a more significant income through federal sources and later state aid, it became less independent in regard to allocations of its income.

Through payments to the Institute, the Delaware Conference contributed about one thousand dollars annually to the Academy during the early years. Such contributions amounted to more than half of the funds that the Institute invested annually in the current maintenance of the Academy. With the coming of federal aid after 1891, the total income of the Academy, excluding special donations, averaged between four and five thousand dollars annually, amounting to the latter sum by 1900.

Records show that with the exception of a few hundred dollars, all of the Academy's income came from federal funds from 1900 until World War I when state aid became a factor. Funds from the conferences were being overwhelmingly distributed for the use of Morgan, the parent school in Baltimore, at the same time that federal monies served as replacements and supplements for conference funds that were once allocated for the Academy in Princess Anne. Keeping spirited campaigns under way, Morgan College increased its income considerably beyond that of its branch in Princess Anne as the years passed.

Indeed, Methodists constantly carried on campaigns to raise funds for Morgan College and its branches. Once again such funds, given to the treasury of the trustees of Morgan College, were of little benefit to the Academy in Princess Anne. At the time that Methodists of the Delaware Conference were proud of their support to the Academy and closely guarded its control, few of them realized that the income from their campaigns was not being used specifically to support the Academy in Princess Anne after the turn of the century. The idea that they were aiding the Academy through the Institute, which gave the first support to the Delaware Conference Academy, continued long after actual support had been directed chiefly to Morgan College proper and its branch in Lynchburg. Notwithstanding, the force of this idea had far-reaching effects upon the history of the Academy. For even though Methodist material support became negligible, there was the insistence that the control and administration should remain in Methodist hands, because the Academy was their school. This idea, often expressed with emotion, gave encouragement to the historic belief that the Academy should continue as a local enterprise, drawing its students, faculty, and administrators primarily from the bounds of the Delaware Conference. Consequently, the Academy drew much of its life from the Eastern Shore, inbreeding itself as a local institution and becoming skeptical of outside control and influence, despite the fact that its source of support was no longer a local affair.

Student fees added to the total income of the Academy. During the first five years, student fees made up a sizable part of the budget; but, as the total income of the Academy increased after 1891, the income from students became proportionately less important despite the increasing enrollment. From the earliest days, records of student accounts were kept at the Academy by the principal, who made periodic reports to officials at Morgan College in Baltimore, Maryland and the Maryland Agricultural College in College Park.

The earliest records of student fees have not been preserved, but responses from many of the former students revealed that they ranged from about eight to twelve dollars per month during the first twenty years. This amount payable on a monthly basis, paid for board, lodging, tuition, books, and laundry. In addition, students who were classified as day students were eligible to eat their meals on the campus.

Physical Plant

The physical appearance of the campus did not radically change during Bird's day. All of the major buildings constructed during his tenure were in use during the early 1920s, and at least two of them were vitally needed and used by the school until 1950. On the other hand, the Academy underwent two very important changes after Bird's administration. In the first place, it became less and less independent as its administration was involved or was disputed by authorities of Morgan College and the Maryland Agricultural College. In the second place, state aid was eventually extended to the Academy, bringing into focus the problems of control and support in spite of federal aid and of the rights of Negroes to a higher education.

Bird's Death

Benjamin Oliver Bird had been in office for eleven years when he tragically, at forty-four years old, lost his life. It happened at about five o'clock on Monday morning, April 26, 1897, having lost consciousness the previous day. His funeral was held at the Metropolitan Church, and a large gathering was present to pay last respects to one of the community's most respected Negro citizens. Bird had always worked with citizens of the community and was careful not to alienate the good will of either Negroes or Whites. W. J. Moore and A. R. Shockley of the Delaware Conference and White, the minister of the Manokin Presbyterian Church, made addresses. Jacob C. Dunn gave a very flowery and rhetorical memorial, but beneath the flattery was an essentially correct appraisal of Bird as being a "man of wisdom and fidelity, who addressed himself to great tasks with heroic courage, quiet energy, and a resolute purpose that at last deserved success."[20] As Dunn correctly realized, Bird had an unselfish desire to lift men through education without a display of power or pomp and without using his office as a clearing house for self-advancement and self-conceit.

According to local tradition, Bird was a faithful worker in behalf of both community and school. Certainly he endeared himself to Negroes of the community, who after his death named in his honor their largest fraternal organization—the B. O. Bird Lodge Number 42, Knights of Pythias.[21] For many years, the school preserved his memory through the "Bird Lyceum," a student literary organization that passed out of existence by the 1930s. On April 19, 1940, one of his daughters, Crystal Bird Fauset, a former member of the legislature of Pennsylvania, dedicated a mechanic arts building on the campus to the memory of her father. Constructed with federal funds, it was dedicated as "Bird Hall." Bird's memory was preserved largely in the memory of men who knew him, because the Academy did not preserve his records. Indeed history has a way of letting the dead bury themselves, while historians have a way of resurrecting them. Bird was buried on the campus, and in later years, some spruce trees were planted along a path leading to the site situated near the woods and branch of the Manokin River. A large granite monument there was inscribed with Bird's hopeful epitaph:

> GOD KNOWS THE WAY. HE HOLDS THE KEY.
> HE GUIDES US WITH AN UNERRING HAND.
> SOMETIMES WITH TEARLESS EYE
> WE'LL SEE UP THERE.
> SOMEDAY WE'LL UNDERSTAND.

A Firm Foundation

Before Bird's death, the school was not only established as an Academy, but it was so well established that the form it took was significant in the development of the University. Until the 1920s, the Academy retained many of the features that were set up before 1900. Even after Methodist financial aid had long ended, the influence of Methodism and its conservative approach to the problems of Negro education continued to influence and direct the life of the Academy.

The effects of this influence upon the curriculum, the faculty, and student body were widespread. The curriculum continued to be primarily classical and literary until the 1920s. Later, when the classics were dropped, it still remained attached to the liberal arts tradition, giving sanction to demands for so-called industrial subjects, which were largely a means to ensure a source of income. The faculty grew in number but was forced to accept the conservative discipline of the Conference and the community. Most of the students continued to come from the Shore, retaining the stamp of character reflected in the background of the region's inhabitants, such as close family ties, educational lags, and poor economic backgrounds. In addition, financial difficulties remained, being increased and complicated by the administration of funds through Morgan College. Without federal or state aid for itself, the Academy carefully guarded the allocated income.

Portia E. Lovett Bird (1897-99)

Bird's legacy continued through his wife who assumed the duties of principal of the Academy upon his death. Portia E. Lovett Bird was born near Berryville, Clarke County, Virginia, on February 10, 1859, and spent her early life on a farm where she gained a lifelong love of nature. Being anxious to give her an education, her parents entered her as a student at Storer College in Harper's Ferry, West Virginia, as soon as she was old enough to leave home; she accordingly graduated very young. After graduation she spent a few years teaching in Rockingham County, Virginia, but most of the years prior to her marriage were spent singing with a company to secure money to build one of the halls at Storer College.

On September 29, 1880, Miss Lovett was united in marriage to Benjamin O. Bird, who would become the first head of the Delaware Conference Academy. In fact, when Benjamin Bird was ordered to the new, untried field in Princess Anne, Maryland, where difficulties and poverty stared them in the face, she never faltered or murmured. Conscious of her husband's pure motive, relying upon his wisdom, and trusting in God, she followed him wherever he led, helping him with all of her energy. As a teacher she excelled, always making clear the subject she taught. What impressed her pupils most was the sincerity of her character and the dignity of her womanhood. Becoming ill shortly after succeeding her husband as acting principal, she bore her sickness bravely and continued to serve. When asked about her hope, she replied, "I attended to that matter years ago." She was often heard saying, "I have no concern about death, it is all important to live well."

At forty years old, death claimed her at 4:25 P.M. on Saturday, November 25, 1899, two short years after the passing of her husband. Her funeral was likewise held in the Metropolitan Church with eulogies given by F. J. Wagner, D.D.; S. S. Jolly; W. J. Moore, and Pezavia O'Connell—all of whom, except Wagner, were members of the Delaware Conference. David H. Hargis read suitable resolutions on behalf of the

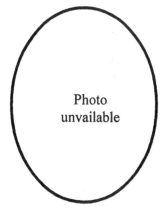

(Figure 4.2)
Portia E. Lovett Bird
(1897-1899)

alumni, accepting a role that he played for the next fifty years.[22] With the exception of the completion of a building for mechanic arts, the campus underwent few changes during the short tenure of Portia Bird.

Dr. Pezavia O'Connell (1900-1902)

Upon Portia's death, one of the most brilliant and colorful figures in the history of the school and of the Delaware Conference was appointed as principal and served two brief but exciting years from 1900-1902. He came to the Academy at the age of thirty-nine with an uncommon degree of formal education and high ambitions. It was his intention to become a bishop of the Church or the first Negro president of Morgan College. He achieved neither and, perhaps in disgust, quit the Conference. He resigned himself to a teaching career that took him to Gammon Theological Seminary, Howard University, and finally Morgan College. Ironically, the Conference officially recommended him for the presidency of Morgan College in 1901.

Born in Natchez, Mississippi, on March 2, 1861, Pezavia O'Connell, at the age of 18, entered Jackson Baptist College. There he won a scholarship to study theology at Gammon Theological Seminary from which he graduated in 1888. For several years thereafter, he was a minister in North Carolina, where he cautiously wooed and married Marie Johnson. In 1893, he became a member of the Delaware Conference and served energetically on various

(Figure 4.4)
Dr. Pezavia O'Connell
(1900-1902)

committees and charges. While a minister of the Bainbridge Church in Philadelphia, one of the most important charges of the Conference, he earned the degree of Doctor of Philosophy from the University of Pennsylvania. He became one of the few Negroes in the nation to hold this coveted degree. Perhaps colleagues envied his achievement and ambition, and O'Connell's temper and straightforwardness hardly assuaged that envy.

An insight into his personality may be gleaned from the recollections of persons who knew him. One of his former students recalled the mannerisms of this volatile, slender man.[23]

Quite impressive as a teacher, O'Connell was a fluent student of the classics who had a flair for etymology. He hated ignorance and despised idleness with respect to students. Frequently, he would reprimand students for wasting their time and constantly urged Negro youth to be progressive, industrious, and thrifty to offset the serious handicap imposed by color and by previous conditions of servitude. For example, O'Connell said that any Negro who lost time in smoking a cigarette was "fire on one end and a fool on the other." On the other hand, O'Connell believed in helping worthy students who gave promise of being somebody. It is thought that he paid much of the expenses of at least 1 student through medical school. Furthermore, he and his wife adopted a daughter when he was the presiding elder of the Salisbury District. They supported her as a natural heir and passed on property to her upon their death. Yet students joked about O'Connell's squeamishness. Even after he was advanced in years, O'Connell never owned an automobile but preferred to ride trolleys and to stay close to his well-stocked library at home. One day, some of his students at Morgan College saw him in a taxi and jokingly remarked that perhaps O'Connell was about to die inasmuch as he was spending money for a taxi. Sadly enough, O'Connell was on his way to a hospital and died that same night on November 26, 1930.

Campus Life

In spite of Dr. O'Connell's vigor and intelligence, life at the Academy was not changed except for a slight increase in enrollment. Furthermore, no changes were made in the course of study; and campus life was not unlike that of Bird's time. O'Connell was meticulous about enforcing decorum and respect for Methodist authority and morality. Like most of his contemporaries, including the Birds, O'Connell insisted upon conformity to the discipline of Methodism and constantly reiterated his beliefs in Methodist fundamentalism.

The Creation of a System

Campaigns carried on in the name of Morgan College and its branches indicated that Methodist zeal for Negro education was still alive in the State at the turn of the century. The campaigns kept Morgan College -- if not its branch in Princess Anne -- alive until the coming of state aid a generation later. These campaigns gave rise to one of the most conscientious and influential individuals in the history of the administration of Morgan College and the Academy in Princess Anne.

John Oakley Spencer became president of Morgan College and its branches in 1902, following the term of F.J. Wagner. Although he came directly to Morgan College from the Hudson River Institute, his appointment was influenced by Goucher, who remembered Spencer for his work at the Anglo-Japanese Methodist College in Tokyo, Japan. With missionary zeal, sometimes with tears in his eyes, Spencer campaigned eloquently and untiringly for support of Morgan College. Often he was criticized and snubbed by Whites for being too active, socially and professionally, in the interest of Negro education. When Spencer died in 1937, he and Morgan College were secure in the history of education in Maryland, and an acknowledgement of his contribution was recognized in a full page of the Baltimore Sun.

During Spencer's tenure, as one campaign ended another was begun. In 1904, Morgan and its branches had a debt of six thousand dollars, which was eradicated the following year by the self-sacrificing efforts of Spencer. Plans were then set up to eliminate a mortgage indebtedness to be financed, in part, by a payment of ten cents by each member of the Delaware and Washington Conferences.[24] In 1907, a few years later, another campaign headed by Spencer was under way for purposes of raising twenty thousand dollars. This campaign was to receive high priority, and all contributions made under the old standing campaign slogan "A Prayer A Day, A Penny a Week," were to go to the new effort to raise twenty thousand dollars to build a domestic science building for the Academy.[25] This hope did not materialize until 1920. In 1908, another campaign was started to raise funds to match a provisional gift of fifty thousand dollars from Andrew Carnegie, the steel baron; and this campaign, substantially aided by contributions from Negroes, was successful.

Such were the special efforts to supplement contributions that annually came through the old Freedmen's Aid collections of the contributing conferences. These efforts were essential to keep Morgan College alive. Normally, without special campaigns, the collections of the Washington and Delaware Conferences, though often made at great sacrifices, were not nearly enough to carry on the educational program of Morgan and its branches. Only a few thousand dollars were coming from the conferences at the turn of the century.

As compiled from the minutes of the conferences, the following collections were made for Freedmen's Aid during the years 1904-07 inclusive:

	1904	1905	1906	1907
Delaware Conference	$ 1,111	1,431	1,381	1,319
Washington Conference	1,792	2,034	2,071	2,147
Total	$ 2,903	3,465	3,398	3,466

Whereas Spencer provided leadership for the first semblance of a college system for Morgan and its branches, Frank J. Trigg was appointed the next principal of the Academy in Princess Anne.

Frank J. Trigg (1902-10)

By the turn of the century, a national movement was well under way for the purpose of developing industrial and agricultural instruction at Negro schools. It is not surprising then that the principal who followed O'Connell devoted a great deal of his efforts to making the Academy more industrial in its educational program. In both experience and outlook, Frank J. Trigg had the qualifications necessary for this type of program. He was a product of Hampton Institute and carried this school's influence to his administration of the Academy.

Trigg was born in the governor's mansion in Richmond, Virginia, on July 31, 1850. Like many other figures in the history of Negro education in Maryland, he grew up in an atmosphere of Civil War and Reconstruction. He was once a servant for John Buchanan Floyd, a former governor of Virginia and Confederate general who was the United States Secretary of War when South Carolina seceded from the Union. A great deal of Trigg's formal education and inspiration came from Union General Samuel C. Armstrong, the founder of Hampton Institute. Trigg spent some of his boyhood on a farm in Virginia, where he lost one of his hands in a thrashing machine. Apparently, the Trigg family

(Figure 4.5)
Frank J. Trigg
(1902-1910)

59

chose to remain with their former masters even after emancipation and the close of the war, for it appears that the former owners gave money to Trigg and encouraged him to attend Hampton, a then recently-opened school for Negroes at Little Scotland near Hampton Roads.

With fewer than four teachers and a score of pupils at Hampton when Trigg entered, he fell under the spell and discipline of Armstrong, whose educational aims shaped the thinking of both himself and his schoolmate, Booker T. Washington. Armstrong's teachings emphasized that his students should have a high regard for the dignity of labor. He taught that his students should teach selected Negro youth to lead their people by example, by getting land and homes. He taught that one should never give a dollar that another could earn for himself or herself. He further emphasized the replacement of stupid drudgery with skilled hands and the building of an industrial system for the sake not only of self-support and intelligent labor but also for the sake of character. Skilled labor and moral character then were foundations upon which Armstrong built his program at Hampton.

Hampton's influence upon the course of Negro education was incalculable. For a half century, Hampton's graduates carried Armstrong's principles to many parts of the nation while Northern philanthropy and Southern white leadership supported "training" or "industrial" schools for Negroes. Hampton gave a philosophy to Negro education; later Tuskegee popularized the idea through its famed president, Booker T. Washington, one of America's most persuasive orators. So far as changing the Negro's socio-economic life, however, it is likely that the idea produced more popular acceptance than it did practical results.

When Trigg graduated from Hampton, two years before Washington, he was indelibly impressed by the teaching of Armstrong. Even thirty years after his graduation, Trigg remembered Armstrong's influence and paid warm tribute to his former teacher, then deceased, in an address before Hampton's graduating class of 1903:

> I take pleasure in referring to General Armstrong as
> my teacher. His Sunday night lectures on moral philosophy will
> never be forgotten by those who heard him. No man who sat
> before him in those days could forget his teachings and efface
> from the tablets of his memory the impressions of that living,
> burning soul of truth and righteousness.

The influence of those lectures has been multiplied many times in the lives of the youth of this Commonwealth through Hampton graduates. The most difficult principles of moral science were beyond the comprehension of the boys, but they believed them, nevertheless, because they believe in their teacher and were willing to practice his teachings by faith.[26]

After graduation, Trigg studied at Norwich Academy in Norwich, Connecticut. Beginning in 1881, he taught a grade school in Lynchburg, Virginia. When the branch of Morgan College opened in Lynchburg, Trigg became the principal in 1893 and held this position until July 1902 when he was appointed to take charge of the Academy in Princess Anne.

The minutes for 1904 document that Trigg was fifty-two years old when he came to the Conference and expressed the hope that Trigg would make the Academy "a second Tuskegee." This hope never materialized, but Trigg was partially successful in turning the Academy's academic program in that direction. The chief changes that came during his administration were made in the educational program rather than in the physical plant.

Academic Program

Trigg's two great interests seemed to have been teacher training and agriculture. Like other Negro educators with baccalaureate degrees, he taught a variety of subjects, including the Bible, Child Psychology, General Psychology, literature, hygiene, and Elementary Methods and Observation. He met with his student-teaching pupils two hours weekly, from two until four o'clock on each Saturday afternoon, grouping the senior class into pairs and requiring each pair to teach one day per week in the preparatory grades.

The normal course of study of Bird's time was altered in order to keep the curriculum abreast with that of other higher schools. Before Trigg's tenure, the entire length of the course of study was never more than five years. Trigg adopted a three to four year plan that made the curriculum both intermediate and secondary. The intermediate course was called the normal preparatory. The academic course was four years in length, embracing both normal and standard courses with an option in the fourth year. Generally, the four-year normal course was selected and, indeed, encouraged. The first class, consisting of nine graduates, to complete the four-year normal course, graduated in 1904.

A photograph of this class is shown below.

At the beginning of his principalship, Trigg's staff consisted of fewer than a dozen members, a complete turnover since 1892. Official catalogues show that in 1903 there were twelve faculty members, including Trigg. Their names and courses of instruction were as follows: Principal, Frank Trigg, A.M., pedagogy, and geography; Matron, Mrs. E. P. Trigg, domestic science; Miss Jeanette Parker, mathematics; Daniel J. Pinkett, mathematics; Ralph A. Marsden, A.B., science; Woodward W. Privott, blacksmithing and wheelwrighting; John L. Richardson, carpentry, joinery, and cabinetmaking; Albert Mebane, B. Agr., agriculture and animal husbandry; Parker E. Moore, printing; James E. Jackson, band music; Samuel H. Fountaine, foreman on farm, market gardening; and Miss Olive W. Wright, domestic science.

With the exception of Trigg, Ralph Marsden is listed as the only teacher with a baccalaureate degree. In addition to science, he taught a variety of subjects, including Greek, Latin, rhetoric, literature, dramatics, and music (boys). Moreover, he gave instruction in physical education and bookkeeping, which shows the extent of the course of study as well as Marsden's overtaxed

(Figure 4.6)
First Four-year Graduating Class of the Academy in Princess Anne.
Seated left to right: Clara Winters, Sarah Coard Davis, Ralph Marsden (instructor), and Jeanette Parker. Standing left to right: Harold Richardson, Annie Coard, Greenbury Howard, Julia Stevenson, William H. Hayman, Blanch Howard, and Anna Handy. (Reproduced from an original photograph courtesy of Mrs. Anna Handy Maddox)

62

versatility. In 1906, Marsden resigned to take a position at Tuskegee Institute. A product of the New York public school system and a graduate of Columbia University, whom one of his students described as "refined and cultured," Marsden was perhaps an anomaly as a member of the staff. He was a northern literary product who may have been irked by the industrial innovations of Trigg or cramped by the limited accommodations of the community.

Beginnings of State Aid

Education was one of the rallying points for the Negro's quest for his democratic rights. Because it held a fascinating and historic attraction for the Negro, the outlook on education was often expressed more dramatically than the Negro's thinking on voting, housing, and employment. Conservative leadership was generally politically safe in its advocacy of Negro rights to an education, but risks were far more perilous when the advocacy of Negro rights was extended to other facets of democratic living. Conservative white leaders, who were openly opposed to the doctrine of equality in such aspects as voting, housing, and employment, accepted the Negro's right to an education with always the qualifying condition (after Reconstruction) that such education would not basically alter the Negro's place in white society. A conservative philosophy was thus imparted to the structure and function of Negro education with the concurrence of Negro and white leaders alike. Remembering antebellum days, Negroes could point out that some education was better than none at all. Whites, remembering Reconstruction days, accorded privileges without power, substituting the Negro's right to an education in place of the total Reconstruction philosophy of Negro freedom. To many Negroes and Whites, Negro education was a panacea; to some it was a palliative.

Yet in time, this conservative approach was challenged by the more radical wings of Negro leadership which, to no small extent, were molded by the social and intellectual forces that were shaping a "new Negro."[27] The Negro became more acutely conscious of his status as a minority group living in the complexity of race concepts and realities, and protests against his status accompanied the renaissance of his consciousness. The Negro sought adjustment in the nation's courts, which often upheld his protest. The Reconstruction philosophy of Negro freedom was invoked by the Negro who never forgot that, like other Americans, he too lived within the orbit of the organic law and the American democratic heritage. Though not always augmented, legal theory and moral suasion were never inextricably rejected by the American Dream of equality, and the Negro began to use these weapons to solve the problem of conservative transience in education and other fields of behavior.

It is not surprising then that the quest for equality in Maryland, though tempered by the bulwarks of conservatism, pointed in the direction of the Negro's participation in democratic living. The rights of the Negro to testify in court, to be admitted to the bar, to vote, to live in less restricted ghettoes, and to share public educational facilities were brought into court. The latter was preeminent in the Negro's thinking about his rights, and the outlook was often measured by the degree of financial aid that the State allowed for purposes of Negro education.

As early as 1888, Negro teachers of Baltimore filed a suit for equal salaries, and several years later some interested Negroes of this city advocated the use of Negro teachers only in Negro schools.[28] A convention of Negroes (all men) met in Annapolis on Saturday, March 19, 1892 and, voting to omit politics drew up a petition to submit to the Assembly. They requested better educational facilities and a manual training school for Negroes. One of the representatives, John Cajay, asked for Negro teachers for colored schools; and Cyrus Sinclair of Cambridge, another delegate, denounced the City of Baltimore for not appointing Negro teachers to colored schools. The delegates voted for a normal school and the repeal of all discrimination laws. Consisting of a cross section of economic classes and forgetting that they had previously voted to omit politics, the delegates pledged themselves to the Republican Party before adjournment.[29]

In February of 1893, there was another convention of Negroes in Annapolis presided over by a local Negro lawyer, Richard E. King. Resolutions were sent to the Governor and Assembly requesting better schools for Negroes. The petition not only requested better schools for the State's districts but it also stated that there was "great need for the establishment of a high school or college in this State for the colored youth, who have not the privilege to attend and study at St. Johns College and other higher educational institutions in the State for white youth that get $31,000 annually from the State."[30]

The petitions were indicative of the Negro's thinking about educational inequalities, but no legal action was taken to force the issue in the courts. There was, instead, reliance upon immediate political changes to effect some of the desired results. Negro voters relied upon the hope of a Republican victory to install some of the changes, but when this victory came in 1896 it did not usher in any basic changes in the state-wide educational program of Negroes.

Baltimore was to acknowledge its first Negro high school, and white teachers were eventually replaced in Negro schools,[31] but the educational system for Negroes in the State as a whole underwent little change in organization and support until the period of World War I. The State gave no additional support to elementary or higher education. In fact, the State's support of higher education for Negroes was practically non-existent until the decade after the turn of the century when funds were given for the establishment of the normal school at Bowie. Only one other grant was made prior to this time; a sum of $2,500 was allotted to the Academy for the construction of a "mechanic arts" building for the "industrial education of the colored people of Maryland."[32] It is hardly admissible that this grant was an allotment for the higher education of Negroes in the same sense that appropriations were made for higher institutions of Whites. Yet being payable to the treasurer of Morgan College, the State's only college institution for Negroes, it was the first grant that the State made for the higher education of its Negroes.

On the other hand, despite the fact that the Assembly gave some support to white higher institutions, it was not predisposed to support and establish a state university for either Whites or Negroes. Additionally, its support of private institutions was not endorsed, and then not wholeheartedly, until after the turn of the century. When Whites themselves, who controlled state funds, were not too favorably disposed to support higher education, it could not be expected that they would give serious attention to the support of Negro institutions. During the session when the Academy received its first grant from the State, the fight against measures to aid all educational institutions was "vigorous," especially in the House of Delegates.[33] State aid to Negro institutions came in noteworthy amounts during periods when Whites themselves considered the feasibility of aid to their own institutions.

However, the principle of state aid to higher education in Maryland was settled well before the turn of the century, though in practice only a few of the older white institutions, privately founded and endowed, were the recipients.[34] Two institutions that were the earliest recipients of state aid were various colleges of the University of Maryland in Baltimore, such as the College of Physic and Medicine, and the Maryland Agricultural College. By 1890, the latter was being appropriated $6,000 annually; within five years, the amount was increased to $9,000; by 1910, the amount was $16,000. Excluding appropriations for buildings, this latter sum remained unchanged until 1916.[35] The University of Maryland received separate grants for its colleges, such as its College of Physic, which was being allotted $3,700 annually in 1890. Altogether, colleges and academies in the State were being allotted about $44,000 annually for maintenance during the early 1890s. In addition to the Maryland Agricultural College and the University of Maryland, some of the schools that shared in the grants were St. John's College, Johns Hopkins University, and Western Maryland College.

Agricultural Extension Program

In Princess Anne, Trigg attempted to reorganize the programs of agriculture. Although he was well aware of the difficulties involved, including the marginal economic status of Negro farmers, he intended to make the Academy a center for disseminating information to local Negro farmers. Specifically, he hoped to encourage home and land ownership as well as scientific chicken raising and dairying. Trigg would place a farmer and tradesman trained at the Academy in every Negro community. This was the influence of Armstrong, preceding by many years the objectives established by the Federal Agricultural Extension Program for Negroes. Although Trigg realized that trained Negro farmers were scarce and that he apparently had difficulty finding them, he finally was able to obtain a former student from Hampton, Woodard W. Privott.

On January 4, 1903, Woodard W. Privott left Hampton and began his tenure at Princess Anne Academy as a teacher of wheelwrighting and blacksmithing. "This kind of work was a novelty on the Eastern Shore and many students came the next term for trades."[36] Trigg and the trustees of the Academy changed the curriculum that year, closing the academic department at 12:30 P.M. and opening the industrial classes at 1:30 P.M. Everybody was required to spend three and a half hours in one of the industrial departments each school day and all day on Saturday from 7:00 A.M. to 4:30 P.M."[37] Further changes followed so that along with his previously assigned duties, Privott was given additional classes to teach: one in arithmetic, one in reading, and another in language. Anxious about his limited training in academics, Privott committed himself to the private tutoring of Professor Marsden to improve his intellect and increase his ability to teach his students effectively. Marsden taught him arithmetic and algebra. Said Privott of Marsden, "This young man is a very nice teacher, much on the Hampton order in his notions; believing it his duty to help those who are less fortunate than he."[38] Privott was successful not only in his classroom but also in his newfound personal life on the Shore; because on Wednesday, September 18, 1907, Privott married a graduate of Princess Anne Academy, Miss Emma Cottman of Quantico, Maryland.[39]

Being a man of moral integrity, Privott excelled in all of his relations, especially with his students, first at Princess Anne Academy and then at Morgan when on March 1, 1913, he resigned from his position at Princess Anne Academy and went to Morgan State College. There he spoke openly, passing on lessons in true Hampton style. One speech was described in Morgan's Bulletin dated February 1915:

> Sunday evening the fourteenth, Mr. W. W. Privott, our instructor in blacksmithing, gave a very interesting address to the faculty and students showing how home training is reflected in every sphere of one's life. In part he said that if the home training has been what it should have been, it will be shown on the ball field, on the tennis court, in the classroom, in the literary organizations, etc., by the absence of that selfish, contending spirit that makes one grab the best for self.[40]

Indeed his home training, being intertwined with tragedy, poverty, and separation from siblings, caused him to be successful. Privott was born in Perquimans County, North Carolina, on May 15, 1876. During his childhood, his mother was widowed, causing the family to be left homeless. As a result, two of Privott's siblings were left with his maternal grandmother while he and an older sister stayed with their mother. Privott began work at a young age and met a student from Hampton who told him about the opportunities there for Negroes who did not have enough money to go to college. Privott worked during the day and went to grade school five nights each week. The following year he sent for a catalogue and was able to attend Hampton on a scholarship.

After Privott resigned from Princess Anne Academy, Trigg was able to sponsor an annual "Farmer's Institute," which was an early forerunner of various farm programs related to agricultural extension programs. In keeping with the philosophy of Hampton Institute, the Farmer's Institute gave practical information through lectures and information to local farmers who attended the sessions. Speakers from the faculty of Maryland Agricultural College and the Farmer's Institute of Maryland were also involved.

Trigg was consistent in his educational philosophy. To him, the task of Negro education was clear. Without "fear and trembling," he taught that the Negro should constantly work toward the philosophy of Armstrong. He gave little cognizance to the intellectual ferment that was being stirred by the young Negro intellectual and Harvard graduate, W. E. B. DuBois. At a conference of Negro educators meeting in 1904, he stated that the Negro must be taught that it is disgraceful not to work; that he must shun the sin of laziness; that he dignifies labor by laboring with his hands as well as his head; and that as the head is trained, the hand becomes skillful and the worker becomes interested in his task and rises above the plain and mere plodder.

The members in attendance represented practically all of the Negro land-grant schools, including W.H. Council of Alabama, Isaac Fisher of Arkansas, Nathan B. Young of Florida, R. R. Wright of Georgia, J. S. Hathaway of Kentucky, James B. Dudley of North Carolina, D. R. Lewis of Virginia, and R. R. Taylor of Tuskegee, Alabama. This conference, attended also by the heads of various Negro mechanical and agricultural colleges, was one of the early forerunners of the conference of Negro land-grant college presidents officially organized at Tuskegee in 1923. Trigg was elected as second vice-president for the next year.

Among industrial Negro educators of his day, who were then the popular leaders in the field, Trigg was favorably recognized. It is likely that his recognition gave a measure of prestige to the Academy in Princess Anne. Based upon its contemporary merits as an educational institution for Negroes at a time when higher education for the Negro was hardly more than a hope or a dream, the Academy held a place of prominence among Negro higher schools of Trigg's day. This prominence, lacking many contemporary merits in the educational field, gave way to the Academy's preeminence as a political symbol in subsequent years.

Trigg left the Academy in the summer of 1910 with high praise for a successful tenure from such persons as John F. Goucher and H. B. Frissell, the principal of Hampton Institute. During his tenure of eight years, he had earned high respect as an able educator on the campus and in the community.

Trigg in Retirement

After retirement, Trigg returned to Lynchburg and reentered service as principal of the branch of Morgan College locally known as the "Morgan Annex." Later in 1917 after a destructive fire at this school, Trigg became the head of Bennett College located in Greensboro, North Carolina. He remained at Bennett until 1927 when David D. Jones, a younger and more resourceful man, succeeded him. Upon leaving Bennett, Trigg retired from active life as an educator, returning once again to Lynchburg where he lived until his death at age eighty-four in 1934.

A great deal of his life had been given to the education of the Negro, but at the time of his death, the "industrial" education of the Negro had long ceased to be a salient outlook in Negro education both locally and nationally. Yet his life spanned a great deal of the American saga. He was born a slave, but he died a free man. As a boy he could remember the "irrepressible conflict" to eliminate slavery. As an old man he heard the pledge of the new deal to eliminate social and economic injustice.

Thomas H. Kiah (1910-36)

Thomas Henry Kiah, a thirty-eight-year-old minister of the Methodist Episcopal Church on the Eastern Shore of Maryland, succeeded Frank Trigg as principal of Princess Anne Academy in 1911. The trustees unanimously approved his appointment and he was overwhelmingly accepted by the Delaware Conference, which passed a resolution in praise of Kiah's morality of character and conservatism.[41] This description of Kiah, coming from the Delaware Conference, a conservative body itself, was fittingly characteristic of the man and his work at the Academy. Kiah grew up under the conservative discipline of Methodism, and his relegation of his philosophy to this discipline was one of the chief factors favoring his appointment. In his report of the Salisbury District, O'Connell praised Kiah's appointment and work: "Order is enforced not as a mere drill but for its benefit to the student in after life. Special attention is paid to the proper relation of the sexes."[42] Methodists felt that Kiah would preserve the character of school life and would not tamper with the mores of the community or the conventions of campus life. Kiah did not disappoint them.

He was a man of great personal honesty and integrity, abstemious in taste and conservative in temperament. He seemed to have cared more for security than for equality, more for privilege than for power. Cautiously he held to tradition, finding contentment and solace in his large family and in the discipline of the ministry. Kiah lived relatively comfortably in Olney for a generation, hardly disturbed by forces that were undermining the very existence of the Academy. In the minds of students, faculty, alumni, and local citizens, Professor Kiah was highly respected, conducting the office of the principal with a show of authority and dignity. Yet Kiah's power was more nominal than actual. He was a good disciplinarian on the campus, but respect for his power was not always shared by his real bosses at Morgan College or the University of Maryland at College Park.

(Figure 4.7)
Thomas Kiah
(1910-36)

Kiah was a product of the Eastern Shore, having been born in Cambridge from the marriage of William and Adelia Kiah. At the age of seventeen, he was sent by the Delaware Conference to Oakville, Maryland, as a minister. Later he served at St. Michaels. He attended the Academy in Princess Anne and graduated from Morgan College with a B.A. degree in 1906. In June 1906, he married Mary Roberta Townsend, who in the course of this marriage gave birth to five boys and one girl: Brewington, Lycurgus, Waldo, Gregory, McQuary, and Rhodelia. Mary Roberta died on October 7, 1919; and on June 8, 1921, Kiah married Cynthia Ola Powdrill, who also bore five children: Cynthia, Thomas Henry, Humphrey, Gwendolyn, and Grace.

Kiah attended summer school on several occasions—Cornell University in 1910 and Columbia University in 1915 and 1930. The higher degrees that he proudly placed behind his name, however, were honorary —A.M. from Wiley College in Texas and Ped.D. from Morgan College.

Campus Life

Under Kiah, student life was not unlike that of Trigg's term. It was regimented in order to conform to the prevailing discipline of Methodist morality, which frowned upon immodest dress, recreation, and social conduct. As was to be expected, dress was prescribed by the authorities. Uniformity of dress was compulsory and was rigidly enforced by Kiah and his matrons. Not only did girls wear white blouses and blue skirts, but also they were forbidden to wear low-topped or high-heeled shoes. Likewise, they were expected to provide a white uniform for work in domestic science. They were also discouraged from using jewelry. Boys were required to wear blue uniforms with a white stripe down the side of the trousers. During World War I as well as shortly afterwards, male students were required to wear army garb. In fact several days after the armistice, Kiah placed an order for men's uniforms, including coats, trousers, caps, and leggings, at the establishment of D. Klein and Brother of Philadelphia. In addition to wearing uniforms, students were expected to supply their own sheets, pillowcases, bedspreads, towels, and other articles that would add to the comfort and beauty of their rooms.

Student employment was liberally accepted. Practically all of the maintenance was performed by students who received room or board as pay, because generally students at the Academy stayed on campus except to travel back and forth to their homes. A few of the student account books that have been preserved show that a large number of the students were employed at various jobs. Fifty-two students, approximately one-fourth of the student body, were employed in 1922.[43] The greater number worked in the dining hall and kitchen. There were twelve waitresses, three of whom served the teachers; two pantry girls; five dishwashers; and twelve other students working in the dining hall and the kitchen in various capacities. The remaining twenty-one student employees were given work as janitors, firemen, launderers, and mail attendants.[44] Kitchen and dining-room personnel were given board; but the other students, except the ironer in the laundry, were paid four dollars per month.[45] Accounts show that in his residence in Olney, Kiah had two girls assigned as workers who were paid a total of fifteen dollars per month. No doubt the girls who Kiah personally selected for this service took pride in the honor of working for the professor as well as the added pay.

Student fees changed little during Kiah's term. Generally, the increases in student fees were only nominal, keeping abreast with the increased cost of living that came during and after World War I. During the school year 1912-13, some of the fees were as follows: board, seven dollars; room, two dollars; incidentals, one dollar and fifty cents; fuel, fifty cents; and entrance, one dollar.

By the end of the War, board was increased to twelve dollars per month and room rent to four dollars. Kiah sent out a circular letter announcing these changes.[46]

An athletic fee of one dollar was subsequently stipulated for soccer or intramural baseball. Both games were popular with students during the first fifteen years of Kiah's administration, and probably some equipment was purchased out of the fee. The administration, however, frowned upon other sports. Athletic and military drills, required of all students, were looked upon as being sufficient to fulfill most recreational needs. Football and basketball were not encouraged as competitive sports; they were not organized into a varsity or intramural program until the late 1920s and early 1930s.[47]

Some track activities, mainly foot races, were held in the month of May; but like football and basketball, this sport existed mainly in name only. Tennis and croquet were played on the campus, but Kiah was not disposed to condone most forms of student and faculty recreation. In fact, Kiah persistently held to the belief that too much recreation was sinful and non-Christian. Consequently, he never permitted a dance on the campus.

Student activities that came near the close of the school year, however, provided many social outlets; and during Kiah's time, these activities were more elaborate than ever before. Farm groups continuously met on the campus, and commencement week was generally one of the most celebrated affairs of the year. The activities were generally stilted, formal affairs that were notable for an abundance of flamboyant speeches and declamations. In 1913, for example, the commencement activities were somewhat different from those of today. Everything began on Wednesday, May 21, with a program of industrial arts in the chapel of the boys' dormitory. Exhibits of class work were displayed, and each department in the trades was represented by a student who read, rather haltingly and nervously, a paper on a selected topic. Later in the week, students in domestic science demonstrated how to bake a pound cake. Other departments, likewise, held student demonstrations, including churning milk, carpentry, and blacksmithing. This was one of the first industrial arts exhibits ever given at the Academy.[48] On Saturday, May 24, a social program was given for students. A few parlor games were played, and there was some group singing but no dancing. On Sunday, students of the B. O. Bird and Eliza Smith lyceums gave a joint program in the chapel. On Monday, S. J. Horsey of Cokesbury, Maryland, a member of the Delaware Conference, delivered the annual sermon at the Metropolitan Church. On the next day, the class gave its declamations in the chapel "amid scenes of beautiful decorations consisting of United States flags, pictures, wild flowers and vines."[49] On the following day, Tuesday, May 28, the alumni met and presented a program. On Thursday, the class was graduated. Forming its line of procession in front of Eliza Smith Hall by two o'clock in the afternoon, graduates and faculty marched down the dirty, familiar county road for the exercises in Metropolitan Church. Spencer presented the diplomas. Ten years later, the activities of commencement week had not basically changed except for the student participants.

Summer school became a going concern during this ten year period, 1913-23. Perhaps the first summer work was conducted during one summer in the late 1880s. Because records are fragmentary, however, it cannot be definitely established when a regular session was held prior to 1913. The session that was held the following year in 1914 was a "marked improvement,"[50] and a planned schedule of activities enlivened the academic work. O'Connell, the former principal and usually a colorful and intelligent speaker, gave an address on the "Grounds of the Negro's Hope." S. S. Jolly, a member of the Delaware Conference, and N. F. Monroe, an instructor at the Maryland Agricultural College, also addressed the session.[51] Then too, rural ministers gave lectures during the summer. Also, classes for rural ministers and programs in agricultural extension were continuously conducted the summers following 1914. Approximately two dozen students, all from Maryland, were enrolled, and nine instructors composed the teaching staff for this session in 1914. It is not known when the last summer session was held at the Academy, but certainly no regular summer session was in operation during the years 1947-50, when the school's entire program was under criticism and scrutiny.

Teachers were paid on a twelve-month basis even when there was no summer session. Their salaries increased in both real and nominal amounts during Kiah's tenure. This increase is not surprising, considering that Kiah served as principal for more than a quarter of a century during which time the Academy's income was increased and Negro teachers in both the State and nation received higher pay than their predecessors of 1900. Compared to salaries of Negro teachers in public secondary and elementary schools in the State, teachers at the Academy were generally paid higher salaries.

Accordingly, Negro teachers in county elementary schools of the State received salaries that averaged about $422 annually in 1920, but teachers at the Academy during that year averaged more than twice this amount. Teachers in Somerset County, receiving the lowest pay of any county in the State except St. Mary's and Calvert, averaged $326 annually for the school year 1920-21.[52] Salaries of the Academy's staff ranged from approximately $364 to about $2,240 annually during the early 1920s. Nevertheless, teachers in most white high and elementary schools of the State were better paid than those at the Academy.

Of the salaries at the Academy, Kiah received the highest, a sum that compared quite favorably with the amount being paid to Negro principals in some of the leading high schools of the nation at that time. No doubt there were some perquisites, including rent that increased his income. Certainly Kiah enjoyed not having to pay rent for the use of Olney or for use of the campus laundry. Although Kiah's salary probably never exceeded $200 per month, the perquisites increased his total income to the extent that he was one of the most prosperous Negroes in the community even though he had one of the largest families to support. He maintained an automobile and dressed well during his tenure. His first automobile, a Cadillac, was purchased a few years before 1920 at a time when Negroes did not commonly own large automobiles. Being unable to drive himself, he kept a chauffeur on hand until his death.

During Kiah's tenure, race relations in Princess Anne were probably at their worst. Specifically, in 1933, the last public lynching in the state of Maryland took place in Princess Anne. George Armwood, a mentally retarded twenty-eight year old black resident of Somerset County, was talked into committing a crime against a white woman for which he lost his life. His accomplice was a white farmer, John Richardson, who apparently escaped serious prosecution. Richardson drilled Armwood on how *he* was to overtake *their* victim, who was known for carrying large sums of money. The two were to split the money afterwards. Thus, Armwood attacked her as she walked on a dirt road near her farm. He failed to get her money, but he did tear her dress from her body in the attempt, after which he panicked and fled into the woods. Discovered not long afterward, she identified her attacker. A manhunt ensued, and the sheriff picked up Armwood shortly after the crime. Sheriff Dryden drove the prisoner to Snow Hill, approximately thirty miles away, to protect him from the angry mob that was beginning to form in Princess

Anne. During the next two days, Armwood was moved two more times and finally back to Princess Anne. There, despite the Sheriff's efforts to stop them, an angry mob, said to have reached numbers as high as two thousand, abducted Armwood from the jail. He was dismembered, stabbed about the face and neck, and dragged by the neck until he was dead. Afterwards, his body was hung from a tree, stripped, and burned. When the crowd was finished, they took the body down and put it on the courthouse yard as a symbol of their displeasure at the court's attempt to protect the prisoner. The criminal deed took all of two and one-half hours to complete, and then the perpetrators went on with their lives as if that night of heightened and intense evil never happened. "Here's what we do on the Eastern Shore!" the mob cried."[53]

Indeed the time, the attitude, and the atmosphere were right for such a heinous crime. The Shore was openly criticized for being primitive. "Writing in his [Baltimore] *Sun* column, H. L. Mencken concluded that it was hopeless to expect any positive changes on the Eastern Shore. The good people with talent and brains had left and the riffraff stayed behind. Anti-lynching bills, Mencken predicted, would never pass the state legislature. "The only way to clean out the area is to reduce its representation in the legislature and let Baltimore take the lead," he wrote.[54] Mencken's judgement provided yet another example of the chasm between the Eastern Shore and the Western Shore.

In an earlier onslaught, H. L. Mencken, in his column in *The* [Baltimore] *Sun*, attacked the Eastern Shore as a depraved civilization "wherein there are no competent police, little save a simian self-seeking in public office, no apparent intelligence on the bench, and no courage and decency in the local press." Characterizing the Eastern Shore as an "Alsatia of Morons," the combative journalist argued that a lynching in 1931 in Salisbury, Maryland was the result of social degeneration that had allowed "ninth rate" men to come to power.

Very little is known about how the incident affected the small community housed at Princess Anne Academy.

Finances

The period prior to World War I, 1912-16, was characterized by a change in the State's policy of aid to higher institutions, and the movement led to the establishment of a state-controlled and state-supported university. The question of the responsibility of the State to support and to maintain a system of higher education became more manifest. Attention as well as controversy was focused upon the Maryland Agricultural College, a semi-privately controlled corporation that had heretofore received a great deal of its support from the State.

It seems that a fire at the College touched off a series of circumstances that led to an investigation and, eventually, of the State's program of educational support. One writer stated that the fire at the College was a blessing, indicating that its destruction may have prompted the State into action in support of better educational facilities.[55] To him, the Maryland Agricultural College was a "sad picture" and a poor excuse for a college. Citing how Whites of Mississippi received more money for higher education than Whites of Maryland, the author pointed out that appropriations were too small. Accordingly, a commission was appointed by a joint resolution of the Assembly in 1912 to assess the relationship between the state of Maryland and the Maryland Agricultural College. By the time the commission made its report in 1914, state support of education (higher and secondary) had become a political issue.[56]

Strong lobbies in support of education began to appear at Annapolis. One of the lobbies, appearing in behalf of the Maryland Agricultural College, was sponsored by the City Wide Congress of Baltimore which enlisted the support of some of the most influential private citizens of the State. Members of the lobby spent weeks and months in 1914 in attempts to secure more aid and a better educational program at College Park.[57] The Assembly appointed a commission, the first in the history of the State, to make a survey of the State's entire educational program. As a result, attempts to aid the Maryland Agricultural College—and, indeed, to revamp the system of education in the State—were not without success. State aid to education was increased and the public school system was changed for Whites and Negroes alike in accord with some of the recommendations made by the survey commission under the direction of Abraham Flexner of the General Education Board.[58]

Specifically, the Academy received its first appropriation for maintenance in 1914 and $500 for each fiscal year of 1915 and 1916.[59] At the session of 1916, the Assembly more than doubled the amount of its previous appropriation for maintenance of the Maryland Agricultural College; it gave the Academy $5,000 and raised the appropriation of the school in Bowie from $7,000 to $10,000. Morgan College received no appropriation at this session.[60] Furthermore, the Assembly of 1916 issued a new charter to the Maryland Agricultural College that indicated the State's interest and control. The College was renamed the Maryland State College of Agriculture. Its board of trustees was designated as the recipient of all federal funds, but the act of incorporation said nothing specifically about the "Eastern Branch" in Princess Anne.[61]

The question of state aid to education again arose after World War I when the school in College Park was incorporated with the colleges of the University of Maryland under a single board of regents. Officials of the newly incorporated body, now styled the University of Maryland, endeavored to make the college a great university. In keeping with this idea, the president of the University made requests for sums that far exceeded any amount previously requested for higher education in the State. In 1922 a sum of approximately three and one-half million dollars was requested, a staggering amount when contrasted to the State's pre-War appropriations for higher education. Governor Albert C. Ritchie, serving the first year of tenure that lasted until 1935, questioned the wisdom of such unusual requests and appointed a commission to investigate state aid to colleges on October 4, 1921. The commission was to make its report in 1924. In the meantime, however, the requests of the University were substantially pared by the economy-minded Governor and Assembly who kept the University's appropriations below the million-dollar mark.

The Governor's commissioner made its report in time for the session of the Assembly in 1924. The Governor and the Assembly favorably received the report; but educators, including the president of the University, denounced it.[62] Carried as a headline on the front page of the Sun, the report advocated the discontinuance of state aid to all colleges except the University of Maryland.[63] It further recommended that state funds be withdrawn from the support of the preparatory departments of all institutions except Morgan College; that funds allotted to the University of Maryland were not to be used for non-resident instruction. Moreover, the commission was opposed to the idea of making the University a great university, indicating that it did not favor the expenditure of large sums for construction and maintenance at College Park.[64]

The Sun stated in an editorial that the principle of the report made "common sense and justice to those who are called upon to furnish the revenues needed for the maintenance of those institutions devoted to what is called 'higher learning'."[65] On the other hand, educators and other interested citizens opposed the findings and recommendations. The president of the University openly criticized the report, reiterating his belief expressed previously that the exclusion of non-resident students from state aid was not feasible.[66] Furthermore, a group of about 100 citizens hurriedly organized and sent a resolution to the Assembly asking that aid be extended to the University. The group included George M. Shriver, a vice president of the Baltimore and Ohio Railroad, and E. P. Cohill, president of the Maryland Farm Bureau.[67]

The Assembly did not adopt the report of Ritchie's commission in full, for state aid continued to go to various higher institutions. Furthermore, contrary to the report, the Assembly appropriated funds to increase maintenance and construction at the University; but the appropriations fell short of the amount envisioned by official plans at College Park for a great university. The University's Eastern Branch was granted $40,000 for the construction and equipment of a building to replace the old boys dormitory that had recently burned,[68] but at no time during the controversy was state aid for Negro education in question. This great debate over the feasibility of state aid to higher education was primarily invoked by the actions of Whites on behalf of institutions for Whites. Ten years later, however, state aid for the higher education of Negroes had become a controversial issue.

Whereas the report to Governor Ritchie in 1924 made only scant reference to Negro education, several reports followed that indicated the State's growing concern with the problem of Negro higher education. The reports became more frequent during the 1930s and their contents, considered in the light of their contemporary background, reflected the dilemma of the State in its attempt to isolate and to resolve the problem of higher education of Negroes. Issues that were not solely germane to education, however, complicated the problem. By joint resolution, the Assembly of 1924 created an Interracial Commission to investigate the problem of Negro education. Later this body was replaced by a Commission on the Higher Education of Negroes, a fact that clearly indicated the growing importance of Negro higher education in the State.

The Commission of 1924 consisted of 13 Whites and 8 Negroes, including John O. Spencer, president of Morgan College, and Carl Murphy, one of the editors of the Afro-American. This Commission made its report in 1927. It recommended equal pay for teachers of the State and the establishment of an "institution of higher learning for Colored people around Morgan College as a nucleus...equivalent in quality" to the University of Maryland.[69] It also recommended that the State make additional appropriations to Morgan. Although nothing specifically was said about the condition of the Academy, the Commission clearly intimated that state aid for Negro higher education was insufficient; that for all practical purposes no state-supported institutions for higher learning of Negroes existed within the State.

Two years after this report was made, the Assembly appointed a special commission to examine the status of higher education in the State.[70] Although the object of this commission was not to examine specifically the problem of the higher education of Negroes, something was reported about Morgan College and the Academy. The Commission requested that Morgan College be granted an appropriation of $8,000; that "some additional appropriation" be made for the Academy to place it "upon a more adequate basis" because "colored boys and girls are not receiving just the type of instruction that should be given at this school."[71] The Commission was reluctant to recommend, as Morgan College suggested, that the State set aside a scholarship fund for Negro students who desired to take higher courses not offered for them by the State. Instead, the Commission lamely recommended that a study be made into the matter of such scholarships.[72] The recommendation to appoint a commission to study the matter of scholarships for Negroes was carried out in 1935—after the State had already made provisions for a scholarship fund.

The scholarship fund was originally designed to use federal funds. An act passed in 1933 shows that the Assembly was inclined to evade further aid to Negro higher education at the expense of Morrill funds which were to be used for "partial scholarships for exceptionally worthy Negro students" to attend Morgan College or out-of-state institutions in order to take "professional courses or such other work as is not offered in the said Princess Anne Academy, but which is offered for white students in the University of Maryland."[73] The act also empowered the Regents of the University to name a board to examine applicants.

This act by the Assembly was unprecedented in the history of the administration of Morrill funds. The idea of state aid through scholarships for

Negro higher education was a recent development, but the idea of the State designating Morrill funds for such purposes had never been passed into legislation.[74] The indication of evasion and misuse of Morrill funds did not pass unnoticed by the Bureau of Education. Members of the Bureau called the matter to the attention of the Secretary of Interior, Harold L. Ickes, who wrote a letter to Governor Ritchie requesting a copy of the Act of 1933 and reminding the Governor that the Department of Interior was charged with the responsibility for the administration of Morrill funds.[75]

It is not known what further action the Bureau took or if a board ever disbursed funds in accordance with this act. However, when the Assembly met two years later in 1935, the question of out-of-state scholarships was again under considerations. The Assembly created a commission to study the matter but established a scholarship fund before the commission made its report. The Assembly's action was timely; for while the delegates were in session the question of scholarships, the disparity in education at the University and the Academy, and the principle of equality in education for Negroes were being debated before the courts. The obligation of the State toward its Negro citizens, consistently evaded in the field of education, was now being argued before the courts in order to compel the State to give more consideration to its program of higher education for Negroes.

Campus Staff

During Kiah's tenure, John O. Spencer was president of the University of Maryland College Park. In addition to his principalship, Kiah was professor of education. Kiah's staff included Barton White, horticulture, botany; John E. Smith, agriculture, chemistry; Robert A. Grigsby, vice-principal, English; Roy L. Cordery, manual training; Charles E. Clark, animal husbandry, poultry; McKinley Wright, ironwork; Daniel J. Pinkett, mathematics, physics; Lida L. Brown, English; Daniel L. Ridout, music; Margaret Bomar, domestic arts; Maslin Pinkett, science; Virginia White, English; Celestine King, secretary; Margaret Smith, matron; and Jessie Calvin, printing. It did not radically change during the remainder of his tenure. The life of faculty members fell into fairly predictable patterns, and if there was dissatisfaction, it did not curtail any faculty member's tenure. It is likely, however, that the staff as a whole openly shared Kiah's philosophy of administration and accepted the orderly but uninspiring ways of campus life. Kiah was known for holding long, regular faculty meetings every Monday night until he grew older and invariably gave long, detailed speeches on matters of student discipline or the condition of the farm. In later years, he was understandably concerned with the shrinking student enrollment; but the precise forces that were tending to undermine the existence of the Academy—its dual administration, inadequate resources, unclarified objectives, and the Negro's quest for equality of opportunity—were omitted at faculty meetings.

The background and work of the staff during Kiah's term of office provided a commentary on life at the Academy. Barton White, for example, came to the Academy as an instructor before World War I and remained on the staff until his death on December 3, 1932. He was a graduate of Hampton Institute where he was trained in horticulture. He seemed to have been well-qualified for his work and devoted a great deal of his time not only to instruction but also to the landscaping of the campus; to the planting of trees, shrubbery, and flowers; and to the maintenance of an attractive flower garden and hothouse that were frequently admired by visitors from the community. According to many observers, the campus was never so physically attractive as it was during White's custodianship.

Roy L. Cordery, also a graduate of Hampton Institute (1910), came to the staff before World War I and remained until the 1930s. He and McKinley Wright performed much of the Academy's maintenance in carpentry, plumbing, painting, and miscellaneous repair work. A native of the Shore, Wright was a student when Cordery was appointed. His industry and ability were appreciated by Kiah, who appointed him to the staff upon graduation in 1917. With the exception of a few years, Wright was employed in various instruction and maintenance positions throughout his career.

Daniel L. Ridout, the son of a Methodist minister, was born in Chestertown, Maryland, on April 21, 1898 to Frances Jones Ridout and the Reverend Archie Ridout. He attended public school wherever his father was assigned as pastor. In 1918, he graduated from Princess Anne Academy whose alma mater was composed by him. There he was an outstanding student who distinguished himself enough to have his photograph published in the Morgan College Bulletin for having written two acceptable musical compositions, "Marching on for Jesus," and "Hail the Risen King." [76] After graduating from the Academy, he attended Morgan College. Because of the death of his father, however, he left Morgan and returned to Princess Anne Academy as the secretary to Principal Thomas H. Kiah. He later joined the Academy's faculty as director of music. He was best known for directing the Princess Anne Academy Quartet.

(Figure 4.8)
The Princess Anne Quartet.
Standing left to right: Brewington Kiah, Sinclair Swann, William "Bill" Pitts, and Cyrus Derrickson. Seated: Daniel L. Ridout.

The quartet traveled, singing in area churches as well as places like Atlantic City, New Jersey. Nevertheless, their days of touring were not free of racial hostility.

In 1920, Ridout met and married Caddie A. Washington, and to this union two children were born, Vivian Ione (now deceased) and Daniel, Jr. Upon leaving the staff in 1924 he entered the ministry, distinguishing himself as a member of the Delaware Conference. After his affiliation with the Delaware Conference of the Methodist Episcopal Church in 1927, he pastored churches in Wilmington, Delaware; Atlantic City, New Jersey; St. Michaels, Maryland; Bridgeton, New Jersey; and Philadelphia, Pennsylvania. He also served as District Superintendent of the Dover District (Delaware Conference) and the Chestertown District (Peninsula Conference).

Dr. Ridout studied at the Ithica Conservatory of Music; at the Sternberg Conservatory of Music, where he majored in piano, theory, and organ; at the University of Pennsylvania; and at Temple University. In 1963, he received an honorary doctorate in music from Allen University in recognition of his outstanding work in the field of church music.

His glorious creation, the Academy's alma mater, has touched the hearts of thousands and will live on in his memory. In later years, Ridout sent his son and namesake – who, like his father, was full of musical talent – to enroll as a student in his alma mater.

Kiah's Dynamic Assistants

Lida Brown and Celestine King were members of the staff in the year of Kiah's death, and both served for many years thereafter. Both came to the staff prior to World War I. Lida Brown, a graduate of Morgan College, served as an instructor of English and language and later as a matron of John Murphy Hall. Celestine King, a graduate of the Alabama Agriculture and Mechanical College, was the Academy's clerk and bookkeeper. Evidently Celestine King, who was a reliable bookkeeper for Kiah, insisted upon the accurate recording of details. It is true that only a few of the accounts have been handed down, but enough have been preserved to show that records were carefully kept at the Academy even though Morgan College was the chief administrative agency. She is favorably remembered by former students as "the Boss" when it came to enrollment. If one lacked tuition money, the only way past her was to be willing to work in such places as the corn field or on the farm.

There is sufficient evidence in the records to show that some of the Academy's expenditures were made locally. A fairly good credit standing was maintained with local merchants and the Bank of Somerset. Bills were submitted for approval to Morgan College, but a great number of small transactions paid from the Academy's available funds. Twice per year Kiah made financial reports to officials at Morgan College, who made decisions in regard to the nature of the Academy's budget. Although Morgan College made the policy that controlled the finances, Kiah was given some latitude in making expenditures for incidentals. This latitude, however, seemed to have been more restricted toward the end of Kiah's tenure. His successors seemed to have had less choice, however, in deciding the amount to be spent or the time and place of the purchase. With the exception of student accounts, the Academy's business office had little business to record or few policies to decide. From a total disbursement of $43,408.74, only about $4,000.00 was payable to local accounts. This fact seemed particularly applicable to the period between Kiah's death and 1950.

"Junior College" Days

Besides fire and finances, another phenomenon threatened the survival of the Academy. The commencing of public secondary schools eclipsed the role of the Academy. Free public education in the counties, though always greatly inferior to the program of the Academy, led to a decline in the Academy's enrollment after World War I. Enrollment in the public schools increased at the expense of the relatively more costly program of the institution. Students began to attend the higher schools in the counties in preference to the more costly Academy. During the school year 1919-20, the total enrollment of the Academy reached 180.[77] Five years later it had dropped to 120. There was a further decline to 96 in 1930-31 and to 44 in 1931-32.[78] From another viewpoint, enrollment in the higher grades (i.e., two-year high school) of public schools increased. By the time Kiah died, the enrollment of Negroes in state-approved public high schools, practically nonexistent outside of Baltimore before 1920, had increased tremendously in such areas of the Eastern Shore as Easton, Cambridge, and Salisbury. Obviously, a great number of the students who attended county high schools were potential enrollees at the Academy.

The rising competition from public secondary schools led to the adoption of a junior college program at the Academy, which seemed to have been Kiah's idea alone. It was hoped that by this means, disaster could be averted. Kiah was interested in setting up a two-year curriculum on the collegiate level, and he contended that the coming of public high schools would justify the change. He opposed the theory that the opening of public high schools would cause the Academy to close. His plan involved a high-school division at the Academy. By adding two higher years of instruction to the curriculum, Kiah thought that students would be induced to continue studying at the Academy. For this reason, the junior college officially opened in the fall of 1925 with four students: Frank G. Fletcher, Horatio W. Jones, Alphonso

Brewington Kiah, and Cyrus W. Derrickson.

> We are small in numbers, but perhaps fortunately so, for we received the best personal attention from our beloved Principal, Dr. T.H. Kiah, and our teachers. Ours was a happy year's work, and we can never forget the pleasant memories of this the most historic year in our school lives.
>
> We returned last fall with the loss of two of our members, Frank Fletcher and Horatio Jones, the former who decided that association with a member of our Academy class of the female sex would be happier than the association with us, and the latter who accepted a position in the public schools of this county. So, though only two in number, A. Brewington Kiah, and Cyrus W. Derrickson, we are happy to have achieved so well and to have the rare distinction of being the first college graduates of our beloved school.
>
> [May] this be only a stepping stone to greater successes [in our] future.

> [Duplicated for the College Class History. Words in brackets supplied because of damage to original.]

Invariably, the first four students came from the secondary grades of the Academy, and, when students applied for admission from other secondary schools, the requirements of admission were loosely interpreted in order to induce enrollment. Records of applicants were not carefully checked and kept, and students were admitted under the guarantee of eliminating deficiencies. It is highly probable, however, that only a few dozen students were ever enrolled in the college at any time prior to 1936. In addition, only a few teachers, a third of whom held no baccalaureate degree themselves and who taught a variety of subjects such as economics, sociology, trigonometry, and algebra gave instruction.

Enrollment, therefore, was not stimulated during the remainder of Kiah's term and continued so until the Academy's revitalized organization of 1947. Needless to say, the junior college idea failed to bring the desired results. In fact, Princess Anne Academy was never approved as such by the State Department of Education or ever acknowledged in American directories of junior colleges. Indeed, the Academy's junior college was a misnomer because the program of the Academy continued to be conducted in much the same manner as previously with basically the same staff, equipment, and methods of administration.

"In 1930, the Board of Regents set aside $600 for scholarships to enable the two-year graduates to attend out-of-state, four-year colleges to complete their college education. In 1935, the Maryland Legislature appropriated $30,000 for scholarships for out-of-state education for Blacks."[79]

Housing and Disaster

Housing was one of the earliest problems in the history of the Academy. From the time of Bird's administration, the problem of adequate housing periodically appeared as enrollment increased or as disaster struck through fire. To begin with, the home of Olney was inadequate as student enrollment increased. With their limited resources, however, the officials of the Academy were unable to construct other buildings in time to meet the growing demand of the Academy's program. Furthermore when this demand was partially satisfied and the Academy's program was fairly well established, destruction of buildings through fire again intensified the problem of housing, eventually focusing attention upon the condition of the Academy. Moreover, the Academy's main physical plant never consisted of more than two or three buildings until 1940, a condition which was exploited when proposals were made to abandon the Academy altogether.

Much of the story of the Academy's physical plant centers on the old Olney home because this building was the main structure on the campus for forty years after its acquisition in 1886. It was used for practically every function that took place on the campus. At various times, it served as the principal's residence and office, the classroom, the dormitory, the dining hall, and the faculty dwelling. It was being used solely as a faculty dwelling as late as 1950. At the time of Bird's arrival, Olney contained about eighteen rooms, including a large room on the first floor that was probably once used by the Haynies as a reception room and library. As the years progressed, Olney was renovated, repaired, and altered to the extent that the original floor plan was changed and a porch was added after 1919.

ALMA MATER

DANIEL LYMAN RIDOUT, SR.

1

To thee, dear Alma Mater,
We raise our grateful song,
For through thy noble teachings
Thou hast made thy children strong;
And thousands still shall praise thee,
All earth shall hear their swell,
And bind our hearts yet closer
To thee we love so well.

2

We love thy spacious campus,
We love thy tow'ring halls.
And hallow'd are the lessons
We've learn'd within thy walls.
Stand thou forever glorious,
Full-rob'd in living green;
Shine thou in endless splendor
Beneath thy trees serene.

Refrain

Maryland, Maryland, Home of Maroon and Gray;
Maryland, Maryland, thee we love alway.
All hail to thee, fair Maryland,
All glory be to thee!
Grow thou in strength and honor
Through all eternity!

Ridout

(Figure 4.9)
University of Maryland Eastern Shore's Alma Mater
written by Daniel Lyman Ridout Sr.

87

Largely with student labor, an annex of frame construction was built adjacent to the rear of Olney in 1887, giving Olney the appearance from a front view of being incongruously constructed of brick and frame. This annex, a two-storied structure, contained about eight or ten rooms.[80] Students often posed for photographs in front of Olney, and an examination of several such photographs shows that the front of the annex contained four windows and a door facing the same direction as Olney. The first floor of the annex was originally used as a dining room and the second floor as a dormitory for boys. After the boys'dormitory was completed, the second floor was used for classrooms, called recitation rooms, and a section of the first floor was used for laundry. The dining hall continued in use until 1919. The annex was the second building that appeared on campus. Its face was oriented to the southwest, the same direction as Olney, and all subsequent plans for buildings were based upon this same orientation.

Olney and the annex never had a central heating plant. The cooking and laundering carried on in the frame annex made both buildings a fire hazard. It is not surprising that a disastrous fire began in the laundry room in 1919. No doubt some students left their laundry to dry near the stove. Igniting other garments, the fire spread rapidly throughout the annex, which was then popularly known as the Domestic Science Hall or the Dining Room. Before the fire was brought under control, it had engulfed the entire annex and most of Olney, endangering some of Professor Kiah's younger children, who were then asleep upstairs in the old Olney home. The fire completely destroyed the frame annex and gutted a great deal of the interior of Olney, including the principal's office and residence. No lives were lost, but the damage was a severe blow to the program of the Academy inasmuch as Olney and its annex were certainly the vital center of campus life in 1919. An account of the fire appeared in the Wicomico News, a publication in Salisbury, Maryland; which, though not generally disposed to report news of the Negro, gave an objective report, indicating the gravity of the destruction.

NEGRO ACADEMY BURNED
Princess Anne Branch of Morgan College
Was Old Landmark

Princess Anne, Md., April 19 — The main building of the Princess Anne Academy, a branch of Morgan College about one half mile east of here, was destroyed by fire early this morning. The fire is supposed to have originated from an overheated stove in the laundry. The school is devoted to the education of colored youths, male and female, and the agricultural course is one of the leading branches taught at the institution. The fire destroyed the administrative offices, recreation room, dining hall, kitchen and laundry. Tentative arrangements have been made to carry on the work for the balance of the school year, ending the latter part of May. There are about 125 boarding pupils at the school.

The building destroyed consisted of a center portion of brick, with two large frame wings. The center portion was one of the old landmarks of Somerset County, and has been known for more than 100 years as Olney Hall. The loss, estimated from $15,000 to $20,000, is partly covered by insurance.[81]

The exact nature of the "tentative arrangements" that were made to meet the emergency is not known. It is likely that the functions carried on in Olney and the annex were transferred to the boys' dormitory and the mechanic arts building for the remainder of the school year; and efforts were made to place Olney, only partially destroyed, in shape for rehabitation. Nevertheless, a temporary building costing about $3,500 was secured through state funds, and the trustees of Morgan College promised to replace the dining hall.[82] The promise of the dining hall, however, did not materialize until 1921 when a brick refectory, costing about $30,000 was completed. This refectory remained in use until 1950 when a third dining hall was erected for the Academy, this time by the State. The grant by Morgan College for the old refectory was the greatest single investment that the trustees ever made to the branch in Princess Anne. Oddly enough, it was the fruition of a promise made thirteen years earlier, ripened by the disaster of fire.

The old Olney home was restored after the fire of 1919, but its existence as a part of the physical plant was continued more as a necessity and adjunct than as a vital center of campus life. The building, however, had not completely outlived its usefulness in housing members of the faculty. It continued to be used for this purpose when, physically, it needed to be renovated for habitation or remodeled as a keepsake for history. Little was done to effect either. It was continuously occupied as a dwelling with only piecemeal repairs being made. Thus, Olney remained standing in the heart of the campus without assurance of its future preservation or respect for its past. Among townspeople, its name was scarcely remembered; among students and faculty, its name was forgotten. Understandably, the slave tradition that surrounded Olney's creation was forgotten, but the new role of its preservation as a dilapidated dwelling was never clarified—unless possibly the Academy's absentee policymakers considered Olney to be good enough for the higher education of Negroes.

Before the Academy could fully recover from the devastating fire of 1919, only five years later in 1924 another fire broke out on the small campus destroying the boys dormitory. It was the second building, built in 1888 several yards north of Olney, constructed on the campus. With a familiar beech tree in front of its entrance, the dormitory was a landmark on the campus. The destruction was not fatal to any of the occupants, all male students, but the problem of housing was accentuated for students who lived in the building.[83]

Constructed of frame, the dormitory contained about fourteen rooms and relieved much of the overcrowded conditions in Olney and the annex. Its first floor housed the chapel and "book room," or library, causing the building to be popularly known as the "chapel" even though the first floor served to some extent as a recreational hall for band and literary concerts. The second floor was used as the boys dormitory. When completed, the building contained no central system for heating, water, or sewage. It had no basement, and the cost of its construction was unknown.[84] Students frequently loitered in front of the building, despite the watchful eye of the principal next door; and in later years when the building was replaced, faculty members took advantage of the shaded area to wash or to park their automobiles.

The fire renewed the issue of housing, revealing once again the inadequacy of the Academy's housing program. Accordingly, the State was asked to provide another building to replace the old dormitory. That the Assembly was in session at the time of the fire facilitated and highlighted the request for aid. With the destruction of the fire fresh in mind, the Assembly appropriated $40,000 for the construction and the equipment of a new building on April 9, 1924.[85] This sum was the largest amount that the State had appropriated for construction or maintenance for the Academy in Princess Anne. Once again the Academy in Princess Anne, by fortuitous circumstance of a disastrous fire, modified its physical plant.

The building that replaced the old boys dormitory was popularly known as the "Administrative Building," being erected on the first land that the State acquired in the heretofore-private landholdings of Morgan College in Princess

Anne. It was a brick structure of three stories, outwardly the most impressive structure on the campus at the time of its completion. It was soon used to replace many of the functions carried on in Olney or in the old boys dormitory. Without many partitions in its original floor plan, the building was eventually partitioned in order to serve many uses, such as dormitory, classroom, principal's office, and library. Several of these functions, including that of the library, were being carried on as late as 1950.

Land-Grant Beginnings

Although federal aid to education in Maryland came long before the founding of the Academy, its existence as a factor in the history of education in the State was premised upon the theory of equitable distribution of funds for Whites and Negroes alike. The Academy became the land-grant institution for Negroes and the Maryland Agricultural College, the land-grant institution for Whites. Contingent upon the equitable distribution of funds between the races, federal funds were a source of valuable support during the early years when state aid for higher education was in its infancy for Whites or was barely existent for Negroes. That the Academy was designated as the State's recipient of the Negro's share of land-grant funds was an expediency that was readily accepted by Whites and Negroes alike.

The first Morrill Act of 1862 established the principle and method of selling public lands for the benefit of education. Sponsored by a Congressman from Vermont, Justin S. Morrill, this act was a Magna Carta in the relationship of the federal government to public education. Generally speaking, the Morrill Act of 1862 provided that public lands were to be sold at $1.25 per acre in lots not less than one quarter of a section; and the proceeds from the sales invested in federal, state, or "safe" stocks, bearing an interest of not less than five percent, were to constitute a perpetual fund for the endowment, support, and maintenance of at least one college where the leading object shall be, without excluding other scientific and classical studies, and including military tactics, to teach such branches of learning as are related to agriculture and the mechanic arts."[86] This act further required that annual progress reports were to be made by the colleges. The apportionment of proceeds was based upon population with 30,000 acres being allowed for each senator and representative in Congress. Maryland's apportionment was 210,000 acres.

Maryland gave their assent to the act but, like other Southern states, designated land-grant funds for Negro education only after the passage of the second Morrill Act of 1890, which was passed expressly to prevent racial discrimination in the distribution of land-grant funds. The act was therefore a step in the direction of granting a measure of equality for Negroes in the field of education.

Maryland was one of only two states to specify funds for privately controlled Negro schools, but the Academy in Princess Anne was the only Negro school in the State that could claim to offer any semblance of agricultural and mechanical subjects required by the land-grant acts. That such a school was already in existence with more than 100 acres of land and with, to some extent, an industrial program was conveniently seized upon by state officials who were unwilling to invest state funds in the construction of any Negro school solely to comply with the demands of the Morrill Act of 1890. Both Morgan College and the Maryland Agricultural College needed funds, and the designation of the Academy was regarded as the most convenient way—and the least expensive way—that the State could continue to receive land-grant funds. Events that transpired during this interim led to the establishment of the Academy as a Negro land-grant institution.

An agreement was signed on December 31, 1890, designating the Academy to receive land-grant funds. The agreement acknowledged the Academy as the "Eastern Branch" of the Maryland Agricultural College. Through this contract, the Academy became one of the first Negro branches of a white college in the history of education in America. The older idea expressed in the Morrill Act of making education of like character for Negroes, losing the convenient singularity of its historic land-grant setting, found new expression in controversy over "separate but equal" or "integrated" education for Negroes.

The contract of 1890 was largely a one-sided agreement that placed the responsibility of providing education of like character for Negroes upon the governing body of the Maryland Agricultural College in College Park. The administration of all land-grant funds was placed in the hands of officials at College Park for the promise of educational and economic facilities similar to those of the white institution. In reality, the promise was an empty one; in the light of history, the contract was an artifice.

Although the contract was only legally in force until April 1892, it

92

served the purpose of mandating the school in College Park as a guardian of federal monies and it opened the Academy as another branch of another school with distant and often indifferent administrative offices across the Bay. The onus of dual control came with the gift of land-grant aid. State and federal officials accepted the contract. On February 25, 1891, Jackson stated in a letter to the Secretary of Interior that the State had made arrangements by contract for compliance with the Morrill Act of 1890. Several days later, March 3, Jackson wrote that he had certified the State to the Treasury Department as being entitled to receive Morrill funds, amounting to $16,000 for the fiscal year ending June 30, 1891.[87]

The Assembly appointed a special committee on education. Its members[88] visited the Maryland Agricultural College but found that legislative duties prevented them from visiting this Eastern Branch. The committee found that the contract was liberal and that it met the approval of officials in Washington. The contract itself was regarded as proof that the College "complied with the requirements of the last Congressional grant in regard to instruction of 'like character' for colored students."[89] The report was adopted, and the Assembly later gave its formal assent to the Act of 1890 on March 15, 1892.

The Academy first received land-grant funds through Morgan College sometime during the year of 1891. The funds were sent to the state treasurer, as in most states, and the treasurer sent the payment to the Maryland Agricultural College, which in turn sent a portion of the fund to Morgan College or during the early years kept it as a credit balance in College Park. It is not definitely known, but it is probable that the Academy's first share, which would amount to 20 percent of the apportionment, was kept as a balance in College Park. In one of the reports of the Maryland Agricultural College, it is noted that large back payments were made for expenses at the "Eastern Branch."[90] It appears, however, that the funds were equitably distributed and that Morgan College regularly received the Academy's share through the Maryland Agricultural College.

By the turn of the century, the share of the Eastern Branch was about $5,000, nearly nine-tenths of the school's total income. With the coming of the Nelson Amendment in 1907, the school's share was eventually increased to $10,000 by 1913.[91] Subsequent federal statutes continued to extend aid to land-grant institutions, but the Academy, along with all other Negro land-grant schools were excluded.[92]

The influence of Hampton and Tuskegee was widespread. "Colored training" schools, aided by the counties and the Slater Fund, were coming into acceptance; and a great number of states, including Maryland, gave cognizance to the movement. The Maryland Assembly, therefore, appointed a commission to study the problem of the halted funds. With high praise for Booker T. Washington and Tuskegee, this commission recommended the establishment of a training school in the State for "colored teachers" and the use of county funds for the industrial education of the Negro. It realized that something should be done for Negroes who were "still wards of the state."[93] About the time that this study was being conducted, the question arose whether the Academy should receive the Negro's share of Morrill funds. The Bureau of Education answered this question decisively in the affirmative.

The president of the Maryland Agricultural College, now R.W. Silvester, entertained some doubts regarding the exclusive right of the Academy to have the Negro's share of Morrill funds. The Commissioner mandated that Nelson funds could only be used by the College and the Academy.[94] Silvester was aware that some persons in the State favored the division of the Academy's share, and he expressed this sentiment in a letter to the Commissioner dated June 24, 1909.[95] The Bureau insisted again, however, that the College and the Academy were the only two schools in the State that could receive land-grant funds. Even as late as 1919, some persons thought that land-grant funds should be shared with the Negro school in Bowie, Maryland.[96]

Since the Bureau was not a law-enforcing body, its efforts to curtail infractions of the use of Morrill funds were based upon moral suasion and upon an occasional threat to recommend discontinuation of land-grant funds. The passivity of the Bureau was of little help in enforcing the "like character" provision of the Act of 1890, either at the Academy or at any other location. Indeed, conditions at the Academy were periodically exposed in reports of the Bureau.

During the age of reform, from about 1890 to 1920, the land-grant colleges emerged into the forefront of American life.[97] For Maryland, the decade after the turn of the century marked the beginning of a new era in the Bureau's interest in land-grant education. The Commissioner of Education, Elmer E. Brown, was of the opinion that the facts should be known about land-grant institutions. He was particularly interested in knowing whether the institutions were complying with the provisions of the law and obtained an opinion from the Attorney General, who assured him that the Commissioner of Education, acting through the Secretary of Interior, was empowered to "ascertain and certify as to whether each institution was entitled to receive its share of Morrill funds."[98] Accordingly, Brown authorized a special survey of land-grant institutions to determine the extent that institutions were complying with the law.

Kendrick C. Babcock and Arthur C. Monohan, specialists in the Bureau, were given the assignment. With the exception of one institution, they visited all land-grant institutions east of the Mississippi River. Their report was made on June 17, 1911. They found that land-grant institutions continued to give "false items" in their annual reports to the Bureau. They found that Negro institutions on the whole, being devoted to academic and teacher training, did not regard agriculture or mechanic arts as the "leading object" according to the requirement of the Morrill Act. They reported that Negro colleges not infrequently gave instruction on a "grade as low as the 4th or 5th of the public schools." Specifically, they found that the Academy depended almost entirely upon federal support and therefore used federal funds for all phases of the school's program.

It is likely that the Bureau's investigation and Brown's threat to discontinue Morrill funds were made known to the authorities at the Maryland Agricultural College. Certainly there is evidence that the Bureau was displeased with land-grant arrangements in Maryland, a fact that caused some apprehensions with respect to Silvester as the president of the Maryland Agricultural College. Accordingly, Silvester telephoned Brown on February 2, 1912 and inquired if there were objections to the continued designation of the Academy as the recipient of Morrill funds. Brown replied the same day, stating in a letter to Silvester that there was no objection to the designation of the Academy. Nevertheless, Brown intimated that the administration of the Academy was questionable. He suggested that a separate board of trustees should be established for the Academy, "which would be more satisfactory than what then existed between the Maryland Agricultural College and Princess Anne Academy."

As an afterthought, the Commissioner decided to examine the contract of 1890 between the College and the Academy. On the next day after his letter to Silvester (February 3), he telephoned the chief clerk in the Department of Interior and requested to see a copy of the contract. Accordingly, the clerk forwarded a copy of the contract with a letter of transmittal. The contract was returned to the clerk on February 7. Thus, attention was focused upon the problem of the administration of land-grant funds in Maryland, but a solution was left open for the future as additional surveys by the Bureau continued to reveal discrepancies in the administration of the affairs of the Academy.

A survey published in 1916, for example, was none too complimentary in its recommendations concerning the Academy. The survey was conducted by Thomas Jesse Jones, a "specialist in the education of racial groups" and a director of the Phelps-Stokes Foundation. Jones made a visit to the Academy in 1915. In addition to giving a statistical profile of the school, Jones made a basic recommendation that "the provision of the land-grant act for agricultural and industrial subjects, though well-taught, were subordinated to literary studies."

A more comprehensive report of the Bureau was completed in 1928 under the direction of Arthur J. Klein, chief of the Bureau's Division of Higher Education. Again the Academy was under surveillance, and the findings were again uncomplimentary. The report concluded that "Princess Anne Academy has not realized to any great extent its possibilities as the Negro Land-Grant College of Maryland," and the Academy's condition was blamed upon the "lack of a vigorous attitude on the part of those responsible for its welfare." Accordingly, the report recommended that the school be placed under an "independent board of trustees in order that it may have the undivided attention of those responsible for its welfare," and that the school be provided with its own president "separate and distinct from the executive head of Morgan College." Thus, once again attention was focused upon the administration of land-grant funds in Maryland, and once again it was suggested that the Academy should have its own board of control.

Even though federal authorities made their position clear and often reiterated their findings in regard to the administration of the Academy, the dual control of the school was not ended until 1936. The authorities of Morgan College and the Maryland Agricultural College seemed to have been more interested in protecting their interests in the Academy than in following or advocating proposals made by the Bureau. In fact, to the extent that the actions of the Bureau continued to be advisory, the two governing institutions continued to accept the status quo of the Academy. The interest of the

Maryland Agricultural College in the Academy lay mainly in the maintenance of the Academy as a means to ensure an uninterrupted flow of federal funds to the State while the interests of Morgan College lay mainly in the protection of its property interests in Princess Anne. To the extent that federal insistence was not a threat to these interests, the officials of both institutions were complacent and evasive to the question of the control of the school.

Accordingly, another contract was conveniently made between Morgan College and the white institution in College Park. In the agreement drawn up in 1919, it was agreed that a "college" should continue "to be maintained and developed" at Princess Anne under the control and administration of the Maryland State College of Agriculture, the legal offspring of the old Maryland Agricultural College. It was further agreed that the property interests of both parties would be respected and used for educational purposes only. A. F. Woods, president of the College in College Park, and Spencer signed the agreement.

Ostensibly, this agreement gave promise of a new deal at the Academy. In reality, however, no basic administrative or educational change was brought about; and the Academy continued to drift as before, stagnant as ever under dual administrations that were aloof and apathetic toward the school's welfare. In the light of history, this contract appeared to have been another dilatory measure—a legal subterfuge—to allay criticism by federal authorities.

One clause of the contract, however, made provision for Morgan College to sell its interests in Princess Anne to the College in College Park whenever Morgan's trustees found the agreement "unsatisfactory." After twenty more years of dual control, both parties began to negotiate again but only after the Klein Report had recommended administrative changes. Both parties agreed in 1928 that all accounts of the Academy should be taken over by the University of Maryland, formerly the Maryland Agricultural College. This agreement was kept, and the University of Maryland in 1928 then began to affect management of the affairs of the school. Nevertheless, settlement of the interests of Morgan College was delayed.

Consequently, officials of Morgan College wanted the University to pay a rental for the use of the Academy's property, but officials of the University insisted that the State should buy the school outright. According to the contract of 1919, Morgan College seemed to have had the better of the legal argument, though neither party had ever kept its promise. Therefore, the bickering of

Morgan College and the University as to whether the property should be sold or rented, according to clauses of the contract of 1919, had more of an academic than a legal basis. After several conferences between officials of both schools, however, the Academy's absentee policymakers made another major decision. On February 13, 1931, a joint meeting of representatives of Morgan College and the University unanimously resolved that Morgan's interests in Princess Anne should be purchased and a rental should be paid to Morgan until the purchase could be concluded.

There was more bickering about the sale price and the rental, but both colleges finally agreed to recommend that the State should conclude the transaction by payment of a sum of $100,000 to Morgan College. Accordingly, the Assembly made the recommendation into law in 1935; and the State became the sole owner of the school in Princess Anne. The sum was to be paid in four annual installments of $25,000, each beginning on October 1, 1935. A confirmatory deed and contract were consummated in Somerset County, formally transferring the Academy to the State "for the use of the University of Maryland" in March 1936.

The transfer of the school to the State brought few immediate results in the program of the school, but its timing coincided with the historic question of the responsibility of the State toward its Negro citizens. More change was stimulated when Donald Gaines Murray, a Negro graduate of Amherst College in 1934, applied to enter the school of law of the University of Maryland (located in Baltimore) on January 24, 1935. He was refused admission and filed his complaint in the local courts. The courts of Baltimore ordered Murray to be admitted, but the University took the decision to the Court of Appeals of Maryland in October of 1935, permitting Murray to enroll in September pending action of the higher courts. The Court of Appeals upheld the decision of the lower courts and Murray was permitted to continue his studies at the University from which he was graduated in 1938.

Arguments in Murray's case reflected contrasts in the approach to the philosophy underlying state aid. The University argued that it was not technically a government (state) agency and as such was not bound to accept students indiscriminately; that the University reserved freedom of action in the selection of its students. Murray's counsel disagreed, pointing out that the University was in reality a state-supported institution and as such, citizens of the State—Negroes and Whites alike—had the right to share the benefits of state aid.

The old Reconstruction Amendment, the Fourteenth, was invoked by Murray's counsel which was aware of the fact that the State had long neglected the support of Negro education and that its University, long a recipient of state funds, had neglected its Negro branch in Princess Anne. It was further contended by Murray's counsel that the Morrill Act of 1890 entitled the Negro to equitable instruction. Instruction at the school in Princess Anne, a part of the University of Maryland, was far from equitable; and scholarships would not suffice. Failure to admit Murray, his counsel argued, was an abridgement of his rights as a citizen without due process for law.

Charles Hamilton Houston, a Negro lawyer of Washington, D.C., who was a graduate of the Harvard Law School, led Murray's counsel, and a young dynamic lawyer named Thurgood Marshall argued the case. Houston devoted a great deal of his professional life for the attainment of Negro rights, conducting a crusade, relentlessly and untiringly, for the Negro's equality before the law. It appears that, though separated by more than a century, Houston exhibited some of the moral courage and ethical qualities that were characteristic in the making of Frederick Douglass, the Negro abolitionist. As few Negro leaders have been unable to achieve since the time of Douglass, Houston skillfully and clearly translated this temperament into a weapon for the rights of Negroes. Whereas Douglass relied chiefly upon persuasive oratory, Houston relied upon his skill and clarity in the delineation of legal concepts. He moved carefully in his legal strategy from an attack upon inequality before the law to an attack upon the accepted theory of separate but equal within the law. He did not live to see the fruits of the latter attack. The case of Henderson vs. The Southern Railway, a case involving the separate but equal theory, was pending before the Supreme Court at the time of his death, April 22, 1950. Upon his death, the Washington Post praised Houston in an editorial as "a crusader for a principle that lies at the heart of American Democracy."

Within the professional lifetime of Charles H. Houston, a profound and significant change took place in the emancipation of American Negroes. He was one of the principal architects of this change. His great gifts as a lawyer were devoted from the beginning of his career to an unremitting battle to win for Negroes genuine equality before the law. Formidable statutory barriers of discrimination on grounds of race crumbled under the skill and stubbornness of his onslaught. It is a tragedy that he could not have lived to see the final victory of the cause he championed and did so much to win.

An outstanding student at the Harvard Law School— he was the first Negro editor of the Harvard Law Review— and later vice dean of the School of Law at Howard University, he served as a special counsel for the National Association for the Advancement of Colored People. He led the successful appeal to the courts in the restrictive covenants cases culminating in a decision by the Supreme Court two years ago that such covenants are unenforceable by either state or federal courts. And he was in the forefront of the effort to secure equal educational opportunities for Negroes in state universities. Whites no less than Negroes must mourn the death of this crusader for a principle that lies at the heart of American Democracy.[99]

Houston lived to see some of the fruits of the Murray case, which created a sensation in educational circles. One of the most widely circulated school magazines, School and Society, carried the results of the case in its February 1936 issue. Moreover, Houston himself wrote an article in the March issue of Crisis, a Negro publication, in which he cautioned the Negro not to shout too soon over the success of the Murray case in opening white universities to Negro students. Furthermore H. L. Mencken, the irreverent literary critic of Maryland, wrote an article for the Sun expressing hope that Murray would be welcomed by white students at the University's School of Law. The May 6 Evening Sun of Baltimore, however, observed that the action on Murray's case would cost the State a lot of money before the thing was over. Generally, the Negro press hailed the decision.

Murray's case was a precedent. It rendered all professional schools in the University System open to Negroes. It was a symbol of the Negro's struggle to obtain equality in education through legal action, and it was a noteworthy precedent for the Negro's subsequent attack upon the iniquities of a segregated system of education for Negroes.[100] Within several months after Murray's victory in the Baltimore courts, the attorneys of Lloyd Lionel Gaines, a graduate of Vashon High School in St. Louis and of Lincoln University, Jefferson City, Missouri, filed a similar suit. The Gaines' case was more celebrated than the Murray decision because it was eventually argued before the Supreme Court whose decision in the case established a legal landmark in the higher education of the Negro. The decision was handed down on December 12, 1938, declaring that the State was bound to furnish "within its borders facilities for legal education substantially equal to those...afforded for persons of the white race, whether or not other Negroes sought the same privileges."

The decision in the Gaines' case was more inclusive in scope than the decision reached in the Murray case. Whereas the Murray case left open the question of the legality of out-of-state scholarships in regard to studies other than those of law, the Supreme Court indicated in its ruling that other studies were also covered by its decision. Chief Justice Charles Evans Hughes, in handing down his decision, referred at length to the Murray case. Other legal suits followed the Murray and Gaines cases, employing substantially the same fundamental pleas for the equal rights of Negroes in higher education. Herman Sweatt filed a suit against the University of Texas and Ada Sipuel filed against the University of Oklahoma. In August 1949, a half dozen suits were filed for Negroes to enter various professional schools of the University of Maryland.[101] Indeed, resort to legal action by Negroes was not an unusual practice by 1950.

A week before Houston's death, the Court of Appeals of Maryland ordered the University to admit another Negro student, Esther McCready, to its school of nursing. This was the second major decision that the higher courts of Maryland rendered in behalf of the admission of Negroes to the University. This decision, headlined by the Afro-American, also made frequent reference to the Murray case which Houston, from his hospital bed in Washington, may have recalled was decided fourteen years earlier. During the interval, Negro students attended the school of law at the University; but the Regents, in giving sanction to the continuation of the Academy, were reluctant to concede the admission of Negro students to the various schools of the University. At a meeting held on graduation day, June 7, 1950, in Princess Anne, the Regents served notice that support would be continued for the University's branch and that the decision of the McCready case would be appealed.

It is difficult to evaluate the effects of the Murray and Gaines cases upon the actions of the State in regard to the higher education of its Negroes, but there is no doubt that legal assaults upon the system prompted a consideration of the problem. Certainly, the coming of the Murray decision coincided with the coming of a new era in the State's support and interest in Negro higher education. Yet with the advent of legal assaults that threatened, if only remotely, to undermine much of the State's traditional, complacent, and conservative approach to the problem, the State's consideration of the problem left much room for doubt and speculation. This was clearly shown in the controversy that developed in regard to the disposition of the old Academy in Princess Anne.

Kiah's Death

Meanwhile, while higher education manipulated the very life of the Academy, students on campus were striking and boycotting classes because they were not permitted to dance. Perhaps unaware of the glass walls surrounding the campus and shielding its inhabitants from the ever frightful, ever impending danger of certain demise, the students threw rocks from within. Kiah's untimely death, however, intervened; and out of respect for his memory, no dance was held during the school year 1936-37. Kiah died at the Peninsula General Hospital in Salisbury on the afternoon of December 30, 1936. He had hit his leg on a wood stove and died from the resulting blood poisoning.[102] His funeral, like Bird's, was held in the Metropolitan Church, and he was interred on the campus. As in the case of many other Negro schools, Kiah's administration of recreational activities lagged far behind currently accepted practices found in a great number of public institutions. The administration's control over the recreational phase of school life—and, indeed, over all other phases of school life—was looked upon as thoroughly undemocratic, suppressing individual initiative and freedom. The Academy sponsored its first dance the next school term.

Kiah drifted with the currents that shaped the destiny of the Academy. During his long term of office of twenty-six years, life at the school became more passive and less controllable by the principal. When Kiah came to the principalship, he found a preparatory school that was well organized and that conducted work on a level comparable to any other higher schools for Negroes in Maryland—as well as many in the nation. The Academy was able to maintain a dual role of preparing students for the secondary level of education while instructing students at a more advanced level. That has been the history, providing access to those who need remediation while maintaining the standard. When Kiah died in office in 1936, however, the school had lost its position as a secondary school and had not gained one as a college in spite of its self-imposed name change around 1934 to Princess Anne College.

Contrasts in school life during Kiah's tenure revealed how far the school deviated from its early mission as a preparatory school toward a land-grant college that existed largely in name only. When he came to the school, the enrollment consisted of about 140 students; when he died, it had decreased to 36. School income more than tripled, but the campus hardly showed any signs of better maintenance or basic improvements. Salaries of teachers increased, but the teaching load was drastically reduced. More funds were spent for agriculture in order to satisfy state and federal demands, but teacher training remained the chief work of the school. On paper, the curriculum was set up for college work; but few measures were taken to make this change a living reality. Plans to make the school a junior college, though well conceived, were stillborn while yet additional plans were being made for a four-year college. During Kiah's term, much of the old life of the school remained while new ideas were not readily received or implemented. Few changes were made in the appearance or function of the school. Vice-Principal Robert A. Grigsby was chosen to fill the gap.

ENDNOTES

CHAPTER 4

[1] This date is given on his tombstone. His obituary, given by Jacob C. Dunn who knew him very well, gives the date of birth as August 14, 1855. See Minutes, 1898, p. 54 et. seq.

[2] Ibid.

[3] The Eastern Shore Steamboat Company and the Maryland Steamboat Company operated regular steamboat service from Baltimore to points along the Eastern Shore during the summer of 1886. The Maryland Steamboat Company, however, was the only company that regularly carried passengers and freight to Deal Island, the route taken by the Birds.

[4] Interview, Joseph Hayman, Princess Anne, Maryland, January 1950.

[5] Minutes, 1898, p. 54.

[6] Dennis, Interview, op. cit.

[7] The date of opening and names of the first students were given by one of the first students, Hampton T. Johnson, a Methodist minister residing in Elkton, Maryland in December of 1948.

[8] Minutes, 1898, p. 54.

[9] Dunn is not listed by Bird in a report found in the Annual Report, Maryland Agricultural College, for 1895 (Hereafter cited as Report (Univ.). Also, Dunn is not listed on the staff in reports for 1891, 1893. However, there is some evidence that he returned to the staff for a short period after 1895.

[10] A memorial to Dunn was read to the Conference, but it was not (contrary to a usual practice) recorded in the Minutes.

[11] Report (Univ.), 1893.

[12] Report (Univ.), 1891, p. 43.

[13] Ibid.

[14] Ibid. In 1895, Bird reported a total enrollment of 130. See Report (Univ.), 1895.

[15] Information from Hampton T. Johnson.

[16] Minutes, 1898, p. 56.

[17] In later years, Hargis established an award in memory of his mother for the best oration in English.

[18] Report (Univ.), 1893.

[19] Nutter, Interview, op. cit.

[20] Minutes, 1897, p. 54, et. seq.

[21] Liber W.J.S., vol. 80, p. 549.

[22] Hargis was instrumental in establishing an alumni association during Kiah's early years in office. After his graduation in 1893, Hargis was active and interested in the organization of the alumni.

[23] Horatio Jones, Interview, May 9, 1949, Princess Anne. Jones was O'Connell's student at Morgan College.

[24] Minutes, 1905, p. 53.

[25] Minutes, 1907, p. 101.

[26] From a speech found in the Alumni Record of Hampton Institute. Major Walter R. Brown, past Secretary of Hampton Institute submitted the speech to past historian of UMES, Dr. W. Augustus Low.

[27] Alain Locke (ed.), The New Negro (New York), 1925. See also Rayford W. Logan (ed.), What the Negro Wants (Chapel Hill, N.C.), 1944, and Robert L. Jack, History of the National Association for the Advancement of Colored People (Boston), 1943.

[28] By 1895, the movement to replace white teachers in Negro schools had gained a prominent place in the Negro's political thinking in Baltimore. For example, the Baltimore Afro-American, a Negro newspaper that was first published in 1892, devoted an editorial (nearly one column in length) protesting against the employment of white teachers in Negro schools, on October 19, 1895. Another editorial on November 2, 1895 urged Negroes to vote the Republican ticket because the candidate for Mayor, Alcaeus Hooper, had promised to discontinue such "mixed schools."

[29] Sun, March 19, 1892

[30] Sun, February 13, 1893.

[31] The Baltimore Afro-American for March 26, 1898 noted that the first colored grammar school under all Negro teachers opened "a few days ago."

[32] Laws, 1896, ch. 261.

[33] Sun, March 26, 1896.

[34] There were dozens of privately supported schools—institutes, academies, and colleges—in operation in the State in the generation following the close of the Civil War. For example, issues of the Sun during the months of September often carried two columns of advertisements of schools with only a few lines devoted to each. See issues of the Sun for September 1872.

[35] The State appropriated $6,000 to the Maryland Agricultural College in 1856. This sum remained unchanged until 1880 when, after some dissatisfaction, the Assembly appropriated "five dollars and no more" until 1888. From 188 to 1894 the original sum was restored.

[36] Privott letter dated January 28, 1907.

[37] Ibid.

[38] Ibid.

[39] Letter, C.C. Reed, dated September 28, 1907.

[40] Morgan College Bulletin, February, 1915.

[41] Minutes, 1911, p.123.

[42] Ibid. p. 88-92.

[43] Account Ledger, 1922, pp. 294-6.

[44] Ibid.

[45] Ibid. 1920, p. 300.

[46] A copy of this letter was found in one of the student ledgers. Although undated, the letter was no doubt mailed several weeks prior to the opening of school, September 27, 1920.

[47] A student ledger for 1924-25 shows that in November of this school year, a collection of only $6.28 was obtained from the sale of football tickets. Printing the posters to advertise the game cost of $9.95.

[48] Morgan College Bulletin, 1913 (June), p.24.

[49] Ibid.

[50] Morgan College Bulletin, 1914 (August), p. 71.

[51] Ibid.

[52] Report (Sup't), 1920, pp. 31, 34.

[53] Maryland's Eastern Shore: A Journey in Time and Place, John R. Wennersten, pp 149-157.

[54] Ibid. p. 155.

[55] Leroy S. Boyd, Maryland Agricultural College (Washington), 1912.

[56] A movement for better schools was given cognizance in the platforms of both Democrats and Republicans, and commissioners of public schools went on record for better pay of teachers. See the Sun, 1911, for September 8, 9, 13.

[57] City Wide Congress of Baltimore, Report of Committee on Maryland Agricultural College, May 16, 1914 (Baltimore), 1914.

[58] Chapter 844 of the Assembly of 1914 appointed the Commission. Its report was submitted to Governor Phillips Lee Goldsborough on December 20, 1915, being published by the General Education Board under the authorship of Abraham Flexner and Frank P. Bachman, Public Education in Maryland: A Report of the Educational Survey Commission (New York), 1916.

[59] Laws, 1914, ch. 721, sec. 113.

[60] Morgan College received its first appropriation from the Assembly in 1918. The amount was $1,000, Laws, 1918, ch. 70, sec. 206. For the biennials of 1920, 1922, and 1924, the amounts were $2,000, $3,000 and $7,000, respectively.

[61] Laws, 1916, ch. 372.

[62] Sun, 1924, January 8, 13.

[63] The colleges to be excluded were Johns Hopkins, Goucher, Hood, Maryland College for Women, St. Johns, Western Maryland, Washington, Blue Ridge, and Morgan.

[64] The report expressed belief that the State's present facilities for higher education were sufficient and that to make a "great university" at College Park would "involve investment ... out of all proportion to the State's resources... and should not be undertaken."

[65] Sun, 1924, January 8.

[66] Sun, 1924, January 3.

[67] The Sun for January 13, 1924 gave a prominent place to the action with a headline entitled, "Citizens Plan to Aid University of Maryland Obtain Funds."

[68] Laws, 1924, ch. 280.

[69] Commission, 1927.

[70] Laws, 1929, ch. 56. This commission made its report in 1931.

[71] Commission, 1931, p. 106.

[72] Ibid. p. 23.

[73] Laws, 1933, ch. 234.

[74] The state of Missouri made some legal provisions for scholarships as early as 1921 and 1929 without, however, arrangements for the use of Morrill funds.

[75] Letter dated May 31, 1933, in records of Department of Interior, National Archives.

[76] Morgan College Bulletin, 1918 (February), p. 27.

[77] Report (Univ.), 1919, p. 145.

[78] Ibid. See reports for years stated.

[79] Ruth H. Young. Campus in Transition: University of Maryland Eastern Shore. pg. 2.

[80] Available records make only scant reference to the building. Wagner mentions the building in his description of the "Delaware Conference Academy" which appears in Bernard C. Steiner, History of Education in Maryland (Washington), 1894, p. 205. In his memorial to Bird, Dunn mentions the fact that the building was completed one year after the school opened, Minutes, 1898, p. 54 et. sec. The minutes of the Trustees of the Institute make no reference at all.

[81] The Wicomico News, May 1, 1919. Known later as the Salisbury Times, this daily publication was among the most widely read publications of the Eastern Shore. The author is grateful to the editors who permitted the examination of copies at the establishment in Salisbury. Records of the local newspaper in Princess Anne have not been preserved.

[82] Report (Univ.), 1919, pp. 120-121.

[83] Letter, Sinclair Swann, Baltimore, November 8, 1848.

[84] As in the case of the annex to Olney, the available records are not very helpful in shedding light upon the construction of this building. It would appear that the Minutes for 1888 would refer to this building, but copies have not been discovered. Furthermore, the minutes of the Trustees of the Institute are not helpful.

[85] Laws, 1924, ch. 280. The appropriation was part of a general construction loan amounting to $2,460,000.

[86] The complete Morrill Act of 1862.

[97] Mails and Files, op. cit.

[88] William Collins, W.J. Hill, J.B. Meredith, M.J. Grove, Charles W. Field, and John G. Rogers.

[89] Journal of Proceedings, House of Delegates, 1892, p. 1028.

[90] Report (Univ.), 1893, p. 11.

[91] The Nelson Amendment provided for an increase of $5,000 for the fiscal year ending in 1908 and an additional $5,000 for the next four years, making a total addition of $25,000 per state to the Morrill Fund. The school's share eventually became $5,000, or

twenty percent of the total increment. Funds were earmarked for expenditure on teacher training in agriculture.
[92] The Adams Act of 1902, the Purnell Act of 1925, and the Bankhead-Jones Act of 1935. Although designated as a "supplementary Morrill Fund" by the Secretary of Interior, February 12, 1936, the latter act, specifically, is not shared by Negro land-grant institutions.
[93] Commission on Industrial Education, 1908-1910 (Baltimore), 1910.
[94] Ibid. Letter dated October 14, 1908.
[95] Ibid. Letter dated June 24, 1909.
[96] Report (Univ.), 1919, p. 11.
[97] George H. Callcott. A History of the University of Maryland. (Baltimore, MD), 1966, p. 228.
[98] This letter, dated February 23, 1911, is found in the records of the Department of Interior, National Archives, op. cit. The opinion is not abstracted in pamphlets of rulings relating to Morrill Acts.
[99] Washington Post, 1950, April 25.
[100] A case in North Carolina preceded the Murray case. Thomas Holcutt applied to enter the School of Pharmacy of the University of North Carolina in 1932. The lower courts denied his admission and his sponsors, regarding Holcutt for a further test case, undertook no further appeal.
[101] Norfolk Journal and Guide, 1949, August 6.
[102] History meeting/interview, May 23, 2000, former student, Roma Jones.

CAMPUS BUILDINGS

at the

UNIVERSITY OF MARYLAND
EASTERN SHORE

Alumni House. (Above) Initially the site of the Home Management Residence, this building was converted in 1992 to serve the alumni association. It was constructed in 1969.

Benjamin Banneker Hall. (Right) Banneker Hall was named for the noted Revolutionary Era surveyor, mathematician, and inventor. This building houses offices for faculty and teaching staff. It was constructed in 1959.

Campus Buildings

Benjamin Oliver Bird Hall. (Left) Built in the early 1940's and named for the first head of the institution, Bird Hall was renovated recently for the offices of admissions, recruiting and financial aid.

The Theodore Briggs and Richard Thomas Arts and Technology Center. (Below) The Arts Technology Center was named for the two former department heads of industrial education. The Departments of Technology and Art and Industrial Education are housed in the building.

111

Lida M. Brown Building. (Left)
This building was named for a
former dean of women at the
institution. It was constructed in
1966.

George Washington Carver Hall.
(Below)
Renovations in 1990 doubled this
space for the Department of
Natural Sciences. It was
constructed in 1972.

Community Center/Office of Residential Life. A cluster of student residences complements this 480-bed apartment complex. The complex was constructed in 1964. It was first constructed to house administration and staff.

Frederick Douglass Library. Named for the self-educated abolitionist, orator, and author who was born on the Eastern Shore, the library boasts a computerized card catalog with links to the collection of other University of Maryland System libraries and a noted African American history collection. Constructed in 1969, the three-story library structure has recently been doubled in size and undergone renovation.

113

Charles R. Drew Student Health Center.
This building houses the medical center where students receive medical
treatment, counseling, and educational services. It was constructed in 1964.

Ella Fitzgerald Center for the Performing Arts. The PAC (Performing Arts Center)
is home for the Department of Fine Arts. This stately building is named for the
internationally acclaimed vocalist and contains a 1200 seat auditorium with a thrust
stage, classrooms and a conference room.

Richard A. Henson Center. This major campus structure was completed in 1993 and contains classrooms as well as 24 guestrooms, and conference and dining facilities for the hotel/restaurant management program. It honors the Eastern Shore philanthropist and prominent aviation chairman, Richard A. Henson.

William P. Hytche Athletic Center. The Athletic Center was named for a former president of the University. It houses two departments, Physical Education and Intercollegiate Athletics as well as classrooms, an indoor track, a swimming pool, a weight room, racquetball courts, and men's and women's locker rooms all fitted with state-of-the-art equipment. This building was constructed in 1998.

Thomas H. Kiah Hall. Formerly the Somerset Jr. High and High School, a 1990 renovation converted this two-story building for the use of the Physical Therapy, Business and Economics, and Mathematics and Computer Science Departments. It is named for a former chief executive of the University.

Murphy Hall. Murphy Hall and Murphy Annex are traditional residence halls that house female freshman. They are named for John Murphy, a former publisher of the Afro-American Newspaper, which was the first national African-American newspaper. Murphy Hall was constructed in 1943 and Murphy Annex was constructed in 1964.

Nuttle Hall. Nuttle Hall is named for a former member of the board of regents, Harry H. Nuttle. Female freshmen are housed in this traditional residence hall. It was constructed in 1973.

The President's House. This elegant home on the edge of the campus is the residence of the university's president and the president's family. It was constructed in 1964.

117

Charles Clinton Spaulding Hall. This building bears the name of the noted black business leader from North Carolina. This one-story structure houses the Department of Poultry Technology and Management. It was constructed in 1963.

Student Apartments. These apartments house sophomore, junior, senior and transfer students. There are six apartment buildings, each containing four six-person apartment suites, in the complex. The complex was constructed in 1980.

Student Development, Cultural, and Recreation Center. Simply called the SDC by students and staff, this building houses the offices of the Student Government Association, the Counseling Center, Career Planning and Placement, Cooperative Education, Basic Skills as well as the Chapel, an assembly room, a game room, a snack area, and the campus bookstore. It was constructed in 1976.

Student Services Center. One of the newest structures on the campus, the building reflects the University's commitment to a student-centered campus. It houses the Hawk's Nest, a student dining room; a six-lane bowling alley; a five-hundred-seat movie theatre/auditorium; a grand ballroom; game rooms; lounge areas; and a host of student, staff, and administrative offices. The building will be the new home for the Student Government Association, the Counseling Center, Career Planning and Placement, Cooperative Education, Basic Skills, the chapel, the post office, and the campus bookstore. It is scheduled to open July 2001.

Henry O. Tanner Hall. The airway science program is located in this structure, which is named for the accomplished black artist from Pittsburgh. Tanner Hall was constructed in 1963.

J. Millard Tawes Gymnasium. The building, constructed in 1996, was named for a former Maryland Governor, Milliard Tawes, who was born and raised in the nearby town of Crisfield. The adjoining Clifford "Cappy" Anderson Track, named for a former coach, was renovated in 1992.

Frank Trigg Hall. (Left)
Trigg Hall is named for the fourth
head of the institution. This four-
story Colonial Revival structure
houses the Department of
Agriculture. It was constructed in
1954.

Joseph Robert Waters Hall. Waters Dining Hall houses the cafeteria and
dining facilities for students. It is a two-story structure, which honors one
of the institution's founding ministers. It was constructed in 1950.

WESM/93.1 FM Radio Station. The University's 50,000-watt station has been broadcasting since 1986 and brings a welcomed jazz and contemporary music format to listeners within a 75-mile radius of the campus.

John T. Williams Hall. This building was renamed for one of the former chief executives of the University. It houses administrative offices to include the offices of the president, the vice presidents, the comptroller's office and human resources. Constructed in 1940, it was originally named Maryland Hall.

Campus Buildings

John Alfred Banum Wilson Hall. This two-story Greek Revival building is the home for the Department of English and Modern Languages and the Education Department. Named for one of the founders of the institution, the building is also the site of the new telecourse production studios.

UMES Farm. The farm contains approximately 400 acres of land, which are used for laboratory and experimetal purposes. Dairy barns, a milk house, poultry units, swine shelters and greenhouse facilities are all located on the farm.

Campus Buildings

UMES Farm Scenes

UMES Farm Scenes

124

UMES Farm Scenes

UMES Farm Scenes

CHAPTER FIVE

FROM MARYLAND STATE COLLEGE
to the UNIVERSITY of MARYLAND
EASTERN SHORE

(Figure 5.1)
Early years on campus of Maryland State College

Robert A. Grigsby (1936-47)

Born in Lynchburg, Virginia, Robert Grigsby began his career as a history teacher in Princess Anne, Maryland at Princess Anne College. A conservative and a quiet bachelor as well as an alumnus of Morgan College, he shared a great deal of Kiah's confidence in the College and became the school's vice principal after several years. Extremely loyal and at times somewhat timid, he was elevated by officials of the University of Maryland to the headship of the school after Kiah's death. With an official title of acting dean (according to school catalogues), Grigsby presided at the school for ten years. In reality, he was hardly more than an adjutant for the regents of the

126

University of Maryland, which by this time was the sole governing body of the school.

The 1930s were difficult years for higher education and for Princess Anne College for a number of reasons. Dean Grigsby's tenure would see hard times because of the Great Depression and later, World War II. For students, black as well as white, who were fortunate enough to graduate from institutions of higher learning, jobs were scarce, and racism was at its peak. All of this colored the mood of the students and the direction of the college as well as all of higher education.

(Figure 5.2)
Robert A. Grigsby

The Commissions

At the College, high school subjects were gradually eliminated from the curriculum. The first year of high school work was discontinued after 1930. So the catalogue of the Academy for 1936, for example, showed that there were only three students in the high school division. After some criticism in the early 1930s, the Academy finally published a catalogue of its program, separate from that of Morgan College. The first catalogue appeared in 1932 as the Catalogue of Princess Anne Academy. Within a few years, the word "College" was substituted for "Academy" in the title, and the publication was continued with this change until 1946. From 1946 until 1950, the Academy published no catalogue.

After 1938, no high school students were carried in the catalogue's register. Furthermore, it was not until 1938 that a collegiate senior class was listed, showing that during the early 1930s a formal four-year college curriculum was being undertaken at the Academy. No aspect of the school's collegiate program, however, was ever recognized by responsible educational agencies, thus the school continued to be recognized only as an accredited high school of the State.[1] One year earlier in 1937, a special commission chaired by Judge Morris A. Soper [a Federal judge in Baltimore and trustee of Morgan] pointed to the continued neglect of higher education for Blacks. The Soper Commission was originally appointed by the Assembly, in session at the time of the Donald Gaines Murray decision in 1935, to investigate the matter of scholarships.[2] In light of the condition of Princess Anne College, a task force was formulated by the Soper Commission on the Higher Education of Negroes in Maryland to study the resources and curriculum made available to both black and white schools.

At the time, there were only two state schools for Negroes in Maryland: Bowie State Normal School and Princess Anne College. The task force found that neither of the two was up to par, but Princess Anne College proved to be in the worst condition. Unfortunatley for Princess Anne College, the Soper Report proved to be the beginning of a deep-seated, age-old rivalry between Princess Anne College and Morgan State Normal School—a rivalry that mortal enemies would use to "pit the two against each other for power, control of Negro education, and money."[3] "The Soper Report proposed 'that in comparison with the provisions for higher education of the white people, the State is far in arrears of reasonable and justifiable provisions for the colored people of the State. ... In its present condition, it is no credit to the State; thus as an alternative, Princess Anne Academy could be converted into 'a high school with special emphasis upon vocational training.'"[4]

Public higher education throughout the State for white students included programs in agriculture, commerce, industry, engineering, library science, and home economics; yet for Blacks, Princess Anne College offered a curriculum in agriculture with only four courses in industrial arts. Business courses were offered in four white colleges but none in black colleges. Home economics was offered in both black and white institutions but was greatly underfunded in the black institutions. Vocational training was offered in the white institutions but not in the black colleges. With the exception of the University of Maryland Law and Nursing Schools, there was really no opportunity for Blacks to attend graduate or professional schools in the State. Teacher training was provided for Blacks in elementary education, but Morgan College was the only institution for training secondary school teachers. Provident Hospital in Baltimore was the only institution that existed for the training of black nurses while twenty-seven institutions existed for training Whites. Additional opportunities not available to the black population included study in the medical, dental, and pharmaceutical professions.

Prior to the findings of the Soper Commission, "H. L. Mencken of the Baltimore Sun, in a series on the University of Maryland, described Princess Anne Academy as 'a one-horse institution on the Lower Eastern Shore,

ostensibly of college grade but actually little more than a glorified high school
. . .. It is so small that, despite the modest total expense of operating it, the
cost per student is higher than that of any other school of the university.'"[5]

The Soper Commission in its final report recommended that the
University's black branch at Princess Anne be abandoned; that the State should
make either Morgan, Coppin, or Bowie a state institution that is upgraded and
placed under a biracial board; and that scholarship aid for black students be
increased. The Assembly that received the report appointed a "special"
commission to study scholarships for Negroes.[6] This commission, making its
report in 1939, likewise pointed out that State support was inadequate. With
the exception of work carried on at the schools in Bowie and Princess Anne,
neither of which "by any stretch of the imagination" offered equivalents of the
University of Maryland, the commissioner observed that Negroes could not
attend state-supported institutions in the State.[7] This fact was obvious and
hardly warranted special observation. The commission did recognize, however,
the implications present in the fact that the Murray and Gaines cases brought
the matter of scholarships pointedly to the attention of the State.

Subsequent commissions were appointed with every one consistent in
painting the school in the worse possible light. Nevertheless, Byrd held on to
Princess Anne College; but in 1939, the State assumed full control of Morgan
State College.[8] Princess Anne College continued to struggle while Morgan
State Normal School became a state college, placing Morgan and Princess
Anne College in true competition — this time for state monies and for students.

Most drastic was the assertion of the Soper Commission that "Princess
Anne Academy had far better be abandoned than continue its present pretense
as a college. It was not now a four-year college worthy of the name, and
indeed it had never been a junior college of sufficiently high standard to serve
its students effectively or to represent the State."[9] Ironically, the anomaly of a
college not "worthy of the name" but at the same time being supported from
public funds reflected more upon the larger forces underlying federal and state
policy than upon the leadership therein. These forces were both national and
statewide in scope and revealed some of the problems surrounding the minority
status of the Negroes in their quest for educational opportunities. The question
of what should be done with this pretense of a college was closely associated
with the question of what should be done about the higher education of the
Negro at national and state levels. History gave no answer, and the dualism

that underlay the control of the school complicated the dilemma, permitting the school to drift as a questionable entity for more than a generation. The existence of the school was a convenient means of exploitation by interests that conflicted over such issues as the necessity of federal and state aid pertaining to the Negro and the Negro's right to equality in education. Kiah, in a larger sense, had been a powerless victim of forces that he accepted but did not create or control. Federal land-grant aid was one of these forces.

World War II intervened, but the study of Maryland's aid to Negroes was resumed in 1945 when yet another commission was appointed.[10] Reporting in 1947, the Marbury Commission made one of the most comprehensive studies ever made of higher education in the State. In regard to the higher education of the Negro, the commission uncovered few unknown facts but made new proposals. Specifically, in regard to the school in Princess Anne, it simply restated verbatim most of the findings reported by the commission that reported in 1937. It did, however, propose the abandonment of Princess Anne as a land-grant institution.

Like other commissions, the Marbury Commission recommended that better facilities be extended for Negro schools, but sanction was given to the continuation of the "separation of the races."[11] This sanction was made over the protest of a minority report submitted by a member of the commission, Carl Murphy, an editor of the <u>Afro-American</u>. In fact, during the next two years, this editor's newspaper frequently quoted and hailed many of the facts and recommendations submitted in the majority report, called the "Marbury Report," when a widespread attack was being made upon the school in Princess Anne. Ironically, beneath the facts of the report lay the principle of segregation, which the <u>Afro-American</u> chose to ignore in its attack on the so called "Jim Crow" school in Princess Anne.

In general, white Southern legislators were questioning the need for higher education for Negroes in the first place, while white legislators in the north supported all efforts to educate them – at least in principle. In addition to the regular struggles, segregation, though embraced by the Whites, was the disgust of the Black communities, who were embittered by the idea of government-controlled segregation.

For more than 20 years, several commissions of the State and Federal government devoted a great deal of their energies to the matter of state aid to Negro higher education. The reports were fairly consistent in stating that state aid was inadequate and that the control of the Academy should be vested in its own board of trustees. Other proposals, however, showed less consistency of thought. There were proposals to increase and to decrease state aid to the Academy, to provide out-of-state scholarships and to admit Negro students to the University on a limited basis, and to abandon the Academy or to alter its mission. Consistently, there were proposals to make further study of the problem, prolonging the investigation of commissions while officials of the State pondered and procrastinated about a solution and a possible course of action.

A course of action prompted by the studies and coupled with legal victories, led to increased state appropriations for Negro institutions. Appropriations consistently increased in the years following the Murray decision, being almost doubled for Morgan and the Academy during the years 1935-1939. For example, Morgan College was appropriated $35,000 in 1935 and $60,000 in 1937 with an additional $15,000 "contingent upon the acquisition of Morgan College as a State College."[12] The Academy's appropriations were increased from $15,513 in 1936 to $25,983 in 1938. The latter appropriation for the Academy remained unchanged until after the end of World War II when the State, in making plans for its post-war reconstruction, gave additional sums that were staggering when compared with the support of pre-war years.

Land-Grant Status: A Guarantee of Survival

In 1936, Robert Grigsby attended an annual Conference for Presidents of Negro Land-Grant Colleges. There he learned that all 1890 schools had very small enrollments in agriculture. In addition, it was made known that the Department of Agriculture had no interest in Negro land-grant education or in the plight of the Negro farmer and agricultural agents in the South. This was a political move by the Department to get Southern political support. "Thus did Princess Anne College experience a phenomenon little understood at the time – the expansion of the land grant [sic] mission to provide an agricultural education to students who did not want it, to please Washington officials who were apathetic at best, to satisfy state officials interested solely in racial segregation and white supremacy."[13] Accordingly, not one system of checks and balances existed to assure that at least the pretense of support was carried out. The State merely provided a meager amount of funds to Princess Anne College for agricultural education while the U.S. Office of Education remained powerless to get the needed information (i.e., statistics) to monitor how well the school was doing.

To some, Princess Anne College was merely a place to house Negroes to keep them from darkening the ivory halls of the white colleges in Maryland. In February 1937, the president of the University of Maryland, Harry C. Byrd, unwilling to lose land-grant status, eloquently described the sentiments of the day saying, "If we don't do something about Princess Anne, we're going to have to accept Negroes at College Park, where our girls are."[14] Thus, he lobbied by default to build up the Eastern Shore branch. Before his noble gesture, the State did no more than it absolutely had to in facilitating the Negro. Consequently, the Negro's educational opportunities were token, and the facilities were well below standard. By law, the State had to provide four walls and a roof as well as to offer a liberal arts education; teacher training; pre-professional areas of law, medicine, and engineering; business; and creative arts. In reality, the Negro's substandard situation was fashioned to compel him/her to teach and to be taught at an elementary level.

Under Grigsby the land-grant mission guaranteed the school's survival; but oddly enough, while it pleased the Whites, rural Blacks felt humiliated by the thought of being trained to do what slavery had at one time forced them to do. "Ironically, while Maryland Negroes starved in rural poverty during the Depression, students at Princess Anne College pursued the study of Latin and Greek."[15] Nevertheless, the land-grant mission attracted middle-class students who had previously "shunned these schools as institutions for the culturally deprived."[16] The year was about 1938 when the college offered four-year degrees in agriculture, home economics, home economics education, mechanical arts, mechanical arts education, and a two-year junior college course in arts and sciences. It is important to note that Dean Grigsby was able to report that "students had passed with but little difficulty to the junior year of Howard University, Morgan College, and Claflin University from the arts and science curriculum. In addition, fourteen teachers with master's degrees were added to the faculty and three assistants joined the administration, one of whom was the school nurse. The library bought over $5,000 worth of books."[17] Princess Anne College was holding its own when disaster struck in the form of yet another cruel fire.

Physical Plant

One way to measure the growth of an institution is by its physical plant. By this criterion, the school saw no primary growth for forty years after the turn of the century. Excluding buildings that replaced those destroyed by fire, the physical plant of the school underwent few changes from the time of Benjamin Bird until 1940. A greenhouse, located not far from the entrance of the campus, was partially destroyed by fire in the early 1930s.[18] Furthermore, a teacher's dwelling, containing about eight rooms and located on the Morris property acquired in 1890, was completely destroyed by fire some time after 1937.

For the greater part of its history, the school was housed in accommodations that were constructed before 1900. A few minor structures were built after this date; but again, major construction included the replacement of buildings that were destroyed by fires. One of the minor structures constructed during World War I was a teacher's dwelling containing about six rooms. It was known as the "White House," in remembrance of Barton White, one of the teachers who lived in the building for many years. This building was in use in 1950 and was occupied by the George Hunter family, who came to the school in 1948. Another dwelling, once occupied by Justine Clark, was built during World War I. Three garages, one costing about $600, were erected a few feet from the dining hall for the principal. A small greenhouse, a barn, and several poultry houses were also built after the turn of the century.

Until 1940, the school obtained its water supply from pumps located on the campus. The water tower was built during the period of World War I, and mechanical pumps were installed beneath a shed that stood near the center of the campus. It is thought that electric power was first introduced into the dormitories and dwellings during the period of World War I. Prior to this time, students read by small kerosene lamps that were refilled twice weekly and required to be put out by 10:00 P.M.

No roads or walks were paved before 1940. The county road leading to the campus, the driveway, and the walks on the campus were all dirt until after 1940. Indeed, before 1940, the physical plant of the school was more reminiscent of the nineteenth century than of the twentieth century. In 1941, however, the physical plant was radically changed with the addition of three brick structures acquired from the Federal government through the Works

133

Progress Administration (WPA) to house mechanical arts, administration, and physical education. The buildings became the nuclei of campus life, absorbing many of the functions that were carried on in the "Administration Building" and the old "Mechanic Arts Building."

The building for administration, containing nearly a score of rooms that were used for offices and for instruction, was Colonial in design. The building for mechanics, also Colonial in design, was somewhat smaller. The gymnasium, containing the power plant, was Georgian in design. Comprising one of the three WPA building projects in Somerset County, the buildings were officially dedicated in a ceremony held on April 19, 1940. The president of the University of Maryland; and Crystal Bird Fauset, daughter of Benjamin O. Bird, delivered speeches.

Although seldom referred to by their proper names, the administration building was designated as Maryland Hall, the new mechanic arts building as Bird Hall, and the gymnasium as Kiah Hall in honor of the school's fifth principal, Thomas Henry Kiah.

(Figure 5.3)
THREE WPA BUILDINGS
Showing left to right: Bird Hall, Maryland Hall, Kiah Hall

In 1941, a tragic fire consumed the old Mechanic Arts Building, the fourth major building to be constructed on the campus. Work on this building, sometimes referred to as the Mechanics Building or the Industrial Arts Building, was thought to have begun in 1897 but completed in the spring of 1899.[19] It contained ten rooms and covered about as much ground space as the first boys dormitory, 17ft. x 35 ft. The cost of the building, including equipment, was $5,000. Half of this amount was contributed by the State Assembly as the first grant that the State made to a Negro institution of higher learning.[20]

As its name suggests, the building was used to house the trades program, chiefly printing and carpentry. The printing shop was located at one end and the carpentry shop at the other. The second floor served as a boys dormitory both before and after the original boys dormitory burned in 1923. It seems that power was introduced early in order to drive the printing presses.[21] Though the presses never printed the Minutes of the Delaware Conference as proposed, they were used to print school programs and the Morgan College Bulletin.[22] The printing shop continued in operation until the 1930s, but the Morgan College Bulletin was not printed after 1924.

For a long time, the old Mechanic Arts Building had been a fire hazard. Its burning in 1941, forty-four years after its completion, brought one of the greatest disasters that the campus ever witnessed. Tragedy and irony were mingled in the drama, for once again, in the wake of disaster, another building was erected to replace the one destroyed by fire. It is almost a truism that the physical plant of the school grew out of disasters and emergencies.

On March 31, 1941 the Salisbury Times carried a sensational banner headline across its front page that relegated news of the war in Europe to a secondary position.[23]

THREE DIE IN PRINCESS ANNE FIRE

Italian Warships Sunk, 1500 Seamen Lost

On the following evening, April 1, the above headline was updated to read:

FIFTH DIES IN PRINCESS ANNE FIRE

The persons who perished in the flames of the old Mechanic Arts Building were not students but workers of the National Youth Administration (NYA) or WPA projects who lived in the community. Instruction in mattress-making, under the supervision of Justine Clark, a faculty member, was being given on the third floor while the lower floors of the building were used for storing materials and equipment. The project provided training and part-time employment for needy students and women as well as mattresses for the economically deprived residents of Somerset and Wicomico counties. On the day of the fire, classes were being conducted by Mrs. Edna G. Waters of Upper Fairmount. Mothers who brought their children along were in attendance. Altogether, about fifty-five persons were in the building when the fire began.

According to eyewitnesses, the fire started when two young men, Melvin Johnson, 21, of Quantico and Carpenter Hayward, 20, from Princess Anne, moved a heater to one of the third-floor rooms. As a result of the move, the heater exploded immediately injuring the two men. The flames, fed by the highly combustible material used in the mattresses, spread rapidly. The only stairway was soon engulfed, trapping many of the victims who were blinded by smoke and fumes. Some made their way to the windows and leaped, sustaining varied injuries, two of which were fatal. Edna Waters, the instructor, made her way to a window and was seen clinging to a sill, holding a baby she had rescued. A student climbed the burning building and took the baby, but before he could return Edna Waters, already burned and tired, lost her grip and fell, fatally injuring herself.

The scene at the fire was one of excitement and panic, of drama and pathos. A crowd gathered, most of whom were unwillingly helpless onlookers. Mothers roamed through the crowd frantically searching for their children. Some relatives were present, tense and eager, worrying if any of their kin had been destroyed in the inferno. McKinley Wright, a faculty member and one of the first persons to see the blaze, made heroic efforts to rescue those who were trapped in the small, atticlike mattress workroom. Volunteer fire fighters from Princess Anne fought the blaze for nearly five hours. By evening, when

136

the flames were under control, only portions of the walls remained standing. The damage was estimated at about $4,000.

More than a score of persons were treated for injuries at the Peninsula General Hospital in Salisbury where the first floor was cleared for accommodations and physicians were called for the emergency. Five died from injuries sustained that day. In addition to Edna Waters, 31, of Upper Fairmount, those who died from injuries were Letitia McBride, age 60; Emma Wright, age 38; and Anna Jones, age 58 (all from Chance, Maryland); and a six-year-old son of the Reverend J. H. Spence of Dames Quarter. Two persons were charred almost beyond recognition. At least eleven were seriously injured, including Charlotte Reid of Wetipquin, age 16, with fractures in both legs; Irma Gaines of Sharptown, age 17, with a strained back; Louise Bailey of Salisbury, age 17, with a fractured pelvis; Lucy Miles of Quantico, age 18, with a fractured pelvis; Alice Wright of Chance, age 40, with a punctured liver; Tresia Beckett of Chance, age 45, with a fractured arm; Elma Spenser of Dames Quarter, age 30, with fractures in both legs; Frances Spenser of Dames Quarter, age 1, with a fractured skull; Leola Graham of Quantico, age 21, with fractures of the pelvis, nose, and heel; Ethel Taylor of Wetipquin, age 17, with a fractured back; and Geraldine Pinkett of Salisbury, age 20, with fractures of the left arm and right leg.

Many others were treated and released from Peninsula General Hospital including a six-month-old baby described only as "Baby Wright" of Chance; Doris Mae Dashiell of Hebron, age 18; Victoria Stanford of Sharptown, age 17; Eva Roberts of Dames Quarter, age 48; Elsie Mae Snows of Salisbury, age 17; Pearline Taylor of Wetipquin, age 18; Martha Beckett of Hebron, age 16; Aileen Bailey of Salisbury, age 20; Eva Evans of Chance, age 19; and Ermenia Goslee of Mardela, age 17.

Dean Robert Grigsby, Fire Chief Raymond Carey, and H. F. Cotterman of the University of Maryland Extension Services as well as other University of Maryland authorities were available to lend support to the families and to assist with the investigation. Dr. Henry M. Lankford, Somerset Deputy Medical Examiner, remained on the scene to make proper identifications.

The news carried by radio reported that the fire began in an old dormitory, which was partially true, and that there were fatalities. It is not surprising then that parents who heard the broadcast hurriedly contacted the school in order to learn if any of their children were caught in the fire. Federal authorities also wanted to know the cause of the fire and promised an investigation.

News of the disaster also reached the state legislature. It is likely that some members of the legislature first heard the news by radio, for the fire occurred on the last day of their legislative session. Before the legislature adjourned the next morning at approximately seven o'clock, it voted for funds to replace the "old dormitory" that had burned. Without having previously given any thought whatsoever to a building appropriation to the school during this session, the members of the Assembly hurriedly included an appropriation of $100,000 as part of a $2,117,000 bond issue. This was more money than the State had ever given at any one time to the school. Without a doubt, many of the legislators who voted for this measure thought erroneously that a dormitory had burned and that regular students were among the casualties.

Fortunately, however, none of the enrolled students of the Academy were involved in the fire. In spite of this blessing, the devastation still had a major impact on the campus community. One of the victims, Charlotte Reid, found a friend forever in a student named Blanche, who consoled Charlotte and afterwards, spent many hours with her during her long-term period of recovery in the hospital. As Charlotte reflected upon the tragedy and her narrow escape, she remembered the early morning hours of Monday, March 31, 1941 as jubilant and tranquil as the employees worked in various areas of the old Mechanic Building but the noon hour as a drastic instantaneous turn of events. She described her experience with the following words:

> *The familiar saying about March coming in like a lion and going out like a lamb reversed its role. Screams and excited voices and yells joined in unison the words, "Fire! Fire! Fire!" Rapid, roaring, yellow flames prevented us from descending the steps from the third floor. Wailing sounds of sirens and honking horns were heard.*
>
> *What could we do in such a situation? We were trapped! We had three choices. We could jump out of a window, descend an old rickety ladder, or burn to death! I chose the first option very hesitantly. When I felt the heat coming through the floor and through the soles of my shoes, I knew it was time to make haste! I saw a window with a*

tiny roof below it. I made my way out of the window and jumped on to the roof while spectators down below me shouted, "Jump! Jump! Jump!"

I spotted the chef from the college who assured me he would catch me. He was really my assurance and incentive, so I leapt from that third story roof and landed on the ground. As I looked around in a dazed state, I did not see the chef anywhere. While waiting to be carried to the hospital, I was told that a few seconds after I leapt the roof collapsed. Some time after that, I came to realize that the chef was never there at all. I must say the following words from the bottom of my heart. "Thank you, Lord!"

At the age of 16, I sustained severe compound fractures in both ankles that left permanent scars. Others around me had gruesome injuries such as broken backs, necks, legs, elbows, hips, and pelvises. I regret the fact that lives were also lost as a result of the 1941 fire. May they rest in peace from their labors on earth.

Ambulances and private cars rushed the injured to Peninsula Hospital in Salisbury, Maryland. The men's ward was being renovated; but when we were rushed there, workmen had to stop immediately in order for us to occupy it. What a hustle and a bustle to assemble beds and equipment to attend to our urgent needs. What a day!

I was among three others who were the last to be discharged on Monday, June 30, 1941, three months after the fire. I still couldn't walk.

What a day, and what an extreme privilege to acknowledge my gratefulness to God for my life and for my ability to walk in the year of 2000.

Certainly, the disaster focused attention upon the school which, ironically, gained its third dormitory for girls—John Murphy Hall—as a result of the tragedy that surrounded the destruction of the old mechanic arts building.

(Figure 5.4)
The Old Mechanic Arts Building.

The War Years

Princess Anne College was deeply affected by World War II (1939-45). While well-wishers in Princess Anne looked for growth in the areas of race relations, the school became involved in the war effort. Consequently, the curriculum was changed to complement the needs of the community. Princess Anne College offered extension and resident classes in food production, food conservation, farm machine repair, and lectures on bomb protection and first-aid demonstrations.[24] Regular courses were discontinued as the number of students, faculty, and staff decreased because of the draft. "Dean Grigsby was proud and pleased to report that 'through increased efforts of faculty, students, alumni, and all others interested in the welfare of Princess Anne College, the institution maintained a full-time schedule' during the early months of the war."[25] By 1944, however, enrollment had actually decreased to fifty students, but just one year later the end of the war brought promise of better days. Preparations were made to accommodate former students as well as new students. The catalogue advertised Princess Anne College as having "Home-like Surroundings, Healthful Climate, Modest Expenses, No Out-of-State Fees and a Post-War Curriculum."[26] In addition, scholastic and community activities increased as well as athletic activities, bringing the community in contact with the school.

In the area of agriculture, the school purchased 100 acres of land to be used by students, livestock, and poultry. The school purchased a cow, a bull, and sows to improve herds. Fruit and vegetables were used and canned for student consumption. Dean Grigsby was hopeful that such agricultural activity would spark "a supportive program in practical and scientific farming" for Princess Anne College.[27] In addition, "Princess Anne College acquired several thousand dollars worth of hand tools as well as two electric welders from the War Assets Administration along with cast-off machinery from the School of Engineering of the University of Maryland."[28] It was a new day for the College; but because of the anticipated increase of enrollment in the University System, Governor Herbert O'Connor appointed a commission to study again higher education in the state of Maryland. Once again the commission was comprised of nationally known educational experts; and an affluent attorney, William Marbury, chaired the committee. The commission was directed to create a strategic plan for higher education in Maryland during the postwar era. The issue was that " . . . Maryland youth had a very low rate of enrollment in higher education compared to other states."[29] The onus was on the public institutions, under which classification Princess Anne College fell, to solve the problems of low enrollment and to fill the need for industrial education. "Maryland, it noted, historically had viewed higher education as the task primarily of independent institutions with public sector institutions filling the gaps."[30]

The Marbury Commission's recommendations concerning higher education were released early in 1947. "It lamented the State's consistent 'policy of providing higher educational facilities for Negroes which are inferior to those provided for Whites.'"[31] Princess Anne College was compared to other state land-grant colleges, all of which had larger enrollments and more income. The State was strongly encouraged to take the land-grant mission seriously and to develop a strong program in one institution rather than spreading out the funds in weak programs in several institutions. That meant either Princess Anne or Morgan. For Princess Anne, specifically, the recommendations included building dormitories and a dining hall, constructing faculty housing, improving agricultural facilities, expanding library facilities, and paving walks and drives because students had to walk through mud and water to get to classes.

Princess Anne College was criticized for a number of reasons. There were no Ph.D.'s on the faculty, more than a quarter of the staff lacked master's degrees, instructors were limited in scholarly preparation, and the turnover was high. Certainly, the integrity of the College was on the line. "On the other end of the spectrum, Morgan State College emerged as the great Black hope. More centrally located near the Negro population of the State and already having "developed relatively strong departments in science and other fields, which are necessary for the support of an effective program in technical subjects such as agriculture, home economics, engineering, and industrial arts," the Marbury Report suggested "transferring the land-grant program to Morgan in Baltimore."[32] In response, the Blacks on the Eastern Shore—students, faculty, and community alike—went to Annapolis to protest.

The institution was still referred to as Princess Anne Academy in the Marbury Report, a telltale sign that higher education refused to see the institution as anything but a college-preparatory school at best. Needless to say, the Marbury Report left Princess Anne College fighting for survival and again competing with Morgan College, this time to be the land-grant school for Blacks in the state of Maryland. According to one writer, "the Marbury Report was politically difficult to accept, but it remains the finest, most scholarly and candid analysis ever made of Maryland's higher education situation."[33] Conversely, another writer described it as somewhat of a failure:

> In many ways the Marbury Commission Report was a failure because it was too bold. A report never had a chance which stirred in racial politics, took on the scholarship system, toyed with political ambitions, offended alumni of institutions that might have been closed, made radical suggestions about junior colleges and a state board of higher education, and for all that promised to cost the state millions of dollars. A commission seeking acceptance or acclaim would have been far more timid. On the other hand, at last the important issues were on the table for all to see.[34]

Grigsby retired in 1947 amidst all of the negative light. He slipped quietly out of town without greeting his successor, Dr. John Taylor Williams, or lingering to say or to accept farewells from people among whom he had lived a great deal of his life.

Dr. John Taylor Williams (1947-70)

In an effort to temper the whirlwind of criticism exuding from the stir caused by the Marbury Report, the Board of Regents appointed John Taylor Williams as president of Maryland State College following Dean Grigsby's retirement. Dr. Williams was the second head of the small institution with an extensive, formal education and the first to be given the title president rather than dean or principal. Never before had it been so critical that someone of his status be placed at the helm of the struggling institution. Dr. Williams' terminal degree, garnished with an impressive background, stayed the conflict because the Board of Regents gave him the authority to reorganize the school. Interestingly enough, while the whirlwind reared as many times before all around the small institution in Princess Anne, Negroes were being educated. Maryland State College always fulfilled its mission with whatever tools were at its disposal. Not once did it shrink away from the task of educating Negroes, regardless of the struggle. Higher education, however, insisted on using the measuring stick fashioned for institutions that had every economic and educational advantage necessary for a successful program on Maryland State College.

Born in Minden, Louisiana in 1904, John Taylor Williams was educated in Muskogee, Oklahoma elementary and high schools, Langston University, the University of Cincinnati, and Indiana University. He was a star football, basketball, and baseball player in high school. At Langston University, he was a member of the varsity football, basketball, and baseball teams. For three consecutive years, he was named an All-American athlete. In addition to his athletic career, Williams received his degree with honors as salutatorian of his graduating class at Langston. The master's degree was conferred upon Williams by the University of Cincinnati, and the doctoral degree by Indiana University. In his long career as a teacher and administrator, Dr. Williams served Kentucky State University, Prairie View A&M University, and Langston

(Figure 5.5)
Dr. John Taylor Williams

143

University. When Kentucky State was in its heyday as a small college football power, he served as its head football coach and athletic director. He also served as Kentucky State's registrar and dean from 1928 to 1947.

Dr. Williams was married in 1930 to Jennie V. Williams; and they had one daughter, Lorelle. Dr. Williams had the experience required in every area of educational administration, and it was the hope of the Board of Regents that he could somehow make a difference. Accordingly, Williams insisted that he be given free reign to reorganize and implement the projected program of the school, to choose his faculty, and to change the name of the school. Thus, at the beginning of 1947, the school name was changed to Maryland State College, Division of the University of Maryland at Princess Anne, and the focus was on the reorganization of the school.

What Dr. Williams had in Maryland State College was an institution that was little more than a junior college. It was "poorly equipped, with low enrollments, an understaffed faculty, and a minute budget."[35] As specified in his directive, he reorganized the college curriculum into four divisions: agriculture, home economics, mechanic arts and industries, and arts and sciences. Eventually, capital improvements were made in the areas of classroom buildings, barn and dairy houses, a cafeteria, apartment houses, and athletic fields. These unparalleled achievements were possible for a number of reasons. In one year, Williams managed to double the enrollment and to increase the faculty from eleven to twenty-four. He also did his part in turning Maryland State College into that same type of football power he led at Kentucky State. Thus, Maryland State College was on the map as the most successful historically Black college football program in the country. In addition, Dr. Williams' new faculty and staff consisted of members who came mainly from the faculties of several Negro colleges, including notably Tennessee Agricultural and Mechanical College and Kentucky State College. With few exceptions, the appointees held the master's degree; six held the doctorate.

Nearly half of the old staff was retained while Dr. Williams reorganized. The last catalogue of "Princess Anne College" (1947-1948) lists 23 persons on the administrative and instructional staff, excluding the president of the University of Maryland. Ten of the 23 were retained on the staff, having served at the school for an average of 11.4 years. The remaining 13 who were not retained (excluding Grigsby) had an average length of service of only 2.4 years.

New faculty members were faced with problems of adjustment to the uncertainties that accompanied the reorganization. One of the most acute problems was that of housing inasmuch as many of the staff members brought their furnishings along but were unable to set up their households. Several families experienced the inconvenience of living on the first floor of the girls dormitory, John Murphy Hall, where facilities were often embarrassingly overcrowded. Other staff members lived in apartments on the third floor of Maryland Hall, in Olney, or Eliza Smith Hall. Both town and campus were unable to accommodate the new arrivals during the first year; and some of the projected apartments and cottages, eagerly awaited, were not ready for occupancy until 1949.

The reorganization of the school was publicized. New appointees to the staff were publicized in Negro newspapers largely through the efforts of Charles C. Jacobs, one of the older members of the staff. Moreover, the newly named "Office of Admissions," under the direction of Violet Woods, released a printed circular displaying the "Administration Building" (Maryland Hall) and the "Portico of the Gymnasium" (Kiah Hall). The circular advertised the name of the school in bold type as a four-year "Land-Grant College" offering the bachelor's degree upon completion of course study (22 courses were listed). Prospective students were cautioned to make early reservations for their rooms.[36]

During the early part of his era, much of Dr. Williams' time was consumed with his efforts to perfect an educational plan. He had inherited the task of continuously fighting both closure or merging of the campus. He was revolutionary in his ideas for campus offerings in spite of its small size, cultural background, and remote locale. Sometimes he stood alone and did not seem to mind. Other times he overwhelmed everyone around him with his passion to succeed at whatever the cost. He was great in stature, standing head and shoulders over most men, and strong in character. His efforts were strongest when the school was under the worst criticism.

The positive publicity of the school came upon release of an illustrated bulletin at the end of the academic year of 1948-49. This publication was a highly favorable commentary upon various phases of school life during the academic year, including illustrations and reprints on such topics as administration, faculty, instruction, athletics, and campus life. Although circulated by the "Office of Admissions," the bulletin was edited by John S.

Lash, the new head of the Department of English, who was congratulated by the president for having performed a "splendid" service. The bulletin included many reprints from newspaper articles, and it decidedly excluded any reprint of articles that, in attacking the school, pointed out the controversy over the school's reorganization.

There was much unfavorable publicity of the school's new program. Both the Negro and white presses of the State freely attacked the school, and repercussions from the attacks extended to circles outside of the State.[37] The white attack was led by the Baltimore Sun and the Negro attack was led by the Afro-American. Their targets were frequently the school; the University of Maryland; and Harry C. Byrd, the president of the University of Maryland. The criticism cut across political, economic, and social issues. An analysis of the criticism as revealed in the Baltimore Sun and the Afro-American shows several categories of thought:

- the size of appropriations made for the University and its branch (now called a "Division") at Princess Anne;
- the financial and budgetary policies of the University;
- the influence, power, and attitude of Harry C. Byrd, "the most powerful man in the State;"[38]
- the control of higher education of Negroes in Maryland;
- the democratic rights of Negroes in Maryland; and
- the democratic rights of Negroes in face of the theory and practice of segregation.

It appears that criticism by the Sun was centered mainly in the first four categories. The Afro-American seems to have spread its attack in all categories with its heaviest concentration upon the "rights" of Negroes to educational opportunity. The attack by the Sun seems to have been in keeping with the traditional policy of the paper in regard to the careful spending of the taxpayer's money. The attack also reflected the paper's old feud with Byrd in his conduct of the affairs of the University. Whereas the Sun steered fairly clear of racial issues,[39] the attack by the Afro, on the other hand, pointed out the problem of Negro leadership within the framework of a predominantly white society. Traditionally advocating the necessity of more state aid for Negro institutions, specifically for Morgan State College since 1939, the Afro likewise advocated the removal of barriers for the admission of Negroes to the University of Maryland, pointing out that Byrd's attitude (controlled segregation) and influence in the movement to reorganize the Academy were prohibitive factors in the Negro's quest for equal rights in education.

The attack by the press is illustrated in captions of news articles. During one period attacks by the Sun were published almost daily, being carried out mainly by two staff writers, Anne Hutchinson and Thomas O'Neill. One article by O'Neill, appearing in the November 19, 1947 issue, was entitled "Branch at Princess Anne Rated Worst Land-Grant College in U.S." Also, in January of 1949, a series of articles by the same author discussed various aspects of the University's program. One article in the series focused on "inadequacies" at Princess Anne. In February of the same year, O'Neill submitted ten questions to the Board of Regents of the University whose replies occupied an entire page in the Sun. O'Neill's eighth question asked, "Do the regents expect the present steps at Princess Anne to persuade the court that Negroes need not be accepted at College Park?" The Regents hedged in answering this question, stating that the University was not opposed to better opportunities for Negroes in higher education. Some of the captions from the Sun and Afro are shown below.

From the Sun:
- ✔ U. of M. $20,913,392 building program cut to $3,027,600 by state planning group (banner headline).
- ✔ Princess Anne College projects of $3,755,000 omitted entirely (sub-headline), January 27, 1949
- ✔ No Students Ever Flunked This School (i.e., Princess Anne), February 27, 1949.
- ✔ Byrd's data declared incomplete despite his assurance to Regents, March 20, 1949.
- ✔ Byrd Successful in 16 Years in Fight (i.e. to keep the University's budget under his control), March 16, 1949

From the <u>Afro</u>:

- ✔ Marshall Urges War on Md. U. Color Bar (i.e. Thurgood Marshall, counsel for the NAACP), March 29, 1949
- ✔ Our 'Do-Nothing' Legislature Leaves But One Alternative (i.e. to file legal suits), April 9, 1949
- ✔ Byrd Plotted Anti-Morgan Move (banner headline), February 26, 1949

Needless to say, Dr. Williams had walked into a hornet's nest of sorts. During his first couple of years in office, recommendations ranged from converting the institution into a prison to turning it into a research poultry farm. At one time closure was only one vote away when a black Senator, Verda Welcome, took the floor of the legislature and fought against the closure of Maryland State College. Senator Welcome was the first Black female to be elected to the Maryland General Assembly. It was she who coined the phrase "the step-child of the University of Maryland" when referring to Maryland State College, and the reference is still used by some today. Truly the College was the stepchild. At the time of Dr. Williams' appointment, College Park had a ten-year history of falling criminally short of dispensing the appropriations guaranteed to its land-grant branch in Princess Anne by the second Morrill Land-Grant Act of 1890.

In addition, the University of Maryland had adopted a system of awarding Negroes out-of-state scholarships as opposed to educating them in the white state institutions. This practice was passionately criticized, placing the onus back on the University of Maryland to provide education for the Black citizens of Maryland. Because the University of Maryland was not in the position to lose the state funds afforded it in hosting a land-grant institution, Byrd set out to relieve the neglect and to steady its battered subsidiary, Maryland State College. In no uncertain terms, however, educational experts and commissions maintained that putting resources into the institution was purely a waste. Nevertheless, influential politicians started pouring money into the conference to make sure that Maryland State College would be a stronger institution. "State appropriations for Princess Anne rose from $116,367 in 1948-49 to $429,768 for the following year.' In addition, Princess Anne benefited from a $3,450,000 building program to rectify a great many needs of the physical plant."[40]

From there, "Williams' strategy involved three main tactics—the development of a successful agricultural program, the establishment of a federal ROTC program on campus, and the creation of winning athletic teams. These endeavors, Williams hoped, would attract students, federal monies, community support, and statewide recognition."[41]

Athletics

The school was first favorably publicized through the spectacular success of its football squad, which was coached by Vernon McCain, Robert White, and J.C. Coffee, who had recruited several of the key players. With the active interest of the new president, himself a former football athlete and coach, the success of the athletic program was undoubtedly a source of morale for both faculty and students. Being denied admission into the regional Negro athletic conference, the coaches and members of the athletic committee contracted for games elsewhere. Consequently, the football squad played the teams of several white colleges for the first time in the history of the school— and indeed in the history of collegiate athletics. The football and the basketball squads were even more successful during the next school year, 1949-1950, piling up large scores against teams of well-established institutions. The Negro press selected and honored one player, Sylvester Polk, as an All-American.

White and Coffee resigned from the staff in 1950, and Coach McCain carried on the program. "When Coach McCain came to Maryland State College (MSC) in 1948, he was to serve as the head football coach, the head basketball coach and the athletic director." It was quite an undertaking for a "humble, 5-foot-5 man, who never cussed or missed church," but Coach McCain had a successful career in basketball as well as in football. He built winning teams and created a firm underpinning for sports on the campus. Although he was not world-renowned, he was the star of athletics in his own community and to every team with which he competed.

Coach McCain's teams were impressive, so much so that they gained the attention of Sports Reporter Ed Nichols, who wrote for the Salisbury Times. Nichols attended all MSC games and wrote such glowing descriptions of the team's plays that the gym was full an hour before each basketball game started.

149

Most of the fans were Whites, and seats were often sold out before MSC students could arrive at the gym. Sam Seidel, a basketball coach at Wicomico High School, located less than twenty minutes from the College, made arrangements to bring his players to the practice sets of the MSC team. As a result, during the following spring, Seidel's team won the state championship. Then, in the summer of 1950, Seidel managed a baseball team and decided to add players to his roster. All of the players that he decided to add were Maryland State College students, and they were black. The other teams protested and cancelled their games against the baseball team. Consequently, Seidel resigned.[42] MSC continued to be successful and was admitted to the Eastern Collegiate Athletic Conference (ECAC) in 1950, to the Central Intercollegiate Athletic Conference (CIAA) in 1954, and into the National Athletic Intercollegiate Association (NAIA) afterwards.

(Figure 5.6)
Football at Maryland State College.
The 1966 Hawks, from left to right (1st Row): J. McGriff, A. Shell, R. Taylor, M. Cropper, H. Brown, C. Kennedy, N. Collins, W. Thompson, W. Frantklin, L. Clay, F. Sumpter, J. Hairston, P. Shuford, C. Stukes. 2nd Row: E. Stephens, L. Kindred, G. Pettigrew, A. Gamble, A. Huff, T. Gray, B. Davis, J. Duncan, E. Williams, W. Belk, R. Baylor, R. Banks, W. Caesar, B. James, T. Stevenson, J. Walls. 3rd Row: R. McCullough, C. Harley, W. Lawrence, A. Laster, G. Irons, G. Masseaux, N. Roundtree, W. Spann, J. Wright, J. Williams, W. Greenfield, R. Garrett, R. Kirksey, J. Williams. 4th Row: L. Sharp, G. Cephas, B. Johnson, G. Cook, L. Acker, M. Alston, C. Parsons, C. Brown, R. Friston, T. Hairston, P. Howard, C. Anderson.

In 1964, Coach McCain retired from athletics and served as assistant professor of mathematics. He was indeed a legend in his own time. It is noteworthy that for every year from 1960 to 1971, one player from the University entered the professional football league, making the name Maryland State College synonymous with victory (See Exhibit H). John Taylor Williams would have it no other way. In 1976, Coach McCain retired from the University.

(Figure 5.7)
Coach
Vernon "Skip" McCain

An Assessment of the Influence of Coach McCain

The winning tradition of football at Maryland State College spilled over into other disciplines as well. Track Coach Clifton J. Anderson (Cappy), a native of Cape May, New Jersey, also created winners. He came to the University of Maryland Eastern Shore in 1960. He was "a graduate of Indiana University (IU), and received his B.S. and M.S. degrees on the Bloomington campus. Following his academic and athletic career at IU, he entered professional football where he played with the Chicago Cardinals (currently St. Louis Cardinals) and the New York Giants. As a track and field specialist at MSC, he trained Charlie Mays and Benedict Cayenne, who later became two 1968 Olympic stars. "In 1961, 1962, and again in 1963, Cappy's men out-jumped and out-ran all other teams in the Central InterCollegiate Athletic Association (CIAA). He was dedicated to 'modesty, gentility, hard work, and superlative performance'."

(Figure 5.8)
Coach
Clifton "Cappy" Anderson

With Baseball Coach Harold Gray, winning was also a tradition. The Maryland State College graduate was a member of three CIAA championship gridiron squads as well as two championship baseball teams. As a baseball player, he once led the nation with an incredible .535 batting average. He played professional football in the Continental League with the Norfolk Neptunes and the New York Titans. In 1969, he returned to Maryland State College where he joined the athletic staff."

(Figure 5.9)
Coach Harold Gray

As athletic director, Coach McCain had an immeasurable influence on many MSC coaches, and thus had an immeasurable influence on the successful athletic program at Maryland State College. Some of the coaches he influenced most are listed below:

Coach Nate Taylor Basketball Coach	**Coach William Smith** Football Coach
Coach Kirkland Hall Baseball/Basketball Coach	**Coach Earl Banks** Football Coach
Coach Clifford "Cappy" Anderson Track & Football Coach	**Coach Roosevelt Gilliam** Basketball Coach
Coach John Bates Football Coach	**Coach Robert "Bob" Taylor** Football Coach
Coach Harold Gray Football Coach	**Coach Lois Smith** Basketball Coach

From Maryland State College to UMES

The following former athletes represent the caliber of athlete who attended and graduated from the University of Maryland Eastern Shore.

Art Shell
Football, Basketball 1964-1968
NFL Career 1968-1982
NFL Coach 1989

Marshall Cropper
Football, Baseball 1962-1966
NFL 1967-1970

Benedict Cayenne
Track 1965-1969; Olympian 1968

Calvin Martin
Football 1947-1950

Carl Hairston
Football, Basketball 1972-1975
NFL 1979-1991; NFL Coach

Charles J. Holmes
Football 1958-1962; NFL 1962

Sherman "The Tank" Plunkett
Football 1952-1957
NFL 1960-1968

Sylvester "Swifty" Polk
Football, Basketball 1947-1950

Talvin Skinner
Basketball, 1970-1974

Curtis "Curt" Gentry
Basketball, Baseball, Football,
Track 1962-1966; NFL 1966-1968

Charles Stukes
Football, Baseball,
Basketball 1963-1967
NFL 1967-1974
Honorary Coach, Special Olympics

Clem Martin
Football 1941-1945

David Riddick
Basketball 1957-1960

Earl Rogers
Track and Field 1962-1965

Edward "Eddie" Williams
Basketball 1962-1965

Edward Gosa
Football 1948-1951

Harold Rush
Basketball, 1948-1952

Theopolis "Sonny" Lloyd
Basketball 1953-1956

William "Bill" Thompson
Football, Baseball 1965-1968
NFL 1969-1981
Colorado Sports Hall of Fame, 1985
The Broncos Ring of Fame, 1987
Piedmont Hall of Fame, 1996

Emerson Boozer
Football 1962-1966; NFL 1970-1975

Harold "House" Gray
Football, Baseball 1957-1962
Coach 1974-1977; NFL 1960

William "Shorty" Gray
Football 1957-1960
Canadian Football League 1961
Continental Football League
Defensive Coord. -UMES 1974-1977

Russell "Russ" Rogers
Track and Field 1956-1960
Coach - U.S. Olympic Teams

Charles "Charlie" Mays
Track and Field 1959-1962;
Olympian 1968

Ira Smith
Baseball, 1986-1991

Jake Ford
Basketball 1967-1970

John "Red Ball" Sample
Football, 1954-1957

Kennie Simmons
Basketball, 1975-1979

Levi Fountain
Basketball 1967-1970

Monica Felder
Basketball 1984-1988

Ralph LeCount Hodge
Baseball 1954-1958

Roger "Nyack" Brown
Football 1956-1960

THE GOLDEN YEARS OF THE HAWKS 1947-1975 . . . [43]

FOOTBALL		BASKETBALL	
YEAR	AWARD	YEAR	AWARD
1947	9-0-0	1955-1956	CIAA Champs
1949	8-0-0	1969	NAIA Finals
1950	8-0-0	1973	NAIA Finals
1952	8-0-0	1973	MEAC Champs
1954	8-0-1	1974	MEAC Champs
1955	8-0-0		
1957	8-0-0	Quarter Finals	NIT
1958	8-0-0		
1960	7-0-1		

BASEBALL	
YEAR	AWARD
1954-1958	CIAA Champs
1960, 1966, 1967	CIAA Champs

PENN RELAYS	
1965	1st Place in 440 Relays

NATIONAL INDOOR
1967

TRACK	
YEAR	AWARD
1961-1963	CIAA Champs
1966-1968	CIAA Champs
1961	South Atlantic AAU Indoor Champs
1961	NAIA District Champs
1962	NCAA National Champs
1963	NAIA National Champs
1964	NAIA District Champs
1965	NCAA Regional Champs
1962-1964	All 1st Place Awards George V. Brown Memorial Relays

NATIONAL COLLEGIATE
ATLANTIC COAST REGION
1962, 1963, 1964

The perfect compliment to top athletes were top fans, and MSC had both. Of all MSC fans, Gail Aikens was one of the most dynamic. She cheered for MSC athletes before, during, and after the games.

Campus Life

During the Williams era, campus life changed, and yet it remained the same. For example, chapel was still mandatory; students were strongly encouraged to be modest in dress; and men were expected to be gentlemen and women, ladies. Accordingly, profanity was not tolerated. Dr. Williams, micromanaged every segment of campus life. He was very much involved

155

with the alumni and with campus activities, including homecoming.

As a testament to his style of leadership, however, the campus flourished with Greek as well as civic, academic, service, Christian, and sports clubs and organizations. In 1948, Miss Amelia Merchant was named Miss Maryland State College, the first in the history of the University (See Exhibit G). Likewise, in those days students with extraordinary talent graced the campus, and they lived the lives of rising stars with all its glory and tragedy. A young man named Clifford Brown emerged as the star trumpet player in the Maryland State College Jazz Band.

(Figure 5.10)
Miss Amelia Merchant

That jazz band as well as the Maryland State College Choir (see Exhibit J) performed all over the Shore. One tragic night, June 4, 1950, two members of the group were killed in a car accident while returning from a performance at about three o'clock in the morning. The driver, who was not a student, lost control of the car near the high school in Princess Anne. Sam Turner, who was to graduate in three days, and piano player Wanda Shevendry were killed. Clifford Brown, also an athlete at MSC, suffered a broken pelvis and was told he would never walk again. Fortunately, he did walk again and went on to become one of the greatest trumpet players in the world. Tragically in 1956 at age twenty-five, Brown along with his new piano player and the piano player's wife, was killed in a car accident just hours after his last memorable show. They were on their way to Chicago after a Music City performance in Philadelphia.

On the business side of things, the Maryland State College Student Council had two of its best years during the J.T. Williams era. During the 1950-51 school year, the student council initiated as well as sponsored "Good Will Tours" into every black high school in the state of Maryland. This group also initiated exchange programs with Salisbury State College and Washington College of Chestertown. During the 1951-52 school year, the same group started gala homecoming celebrations, including the very first homecoming parade. Daniel Ridout, Jr. was president of the council the school year, 1951-52.

(Figure 5.11)
Maryland State College Choir, 1949-1950
Director Clarice J. Michael is not pictured.

(Figure 5.12)
Maryland State College Student Council, 1950-1951. Pictured left to right -- 1st Row:
Bishop Wayman, Mary Smither, Helen Timmons and Woodrow Hall (President); 2nd Row:
Dean Harris (Advisor), George Boston, Felix Lacy, Daniel Ridout, Jr. (Vice President).

(Figure 5.121)
Faculty and staff rehearse for a campus-wide talent show.
Left to right: Professor "Fess" Richard H. Thomas, Dr. E. W. Waters, T. Waldo
Kiah (son of past president), Gaston Finney, and Sherridan A. Parks.

Most notable was the latter part of the Williams era, which was one of
political and social unrest. It was the early sixties, and students were especially
involved in the Black Power movement. Consequently, they participated in
demonstrations on campus as well as off-campus. Specifically, students
actively participated in sit-ins and picket lines on campus to communicate
their displeasure with some administrative decisions. Their issues varied, but
all of them were centered on the civil and social rights of the Negro and of the
student. On the contrary, Dr. Williams was known for his opposing position
regarding the rights of students, which was best explained in his words
immemorial, "My way or the highway," and he remained unrelenting in his
philosophy.

Generally, the campus had a familylike atmosphere with Dr. Williams
providing absolute, patriarchal leadership. He was a strict disciplinarian, and
students knew that they could be sent home for violating the rules and
regulations, such as leaving campus without checking out, violating curfew,
and using profanity. Dr. Williams was so determined to have order that during
the full term of his appointment, he was the chair of the Student Life Committee.
It was one of several committees for handling light violations. Students were

aware, though, that with most violations that were handled by the Student Life Committee, the chances were more than likely that the violator would be sent home while any committee other than "Student Life" was less likely to send a student home.

The responsibility of the fatherlike administrator was far greater than imaginable and far greater than the average student could comprehend. In his hand lay the well-being of every enrolled student of the campus community, which was larger than ever and more diverse. From the students, he insisted upon spotless deportment, unerring accountability, and responsible management. His demands went a long way to insuring the safety of every young man or woman inserted into the peculiar dimension called the Eastern Shore. No doubt, Dr. Williams was charged with giving parents, at one time or the other, peace of mind. In light of the atmosphere of racism, discrimination, and the threat of violence, his responsibility called for desperate measures; and he was the one to meet the challenge.

On the other side of the spectrum, Dr. Williams supported the students in their political activism off campus. The sixties offered a different kind of fight to the consciousness of the strong student. With it, their strength and purpose was tested beyond anything they had ever experienced in the town of Princess Anne, Maryland. In the summer of 1963, the Princess Anne Biracial Committee published a desegregation agreement that, in principle, was meant to afford the black community admission to and service in any business in Princess Anne, Maryland, including the restaurants. No doubt the nationwide movement, represented in the form of lunch-counter sit-ins, boycotts, civil rights demonstrations, and marches, influenced the disposition of the small company of students at Maryland State College. Certainly emotions ran high, and convictions ran deep; and in the scheme of things, students on the campus took their stand in the ongoing, national struggle for the equal treatment of the black citizens in America. Indeed, the small campus, specifically the Class of 1963-64, caused a major change in the town of Princess Anne where, up to that point, many battles had been lost.

The struggle in Princess Anne began when Maryland State College students, who seldom frequented the local restaurants, learned that two of them had reneged on their agreement to serve Blacks. One of the restaurants had acquired a new owner who did not feel bound by the previous owner's agreement. Johnny Wilson, an aggressive young student at MSC, went into the small town to survey the situation. He found it to be exactly as it was reported.

The black townspeople in Princess Anne basically accepted the situation as the business of the day. The college students, however, were deeply disturbed by the implications of the revocation. Thus four brilliant students, who were committed to nonviolence, organized a protest that followed the same pattern as the protests staged in the Deep South in places like Montgomery, Alabama; Jackson, Mississippi; New Orleans, Louisiana; and Birmingham, Alabama, to name a few. The first of the four, Johnny Wilson, was raised in Princess Anne while Addison Cash grew up on the Eastern Shore of Virginia, Warren Morgan in New York City, and Curtis Gentry in Ohio. Under their direction, on February 20, 1964, MSC students went into the town of Princess Anne as a group to seek service at all of the local restaurants. They received service at all of them except two, Tull's and Muir's. The students retreated and met together on campus to discuss their strategy. The following day they went back to Tull's where white customers blocked

(Figure 5.13)
Student Leaders in 1960 Protests.
(Picture reproduced from the *Evening Journal*, Wilmington, Delaware, Friday, February 28, 1964)

the entrance so that the approaching demonstrators could not enter. Someone called the state police, who showed up with two vicious dogs from the K-9 Corps. True to form, the police and their dogs joined the irate customers in blocking the door of the restaurant. Needless to say, there was a lot of confusion, pushing, and shoving. During the scuffle that ensued, the restaurant's door hinge was sprung. The students left the scene and returned to the campus without further incidence.

In what appeared to be an effort to divide and conquer, the authorities singled out Wilson, the most passionate of the group; and Tull, the owner of the restaurant, swore out a warrant for his arrest. The police immediately headed for the campus, sought out Johnny Wilson, and handcuffed him. The officers placed Wilson in the back of the patrol car to leave the campus. "As everyone looked on in bewilderment, one student moved to the front of the patrol car to lay down in its path. Others followed until there was no clear path for the police car. The unrelenting students demanded that their leader be released."[44] The police were forced to leave the campus one hour later without Johnny Wilson. Later the same day, Johnny went to the local jail and surrendered. By that time, Princess Anne was flooded with state troopers, newsmen with communications paraphernalia, and onlookers. The following day, February 22, 1964, two small groups of students went back to the two restaurants that had refused to serve Blacks and were met with the same opposition displayed on previous occasions.

On Sunday afternoon, February 23, the students marched up one side of Main Street and down the other side to protest the discrimination. Then, on February 24, the violence began. The home of Mr. J. Leon Gates, an accountant at Maryland State and an uncle of Johnny Wilson's by marriage, was bombed; and a cross was burned on the football field in full view of the campus community. Dissension and conflict began to arise between the student leaders, the college administrators, the Princess Anne Biracial Committee representatives, the black townspeople, and later on local politicians. A truce was called until Wednesday, February 26, pending desegregation agreements from the two restaurants.

On Wednesday, the student leaders met with city officials and the Biracial Committee representatives who served as a liaison between the demonstrators and the restaurant owners. Dr. Williams was present at the meeting in support of the student protesters. During the course of that meeting, one of the city officials promised the student leaders that if anything happened to his family, he would go looking for them. Everyone was anxious about the outcome; because if there was no agreement, the students would march. At three o'clock that afternoon, the word came, "We march!" Dr. Youra Qualls, head of the English department, and Ms. Ina Steele, Dr. William's administrative assistant, marched alongside the students.

The student body, as a whole, participated in the demonstrations. They sang "We Shall Overcome," one of the songs of the civil rights movement as they marched the streets of Princess Anne. Gloria Richardson, a civil rights leader from Cambridge, Maryland, joined the students. They marched for about an hour; and then, to dramatize their demands, they decided to sit in the street to block traffic. State troopers showed up and physically tried to remove the numerous marchers but became frustrated. They began to wave traffic on, as cars and trucks approached the scene, in spite of the blockade of students. A truck as well as a school bus barely missed running over them.

On Friday, two days later, the students marched once again in an orderly manner. The troopers were summoned, and they in turn called for the dogs. Some students stood fast and were attacked by dogs; others scattered. One young lady, the victim of a particularly vicious attack, was bitten several times on the right side of her neck. During the attack, the troopers swung their clubs freely at the students, hitting some and grazing others. Said Gentry, "We just told them we could not fight back. We did not fight back even when they were dragging our young ladies down the street. We sang . . . we just sang."[45] In the midst of all of the chaos, the students were repeatedly referred to as "niggers."

Finally, they arrested Johnny Wilson again along with about twenty-seven other students. Curtis T. Gentry gathered the remaining students and returned to campus. There they were treated for injuries such as dog bites, head wounds, and scratches. Two of the more seriously injured students had to be hospitalized. Gentry became the liaison between the students and all concerned with the protests while the others were incarcerated.

Within a half-hour, a small group had regained its composure and started back towards Main Street. An onslaught of water from fire hoses, manned by volunteer firefighters, stopped them. The students formed a big ball to protect themselves from the pounding surges of water. One student fell and went into an epileptic seizure. Dr. Neville A. Baron, the college physician, rushed to administer treatment while the firefighters directed the water at the treatment area, soaking Dr. Baron and the student. William P. Hytche, professor of mathematics at MSC, was in his restaurant, the Hawk's Nest, just a block or two away from the main street when he heard the commotion. He rushed to see what was going on next to his place of business. He saw Dr. Baron kneeling beside the epileptic student, both dripping wet and in danger of getting slammed by the water again. He left the Hawk's Nest and went down the hill to assist Dr. Baron. On Dr. Hytche's return to his restaurant, the firemen turned the hoses on him. The powerful thrust knocked him flat on his back. He later commented:

> I became enraged because the firemen knew me and I knew them, and they understood I was returning to my place of business. I must admit I was angry enough to be violent in spite of my unconditional support for the non-violent movement. Someone asked if I could forgive the firemen. I responded, "Yes, they are forgiven, but I shall never forget what they did.[46]

Letters supporting the students poured in, some from as far away as Denmark and Austria. Some white townspeople urged the restaurants to desegregate to save the town from the ravages of racial unrest; others cheered them on in their segregationist stand. There was so much occurring in the little town of Princess Anne that state troopers patrolled the streets day and night.

By Friday, February 28, 1964, Dick Gregory, an author, actor, and civil rights advocate, arrived to speak to the students. Dr. Williams, who was present at every meeting, asked that the students not meet on the campus in state-owned buildings, because in actuality they were demonstrating against the State. Accordingly, Gregory spoke at the Metropolitan United Methodist Church outside of the college campus that afternoon and again that evening. He urged the demonstrators to boycott the town until there was complete desegregation to include a specific number of Blacks to be employed by local businesses. Until that time, such a request was unheard of in Princess Anne. Dick Gregory rendered financial as well as moral support. His three-hour speech was so powerful and so inspirational that even the media stayed riveted where they stood.

The boycott began the following Wednesday, and the Federal Post Office was the only business not affected. Since the college was the principal source of profit for Princess Anne, the town took notice. A few years earlier, the State had constructed a nonbusiness bypass road that took most of the traffic from the town center, causing a substantial loss of business. It was believed that a boycott would go a long way towards getting the attention of the "movers and shakers." Sam Doane, a black leader in the community, was very instrumental during the boycott. He organized the migrant workers, who "poured into town every Saturday to spend their good money."[47] As a result, the migrant workers stopped spending in Princess Anne in full support of the boycott.

Under the backbreaking stress of this protest, arrangements were made for the student leaders to meet with Governor J. Millard Tawes at the State House in Annapolis, Maryland. Out of all the black schools and students demonstrating, Wilson, Gentry, Morgan, and Cash were the only students invited to sit down and talk with the governor of the State. Dr. Williams, in classic Williams' style, counseled the four to be very professional, to be on their best behavior, to be sure to have their facts straight, and not to demand but to negotiate. They knew that Dr. Williams, in fulfilling his paternal role, would attend the meeting with them. Ironically, the same patrolmen who unleashed the attack dogs on the students during the marches were the same ones who had to chauffeur them to the meeting in Annapolis.

When they arrived at the State Building after what must have been a long and solemn ride, there on the steps stood 100 to 150 students singing "We Shall Overcome." It was a touching sight. Inside, the young Parren J. Mitchell was there on behalf of MSC. At the time, he was the chairman of the Maryland Human Rights Commission. At that meeting, the governor promised to see that the Public Accommodations Act of Maryland, then applicable to Baltimore City and eleven Maryland counties, would cover the remaining twelve counties in Maryland and particularly Princess Anne, which was the county seat. The governor's comments defused the student protests immensely.

Approximately one month later, Warren Morgan and a group of students were on their way to the Metropolitan United Methodist Church just outside the campus on Easter Sunday. They were viciously attacked by a group of white ruffians, and Morgan's face was broken on the left side. Though protests continued to spread far and wide, the aforementioned were the most significant parts of the MSC student protests. Students who were arrested had to go to court. Fortunately, all charges were dropped.[48]

Physical Plant

No serious attempt to pave the pedestrian pathways about the campus were undertaken until 1947 when Dr. Williams assumed office. Throughout most of the history of the school, students and faculty members had to contend with muddy walkways during the rainy season. In fact, prospective students were advised to procure appropriate footwear. The poor natural drainage of the campus, like that of most of the region, added to the difficulties; and at that time, no system of artificial drainage was adopted by the school. Additionally, Maryland State College continued to have its bout with fires.

At the close of the second semester in January 1950, one wing of the second floor of a recently completed boys dormitory was partially destroyed by fire. Later that same year, the construction of a dining hall by the State occurred in the wake of yet another crisis – a controversy over the very existence of the Academy. Before the decade was over, another building burned – a building with a story of its own.

(Figure 5.14)
Maryland State College campus in 1967.
Somerset & Wilson Halls pictured

165

(Figure 5.15)
Delcon Hall in Flames, February 1, 1959

In the early morning of Sunday, February 1, 1959, Delcon Hall was reduced to ashes under the watchful eye of the Princess Anne Fire Department. The building was sixty-seven years old and condemned. Mixed emotions filled all who looked on that morning. "Her frame went up in flames and smoke, but the memories and history of the service rendered will ever be an indestructible shrine in the hearts and minds of many men and women."[49]

Delcon Hall was the third major building to be constructed on the campus and served as the girls dormitory.[50] The exact date of its completion is unknown, but it is probable that the building was dedicated during the fall of 1892 or the spring of 1893 as the Eliza Smith Hall. Of frame construction, the building was designed to accommodate all of the female students, who numbered approximately fifty. Until 1915 it was the most modern building on the campus, containing baths and running water in addition to separate rooms for study, reception, and a teachers' lounge. The minutes of the trustees show that the building was constructed from a donation of $3,400 given by Dexter Smith. Available records do not show how Smith knew about the Academy in Princess Anne, and attempts to uncover circumstances leading to Smith's donation have not been successful.[51] Yet it is definitely known that Dexter Smith and his wife gave the building as a memorial to their deceased daughter,

(Figure 5.16)
Eliza F. Smith whose family gave the first girls dormitory to Princess Anne Academy in her memory

Eliza, whom they loved greatly.[52] For many years a large picture of Eliza was displayed on the walls of the building, but it gave no clues whatsoever as to the place, time, or circumstances surrounding the photography. A year or two prior to 1949, Eliza's picture was removed from the walls and was never replaced. One of the football coaches, J.C. Coffee, rediscovered the picture in its rotting and dusty frame. It has been reproduced here for the memory of the family who gave the school its first dormitory for girls. Eliza's picture was presented to the school when the building was dedicated.

The picture showed that Eliza was an attractive young woman, well-dressed in winter attire with a tight-fitting, striped bodice in plain view beneath a winter coat. Her attire was fashionable in the late 1880s. Persons who saw Eliza's picture often wondered what the subject's connection was with the school. Only a few persons on the campus in 1949 actually knew the location of Eliza Smith Hall which, being unmarked with plaque or inscription, was known popularly as the "Old Dormitory." As late as 1950, the building was being used as a dwelling for faculty members as well as a classroom and a practice hall for music. Hardly any of the occupants knew— or cared—that their building was officially dedicated as Eliza Smith Hall nearly sixty years earlier.

A large frame building, more than twice the size of Eliza Smith Hall, was built within several feet of the first girls dormitory in 1915. For all practical purposes, this building was an annex to Eliza Smith Hall, linked by a corridor several years later. The building was originally used as a girls dormitory, relieving the overcrowded conditions in Eliza Smith Hall, which, by World War I, was too small to house the number of girls, approximately ninety. After 1924, the annex was used to house boys while the girls were removed to Eliza Smith Hall, where they were primarily housed until 1942. Upon completion, the annex cost about $8,000. It was officially designated as Delcon Hall after the Delaware Conference, but this name was rarely used inasmuch as the building was frequently referred to either as the boys or the girls dormitory, according to whatever function it was serving at the time.

Nearly a half-century passed before a third girls dormitory was built in1942. This time the state of Maryland was the donor. Again, in 1944 there was an unveiling of a picture that was later placed upon the walls of the building officially dedicated as John Murphy Hall. The dedication was made because of the fear of an opponent's political weapon—the Negro Press of Baltimore. The dedication of John Murphy Hall was a gesture of appeasement to placate political power. As subsequent years showed, however, the gesture of appeasement failed; for the press continued to attack the school, leaving the name of John Murphy Hall as an incongruous symbol of expediency and perhaps of folly.

Williams "Under Fire"

By 1966, the issue of inadequate and unfair state appropriations began to fester and culminate. Dr. Williams was fed up with the constant neglect that was accompanied by the unforgiving scrutiny of the Board of Regents. "President Williams was 'under fire' from the Regents because a five-year master plan requested by Middle States for the development of Maryland State was late in preparation and lacking in definite goals. The Board complained that President Williams dwelled too much on past problems and not enough on the future . . . The plan drawn up by President Williams was handed back for revision because it 'lacked an over-all statement as to where the school fits into the total State program of higher education.' The Regents also complained that Maryland States' standards were embarrassing to the University and the school should either raise the standards to make it a branch of the University or abandon the school altogether."[53]

During this time, Dr. Williams worked hard to secure an unprecedented appointment with the governor to explore greater funding for the campus. Finally, the governor's secretary called, and at the appointed time Dr. Williams entered the governor's office for an unusually candid meeting. Before the President could bring up any issues, however, the governor picked up a newspaper, put his feet on the table, and started reading. As Dr. Williams talked, the governor read. Suddenly Dr. Williams slapped the paper out of his hands and demanded that he listen.

168

The governor apologized profusely and sat through about twenty-five minutes of issues. Dr. Williams thanked him and left satisfied that the governor had really heard him. Subsequently the governor wrote him a letter about their meeting, but nothing was mentioned about the issues Dr. Williams had discussed. The governor's term expired about 2 ½ years after that meeting, and not a single dollar was appropriated for the campus under his governorship. It is reported that the governor said that he did not care about Maryland State College and that, if it were left entirely to him, there would not be a "damn" school in Princess Anne.

Still Maryland State College progressed despite some unfriendly and unbelievable obstacles and because of some informal friendships. One such friendship came in the form of Senator Welcome, who defended Maryland State College in Annapolis. Concerning MSC, "she charged that the Regents 'have allowed it to rot on the vine. They have channelled millions (dollars) to their other branches and programs at home and abroad . . . but only crumbs to Princess Anne."[54] Again, the question of merger or closure had come to the forefront; but this time, the students learned of the conflict. By May 1967, about one year after its start, the controversy subsided with University of Maryland President Wilson Elkin's declaration that he planned to make Maryland State College an "integral part" of the University of Maryland. MSC students refused to be as hopeful as Dr. Williams, who by this time needed to believe that in the end, his hard work would make a difference. He held on to his hope while the students directed their frustrations at him.

Students lamented the cafeteria food, they complained about the condition of the facilities, and they bucked long-time campus policies. Before the end, Senator Welcome was invited to the campus by students to survey the condition of things. She was appalled at the neglectful conditions she saw. Once she went back to Annapolis, she "called for appropriations to construct a student union, a dormitory, and a swimming pool as well as to build bleacher seats."[55] One senator said, "I am against spending funds for a pool down there. If they want to swim, let them swim in the Manokin River." One would have to know that the Manokin River is a mossy, stagnant creek to appreciate the sarcasm in his statement. The bottom line was that in spite of Dr. Williams' substantial victories, Maryland State College was consistently described as merely mediocre. In truth, Dr. Williams had no funds available to him to alleviate the neglectful conditions Senator Welcome saw. He had spent his entire career up to that point in trying to get the financial support the school needed to go to the next level. All he could do, however, was help the students excel academically with whatever facilities and equipment they were fortunate to get.

Indeed, Dr. Williams was known for encouraging excellence in the classroom from his faculty as well as from his students. As a result, in 1968 a Maryland State College student, Miss Saundra Williams, was named the first Miss Black America. The Miss Black America Pageant was first held in Atlantic City in 1968 as a protest, because until then there had been no black contestants in the Miss America Pageant.

Williams' Retirement

About mid-year in 1970, the underlying current of discontent formed into an explosive situation that led to the forced retirement of President Williams. In essence, the controversy was centered around his leadership style. It seemed that, as time passed, the students grew more and more aggressive and rebellious against the rigid structure of campus life. "On April 7, 1970, a total of 178 students were arrested after staging demonstrations on campus protesting conditions at the school and demanding the resignation of President Williams."[56] The students staged a sit-in, and Dr. Williams and his staff were unable to leave their offices without calling the police. Dr. Williams, was convinced that students demanding his removal had received support at the state level and that he had not been asked to present his side of the controversy."[57] Reportedly, parents and alumni were also a part of the mutiny. "Governor Mandel, Secretary Lee, students, alumni, and parents met in Annapolis to discuss the situation and to form a committee for the improvement of Maryland State. The Governor acknowledged that the college's problems were partially financial and partially a question of leadership. Governor Mandel "all but assured students that President Williams would not be named chancellor of the college when the new system was instituted."[58]

Though Dr. Williams had the support of some, the opposition was overwhelming. Dr. Williams was not ready to retire. Even as late as 1969, he was still working toward the realization of his long-ranged plans to enhance the academic program and the physical plant. He had hopes for that swimming pool that he had been requesting since the beginning of his tenure, and he wanted to build an auditorium and a new science building. Instead, his plans were cut short. Under a cloud of controversy, Dr. Williams announced his retirement on May 26, 1970 and retired on August 1, 1970.

Over the years, Dr. Williams devoted a great deal of his time to the National Association of College Deans and Registrars, of which he was vice-president. During World War II, he was a member of President Roosevelt's Advisory Committee of the United States Armed Forces Institute. Subsequently, he was cited by the Army Secretary and the Navy Secretary for his services as an educational expert. Concurrently with this assignment, he acted as expert consultant to the Joint Army/Navy Committee on Welfare and Recreation, Expert Advisor to the American Council on Education, and Special Lecturer for the Morale Division of the War Department. Williams was a devoted member of Kappa Alpha Psi Fraternity in addition to many clubs and civic organizations including Frontiers, Pyramids, and the Pigskin Club of Washington. He also served on the board of Peninsula Regional Hospital. All of his life, he remained an avid sportsman; golfer, hunter, and fisherman.

"For the twenty-three years that Dr. John T. Williams was president of Maryland State College, the institution in Princess Anne experienced changes touching every aspect of the school's life. Dr. Williams ably guided Maryland State from a struggling, four-year college beset with academic, financial, and political problems to that of being an integral part of the University of Maryland. Dr. Williams' tenure as president was marked by a leap in enrollment, a great building boom on campus, an increase in faculty, and academic recognition for the school at Princess Anne. The combination of a dynamic president with the change in educational philosophy after the Brown versus Board of Education Supreme Court decision in 1954 and the expansion of higher education in general in the 1960s formed the backdrop for the emergence of Maryland State College as a viable institution."[59]

As a result of his influence and involvement in various extracurricular activities, Dr. Williams had a tremendous amount of social pull. Over the years, he was able to get influential guests to address and/or entertain the campus community. Some of the most influential commencement speakers were: Mrs. Franklin Delano Roosevelt (Figure 5.17), The First Lady of the World, 1954; Dr. Martin Luther King, Jr. (Figure 5.18), Civil Rights Activist, 1959; and Mr. Jackie R. Robinson (Figure 5.19), First Black Major League

Baseball Player, 1961. Indeed, Dr. Williams lived long enough to see Maryland State College become an integral part of the University of Maryland in 1970 when the name was changed one final time to the University of Maryland Eastern Shore (UMES).

Less than a year after he retired, Dr. Williams checked himself into Peninsula General Hospital early one Tuesday complaining of chest pains. He died that same day from a heart condition. In his honor Maryland Hall, built in 1940, was renamed John Taylor Williams Hall. Today it is more popularly known as the J. T. Williams Administrative Building.

Captions for photos on page 173:

(Figure 5.17)
Dr. John Taylor Williams escorts Eleanor Roosevelt, then First Lady of the World, as they head the procession in the 1954 graduation ceremony.

(Figure 5.18)
Dr. Martin Luther King, Jr., commencement speaker in 1959. Members of the Board of Regents look on.

(Figure 5.19)
Dr. John Taylor Williams; Mrs. Jackie Robinson, and baseball great, Mr. Jackie R. Robinson.

Selected University of Maryland Eastern Shore Commencement Speakers

(Left) (Figure 5.17)
First Lady Eleanor Roosevelt
1954 Speaker

(Below, left) (Figure 5.18)
Dr. Martin Luther King, Jr.
1959 Speaker

(Below, right) (Figure 5.19)
Baseball Great Jackie R. Robinson
1961 Speaker

ENDNOTES

CHAPTER 5

1   Accredited Secondary Schools in the United States, (Washington), 1934.

2   Laws, 1935, ch. 92.

3   Ruth Ellen Wennersten, The Historical Evolution of a Black Land Grant College: The University of Maryland Eastern Shore: 1886-1970. Thesis submitted to the Faculty of the Graduate School of the University of Maryland in partial fulfillment of the requirements for the degree of Master of Arts, 1976, p. 61.

4   Ibid.

5   Ibid., p. 58.

6   Laws, 1937, ch. 506.

7   Commission, 1939, p.2.

8   Dr. George H. Callcott, The Maryland Education Commissions, pg. 12.

9   Maryland Commission on Higher Education of Negroes, 1937, p.11. Hereafter, references to all State commissions on education are cited as Commission.

10   Laws, 1945, ch. 716.

11   Commission, 1947, p. 361.

12   The Trustees were still having financial difficulties despite the fact that they had disposed of their interests in Princess Anne at a profit (1936). The Trustees held that the College could best be maintained as a State institution and transferred the school to the State in 1939. There was no proviso, however, that Morgan would be obligated to give graduate and professional work that was being rapidly and unrealistically included in the curricula of Negro colleges in other states.

13   Ruth Ellen Wennersten, p. 65.

14   Ruth Ellen Wennersten, p. 60.

15   Ruth Ellen Wennersten, p. 67.

16   Ruth Ellen Wennersten, p. 64.

17   Ruth Ellen Wennersten, p. 68.

18   Report (Univ.), 1933

19   Minutes, 1899, p.57

20   Laws, 1896, ch. 261

21   Minutes, 1897, p. 66

22   It is to be noted that the Bulletin was entered as second-class matter at the post office in Princess Anne, on January 11, 1909.

23   When 200 Negroes burned in a dance hall in Natches, Mississippi the previous year, this paper carried only a short article, a column of about five inches in length.

24   Ruth Ellen Wennersten, p. 69.

25   Ruth Ellen Wennersten, p. 70.

26   Ruth Ellen Wennersten, p. 74.

[27] Ruth Ellen Wennersten, p. 75.

[28] Ruth Ellen Wennersten, p. 75.

[29] Maryland Statewide Plan for Postsecondary Education, Adopted by The State Board for Higher Education July 6, 1978. Pg. 17.

[30] Ibid. pg. 17.

[31] Ruth Ellen Wennersten, p. 76.

[32] Ruth Ellen Wennersten, p. 78.

[33] Malcolm Moos, Director, The Post-Land Grant University: The University of Maryland Report. (The University of Maryland), 1981, p. 131.

[34] Dr. George H. Callcott, pg 13.

[35] Ruth Ellen Wennersten, pg. 81.

[36] The school was later criticized during the school year 1948-1949 for soliciting the enrollment of students, particularly non-residents of the State. However, student enrollment passed the 300 mark, the largest in the history of the school, and, in contrast to former years, a large percentage of the students were non-residents of the State.

[37] For example, the New York Times reported the controversy. A special correspondent, George Streater, visited the State and Reported a column dated from Princess Anne, December 4, 1948. Streater's article was captioned "Negroes Criticize Maryland School" with a sub-title of "Making College of Academy at Princess Anne is called Bypassing of Equal Rights." There were two sectional titles in the column. Under one, entitled "Dr. Byrd States His Positions," the author reported that "Dr. Byrd denied this week that construction of the new college is aimed at denying educational advantages to Negroes and declared that in the other sectional heading, "Head of College is Assailed," it was pointed out that Williams "has been under attack as an interloper brought here to do the bidding of Dr. Byrd."

[38] Byrd was born in Crisfield, Maryland in 1889. He was graduated from the Maryland Agricultural College and later became its football coach. In 1918, he was appointed as vice president of the College and served in this capacity until 1935 when, following an investigation of the University's administration, he was appointed as acting president. On February 22, 1936 he became president, being criticized severely during his administration. See Thomas P. Monahan, "The University of Maryland, a Challenge to Democracy," a mimeographed publication by the author (Washington, D.C.), 1943.

[39] On the noteworthy occasion, the Sun printed a Negro's protest against segregation under the caption "Morgan Professor Threatens to Quit if U. Of M. Takes Over" in the issue for November 21, 1948. The letter (about one column in length) was written by Clifton R. Jones who stated that Byrd's purpose was "to institute in Maryland what he calls controlled segregation." Jones further stated that the school in Princess Anne was a "wasteful expenditure" to taxpayers and an "utter disgrace" to the state of Maryland.

[40] Ruth Ellen Wennersten, pg. 87.

[41] Ruth Ellen Wennersten, pg. 92.

[42] Harold Rush. Story as told in letter from Rush, former athlete and MSC student.

[43] The Hawks on Review, Publication of the University of Maryland Eastern Shore, 1976-1977.

[44] Dr, William P. Hytche, Step by Step to the Top: The Saga of a President of a Historically Black University. pg. 127.

[45] Curtis Gentry, telephone interview, November 30, 2001.

[46] Dr. William P. Hytche, pg. 129.

[47] Curtis Gentry interview.

[48] This ordeal was originally described eloquently in the May 9th, 1964 Ledger, an MSC campus publication printed by the Department of Business under the leadership of the Department Chair, Dr. Vernon Stone.

[49] T. Waldo Kiah, The Hawk 1959, pg. 78.

[50] A small shop was built on the campus in 1891 through "the generosity of friends who supplied the materials, and by the labor of students themselves." It is likely that this shop housed the trades, including the four "male departments" of blacksmithing, bricklaying, carpentry, and shoemaking. This building was "very temporary" but it was the first structure on the campus used for "industrial arts". See Report (Univ.), 1891, pp. 41-42. The instruction carried on in this small shop, hardly more than a wooden shed, was the only claim that the school could show in behalf of industrial education in order to meet the requirements of the land-grant act.

[51] Although the author has no conclusive proof, it may be that the Dexter Smith in question was once an editor and publisher who lived in Boston. For many years a Dexter Smith of Boston, Massachusetts, published, and edited a musical magazine called Dexter Smith's Paper, which became the Musical Record at the turn of the century. The first edition of the magazine was published in January of 1872. An entry card in the Library of Congress for one of Smith's operatic translations (1908) gives his dates as 1842(1)-1909. Smith is not listed in Who's Who (which during his time was no reliable index to outstanding personalities; for example, Goucher was not listed until the later years of his life) and genealogical registers of New England. There is the probability that this Dexter Smith gave the funds for Eliza Smith Hall. Certainly, his dates indicate that he could fit into the known facts. For example, being born about 1842 would make him about fifty years of age at the time the building was completed — old enough to be the father of the young woman after whom the building was named.

[52] Report (Univ.), 1893, p. 45.

[53] Ruth Ellen Wennersten, pg. 104.

[54] Ruth Ellen Wennersten, pg. 105

[55] Ruth Ellen Wennersten, pg. 108.

[56] Ruth Ellen Wennersten, pg.114.

[57] Daily Times Article, April 1970.

[58] Ruth Ellen Wennersten, pg. 115.

[59] Ruth E. Wennersten, pg. 80.

THE PROGRESSIVE YEARS
of
THE UNIVERSITY of MARYLAND EASTERN SHORE

(Figure 6.1)
Two benefactors contribute to Hytche's vision.
Left to right: Mrs. Richard Henson, Dr. Richard Henson, Dr. William P. Hytche,
Dr. Richard Bernstein and Mrs. Richard Bernstein.

The Education of the Negro: Unanswered Questions

The quest for a "solution" to the problem of the higher education of Negroes in the State—and specifically the problem of the "old Academy"—revealed the dilemma and inconsistency in the intellectual approach of Whites and Negroes alike. The idea of aiding segregation on one hand and of supporting the theory of "integration" on the other, were incongruous dichotomies. The intellectual leadership of the Negro, for example, admitted that the "separate but equal" theory of education, unrealistic and costly in its approach, was undoubtedly a practical denial of the fundamental philosophy of equality. Yet this leadership proposed to implement equality in education by increasing materially the permanent effectiveness of segregated Negro colleges. Therefore, the implications of this approach were rejected by critics. They saw the reorganization of the Academy as a threat to Negro equality although they had to admit that the theory of integration was still a nebulous and debatable quantity in the equation of Negro rights. Critics therefore maintained their claim that the school in Princess Anne should not receive state aid because it was a "Jim Crow" stepchild of the white University, a subterfuge to prevent equality through integration at the University of Maryland. At the same time, more state aid was being sought and granted for Morgan State College, itself a segregated institution. The gap between the theory and practice of "separate but equal" remained an appallingly wide one between the Academy and the University of Maryland. The distance of the gap, however, did not invalidate the premise of the theory.

Solutions to the problem came in several diverse and well-intentioned forms. Firstly there was the adoption of out-of-state scholarships for work not offered at Princess Anne or Morgan but given at the University of Maryland. Second there was a more pronounced increase in the amount of state aid to Negro higher institutions, especially at Princess Anne. Third a limited amount of integration was accepted with contemplation of further entry of Negroes at the University. Fourth, sanction was officially given to the idea of regional colleges for Negroes to be supported by joint action of Southern states.[1]

The solution by the State left several unanswered questions that were specifically related to the problem. Higher education considered:

1. Should the school in Princess Anne be abandoned altogether, expanded, or its function redirected;
2. Should scholarships be eliminated or expanded;
3. What is the extent that the State should support the "regional" plan for Negro education;
4. To what extent should the existing educational program for Negroes be coordinated and consolidated;
5. To what extent should the State's program of higher education be controlled by the University of Maryland; and

6.   To what extent should Negroes be admitted to the
      University of Maryland?

Many of these questions were related in varying degrees to one fundamental question: What should be the extent of the State's guarantee of equality of opportunity in higher education, particularly for its Negro citizens? Thus, finding the answer to the question confronted the second half of the twentieth century even as the second half of the nineteenth century was faced with the problem of formal and public education for the Negro.

All in all, the story of Princess Anne's University has its own unique setting. There is, for example, the influence of the Eastern Shore with its geographic isolation and class and family consciousness; the early dual control of the school by absentee boards in College Park or Baltimore wherein resourceful and dynamic leadership at the school was discouraged; the symbolism of the school in contests over state aid and Negro rights; the disasters that came in the wake of destructive fires; the convenient use of the school as a means to obtain federal funds. Certainly the story of the school, like that of the Negro, is marked with many milestones along the road from slavery to freedom—from Reconstruction to integration.

By 1970, however, the heritage of the school, if not its future, had become secure in the history of higher education in Maryland. Unfortunately, the man who stimulated the necessary change was also the man who bore the brunt of the vengefulness often associated with major change. The State acquiesced; they pledged their support while under the weight of a form of peer pressure. Then, they kicked the closest person to them. Consequently, Dr. J. T. Williams found himself on the outside looking in while Dr. Howard Emery Wright took the helm.

Dr. Howard Emery Wright (1970-71)

Dr. Howard Emery Wright, a mild-mannered academic dean, was appointed as the acting chancellor of Maryland State College in August 1970 following Dr. Williams' retirement. He served as acting chancellor of the University for less than a year, making possible a smooth transition of permanent executive officers. He earned his A.B. from Lincoln University of Pennsylvania and his M.A. and Ph.D. degrees from Ohio State University. His capabilities

179

(Figure 6.2)
Dr. Howard Emery Wright
Acting Chancellor, 1970-71

as dean and chief academic officer earned him admiration and support among faculty, students, and staff. In a brief message published in the 1970 college catalog, Dr. Wright's concerns were perhaps best illustrative of his short tenure:

Our chaotic world is in the midst of a revolution, involving all of us. We pass from protest to a program – one of social sensitivity for those seeking equality, justice, and the opportunity for vast improvement. The University is for all the citizens of Maryland who wish to benefit from its offerings as they prepare themselves for leadership, dedicated to change, and improve this troubled world.

Indeed, there was trouble in the world of education and Dr. Wright was in the middle of it. He was able, nevertheless, to nurture the program at UMES and was well respected because of it.

Dr. Wright was best known for his strong interest in the campus library. During his tenure, he was instrumental in the acquisition of the Frederick Douglass Library building with all its necessary equipment and reading material. For a while it was the largest building on campus, and efficiently managed by Jessie Cottman Smith, who twenty years later became the first dean of library services.

As an applicant in the national search conducted by the Board of Regents for a permanent chancellor for the University of Maryland Eastern Shore, Dr. Wright left office when Dr. Archie Buffkins was selected.

(Figure 6.21)
Dean Jessie Cottman Smith,
first dean of library services at
the University

(Figure 6.3)
Dr. Archie L. Buffkins
Chancellor, UMES

Dr. Archie L. Buffkins (1971-75)

Dr. Archie L. Buffkins assumed the post of chancellor of the University of Maryland Eastern Shore on June 1, 1971. Dr. Buffkins, a native of Memphis, Tennessee, received his bachelor's degree from Jackson State University, Mississippi, and his master's degree and doctorate from Columbia University. His graduation from Columbia University was followed by his postdoctoral research in higher education administration at the University of Maine, Harvard, Oxford, and the University of Amsterdam. He also did advanced musical study at the Chicago Conservatory of Music. A composer, author, and administrator, Dr. Buffkins previously held academic appointments at Rhode Island College; Texas Southern University; Kentucky State College; Jackson State; Morristown College, Tennessee; and the University of Maine. He was the author of two books – *An Intellectual Approach to Musical Understanding* and *Philosophical Thoughts of a University Scholar*. A relatively young man of thirty-six when he assumed the helm of the University, Buffkins was considered a man of strong views and of consistent actions in support of those views.

One of Dr. Buffkins' main motives in coming to Princess Anne was to "take a traditionally black institution of higher education and develop it into a first-rate multiracial institution, based upon mutual respect for all people with special emphasis on intellectual quality and cultural pluralism."[2] When a federal judge's sweeping desegregation order was issued, an organization purporting to represent 110 predominantly black institutions announced its opposition. Dr. Buffkins stood against them, stating his personal commitment to a "multiracial form of quality education on all levels." He asserted that every school should be a center of learning for all groups of people regardless of their race, color, or creed. Buffkins' vision, however, of a multiracial, multicultural institution was to be a harbinger of the future.

Integration

In 1974, the state of Maryland had the job of desegregating the rest of its public postsecondary schools. Governor Marvin Mandel submitted his plan for desegregation to the Federal Department of Health, Education, and Welfare, and to the Office of Civil Rights. As a result of that plan, a biracial task force was appointed by the Maryland Council for Higher Education and commissioned to coordinate the desegregation process and to "propose ways of enhancing the role and image of the predominantly black public colleges in the State."[3] The commission took on the name of its chairman, Thelma B. Cox. For once, after many, many years, an educational commission recognized UMES as a successful and growing institution of higher learning. "The Task Force recognizes the great strides this Campus has taken in the last three years. It endorses and supports the Chancellor's efforts in establishing this Campus as a showcase multi-racial University campus."[4] In addition, the task force recommended that UMES develop programs that were compatible to its geographic location. The Cox Commission's report was submitted to the Maryland Council for Higher Education on August 9, 1974. Today, the University of Maryland Eastern Shore has one of the most racially and culturally diverse faculty and student bodies in the University of Maryland System.

Physical Plant

Dr. Buffkins was especially dedicated to the development of cultural and performing arts at UMES. It was during his tenure that the Ella Fitzgerald Center for the Performing Arts was completed. Ella Fitzgerald was present as an honored guest at the dedication ceremony of the beautiful facility. Among those appearing at the Performing Arts Center have been such renowned performers as the National Ballet, Rubie Dee and Ossie Davis, the Washington Ballet, Maya Angelou, the acclaimed soprano Patrice Munsel, Peter Nero, and Stanley Turrentine.

Buffkin Resigns

After three years as Chancellor of the University of Maryland Eastern Shore, Dr. Buffkins moved on to assume high-level administrative positions

(Figure 6.4)]
Ella Fitzgerald with Dr. Archie Buffkins at the Dedication Ceremony
of the Ella Fitzgerald Center for the Performing Arts

with the University of Maryland College Park, the Kennedy Center, and
Maryland Public Television.[5] Buffkins succeeded in recruiting talented faculty and
students and in establishing centers of excellence in research on the campus.[6]

Dr. William Percy Hytche, Sr. (1975-97)

Dr. William Percy Hytche was active on the campus of the University
of Maryland Eastern Shore for approximately fifteen years when Buffkins left
UMES. He came to the University, then known as Maryland State College, in
1960 under the presidency of Dr. John Taylor Williams as a professor of
mathematics. Dr. Hytche, like Dr. Williams, was a native of Oklahoma. In
addition, he was the son of a Methodist minister and was the seventh child
and youngest boy from a blended family of nine siblings. He came to UMES
as a mathematics instructor with his wife Deloris and their three children:
Pamelia, Jacqueta, and William, Jr. Dr. Hytche rose through the college's
academic ranks from professor, to chairman of the Mathematics Department,
to chairman of the Division of Liberal Studies, and to dean of students. He
was well known like Dr. Wright and admired by students, faculty, and staff.

When Dr. Buffkins announced his resignation, several groups on the campus led by the UMES Senate recommended Dr. Hytche for the chancellorship. In turn, Dr. Wilson Elkins, as President of the University of Maryland College Park, offered the position to Dr. Hytche, who in July 1975 made the transition from dean to acting chancellor. Four major problems met Dr. Hytche when he took office as acting chancellor: low enrollment, poor program offerings, low morale, and a financial deficit in the athletic program. Besides these problems, there was the major concern that the community needed

(Figure 6.5)
Dr. William P. Hytche

to be united in a partnership with the University because this was the key to survival. Said Hytche,

> *The first letter I wrote on my first day in office was to the chair of the Department of Music, Dr. Gerald Johnson, requesting that a gospel choir be established. This was my first effort to get the community more interested in the University, because I had observed the campus's large turnout for gospel music programs. . . . The second letter I wrote my first day in office was to twenty-eight local leaders in the community inviting them to become a member of a Chancellor's Advisory Council (CAC, later called the President's Advisory Council – PAC). I needed to develop a political base; and along with the invitations, I gave some guidelines as to exactly what I wanted from such a committee.* [7]

Dr. Hytche had had the benefit of riding in the back seat of administration for many years prior to his leadership. Being a true mathematician, he had surveyed the land and considered the best possible solutions for the problems and the people involved. He was, therefore, focused early in the game and determined to do what needed to be done.

"Dr. Hytche continued to build bridges of cooperation with the white community leaders and within a year after assuming office, the tireless math professor scored a significant breakthrough when community leaders led by Abe Spinak, a science administrator at the NASA facility at Wallops Island, Virginia, agreed to serve on a blue-ribbon campus advisory committee."[8] In fact, all twenty-eight leaders accepted Hytche's offer to serve, and the resulting Chancellor's Advisory Committee has been an invaluable asset to the university since its inception.

In 1976, Hytche was appointed permanent chancellor of the University of Maryland Eastern Shore. His chancellorship continued to be rooted in endless efforts to keep the doors of the university open. Because the instability of the campus was a reoccurring problem throughout its history, the Methodist Church and the local community were not totally sure that the institution would survive in spite of its staying power. Consequently, the people of the community did little to nothing to help the campus; they thought the campus would cease to exist.

Every two or three years, the campus would be scrutinized from almost all aspects. One year it would be the number of out-of-state students enrolled, another year it would be poor management of funds, other years it would be an array of criticisms capped with the suggestion to close the campus altogether. The critics came from the business sector and from the white power structure, most of whom had never visited the campus. Their utterances were based only on prejudices, because they had no first-hand knowledge of the campus programs, its infrastructure, or its potential to help those who had no access to higher education. The commissions did the same, except that they were a little more sophisticated. Nevertheless, Dr. Hytche always responded to his attackers and, when possible, invited them to the campus.

It was so hard for the UMES administrators to communicate that the UMES mission was different from that of any other school in the University of Maryland System. No one questioned the cost per student at the University of Maryland at Baltimore or even at Salisbury State University; this would have been a fair and reasonable comparison at the time because their enrollments were comparable to the enrollment at UMES. Their existence was justified, however, based on their missions; but the University of Maryland

Shore has constantly had to defend its existence despite its mission. According to Hytche, "It is difficult to win many games when you are forced to play defense at all times."

Campus Life

Life on the campus of the University of Maryland Eastern Shore was representative of the many educational opportunities available to the Black, the White, the Asian, the West Indian, the African, the upwardly mobile. The percentage of tenured and tenure-track faculty with terminal degrees increased steadily so that by 1996 it had reached 93 percent. In addition, the physical plant was greatly improved during the Hytche administration. Dr. Hytche stated, "I always believed that I could make the campus work. My greatest dream was to be able to walk from one side of the campus to the other without getting my feet dirty and to have a well-lighted campus at night." He was able to see his vision become a reality through his development of a strong political support system in the Maryland State Legislature, earned through his hard work and his outstanding human relations skills.

Dr. Hytche's gentle spirit and kind heart led him to employ a strong concern for students and personnel as well as to support community goals that would strengthen Somerset County, Wicomico, and other Lower Shore Counties. His door and telephone line were always open. With all of his expanding national and international achievements, he never lost the human touch so essential to his administrative and personal persona. In fact, Dr. Hytche's warm and compassionate personality went a long, long way towards the overall success of the University whether in the political or in the social realm.

The man, Hytche, could be found walking the campus at any time during the day in a suit, shirt, and tie and would not hesitate to interact with parents or students. Once, Dr. Hytche got on his knees in his expensive suit to repair a flat tire on a student's bicycle. During the University's annual Thanksgiving and Christmas dinners, President Hytche could always be found carving the turkeys or working behind the steam tables urging students to try a little bit of everything that was new to them. Because he was willing to serve, other faculty members and administrators also volunteered to serve these meals.

Hosting social events at his campus residence was one of his ways to

(Figure 6.51)
Dr. Hytche with jazz artist, Stanley Turrentine,
and UMES Professor of Music, John Lamkin.

unite the University and community. Family picnics and receptions, complete
with the guest-book signings, were memorable. Guests came to the picnics
and parties with the expectation that Dr. Hytche would serve his barbecued
specialty as well as his special oyster dip. Throughout all of these campus
events, Mrs. Hytche remained firmly focused as supportive wife and keeper
of their home.

In respect for the history, Dr. Hytche fostered an exemplary relationship
between the UMES campus and the Metropolitan United Methodist Church.
During the pastorate of the Reverends Samuel Tatem, Simon Stubbs, Elijah
Davis, Carroll Scott, Vaughn Johnson, Gary Meekins, Theodore Day, Walton
Burke, Jessica McCargo, and Charlotte Nichols from 1960 to present, Dr.
Hytche could always be found in the same pew with his wife. President Hytche
was able to meld the history of the campus with the Methodist Church and to
enhance the Wesley Foundation and other church goals with those of UMES.
The annual UMES Sunday at Metropolitan became a primary worship service
with music provided by the university's Gospel Choir and with bags of snacks
given to students for final examination week.

As a rule, Dr. Hytche employed a seven-day workweek with a sixteen-
to eighteen-hour workday. Late involvement at night never resulted in his late
arrival to the office the next day. Seven thirty in the morning or earlier was the

time that he and Dr. John Toll, Chancellor of the System, knew that they could find each other in their offices. As with his predecessors, Dr. Hytche had miles to go and battles to fight with each new day. Most of his battle arrived on the heels of a commission.

The Commissions

According to George H. Callcott, a renowned historical researcher and writer who performed a study on education commissions, "almost every colonial governor or legislature had a commission, or at least a plan, for encouraging education."[9] In 1699, the report of a commission led to the establishment of the first state-supported educational institution, King William's School (subsequently St. John's College), in Annapolis. In 1782, another report led to the establishment of Washington's College. In Maryland, as elsewhere, state-supported colleges for the rich often came before state-supported public schools for the poor. In 1799, soon after the American Revolution, the General Assembly received a one-person commission report, surely the most ambitious educational plan offered in America, developed by Samuel Knox, a Presbyterian minister and educational propagandist. His report called for a free elementary school in every village in the nation with the best students progressing to a free high school in every county; the best high school students proceeding to a free state college; and the best college graduates proceeding to a free university that would be the apex of American culture, to be established, of course, in Maryland. Knox's plan was endorsed by George Washington and Thomas Jefferson, debated by Congress, and received a good-faith appropriation of five hundred pounds sterling. Unfortunately, the enthusiasm of dreamers such as Knox was not matched by the enthusiasm of taxpayers. For a half century or more, people occasionally referred to the Knox Plan, and Jefferson's University of Virginia eventually reflected some of the details of the plan; but of course, this rationalistic scheme was never realized.[10]

Traditionally, educational commissions were appointed because of a politically-motivated idea or emerged from a desire to establish schools, colleges, or in the case of Knox, an entire educational system. Such commissions in the case of the University of Maryland Eastern Shore invariably resulted from racial and political controversy, which served to keep the administration, the personnel, and the students of the University off balance and insecure about the University's survival.

In a study on the structure and governance of education submitted to the governor's task force in 1975, the Leonard H. Rosenberg Foundation Commission explored ways to increase coordination between various sectors of education to better utilize educational resources from childhood through graduate school. The major recommendations of the Commission included:

> ...abandoning the tripartite governing structure and creating individual institutional governing boards; creating a state-level coordinating board for higher education with responsibility for planning, evaluation, budget, program approval and other powers; development of Morgan as an urban-oriented and doctoral-granting institution; and merger of Salisbury State College and UMES into a single regional institution. Additional recommendations included a state-level board for coordinating higher education with elementary and secondary education and administration of the State's financial aid programs by the proposed State Board for Higher Education.[11]

NAACP Representative Rudolph Cane and Theodore Adams, president of the UMES National Alumni Association, testified on behalf of the University of Maryland Eastern Shore and vehemently opposed this Commission's recommendation to merge SSU and UMES.

In 1976, the proposed state-level coordinating board for higher education was implemented.

> This new board, the State Board for Higher Education (SBHE), had the regulatory authority to approve new academic programs for public sector institutions and to make recommendations regarding new significantly amended programs at independent institutions. In addition, SBHE had the power to authorize new degrees at all public institutions and could establish policies for the transfer of students between institutions. SBHE was responsible for developing and maintaining a plan for all postsecondary education, administering the State's program of aid to independent institutions, developing and monitoring the State's desegregation plan for

public institutions, preparing a consolidated capital and operating budget for postsecondary education, and making recommendations concerning campus and agency budget requests.[12]

Then two years after the Rosenberg proposals, the Donaldson Report was presented during the 1977 legislative session. It was related specifically to the University of Maryland Eastern Shore and Salisbury State University and this was probably among the biggest blows dealt to the University.

The author of the Donaldson Report, Mr. Robert Donaldson, was a legislative analyst who analyzed the budgets of certain segments of the State, and the University of Maryland System campuses were under his jurisdiction. He looked at enrollment, the cost per full-time equivalent student, and a number of other variables to help the legislature understand how funds were being spent. In short, his report to the subcommittee of the Appropriations Committee on Higher Education stated that the University of Maryland Eastern Shore (UMES) should merge with Salisbury State University (SSU) or be closed. This report came about with no prior warning, and it hit hard. The Chancellor's Advisory Council (CAC), under the strong leadership of Attorney Tony Bruce, surveyed the report and went to work to protect the University. They rallied together and summoned the help of the community.

All state and local newspapers reported the contents of the document that Donaldson submitted to the legislators. The implications of the report were far-reaching. "The Maryland Senate passed a resolution in 1967 recommending merger with nearby Salisbury State College. In 1975, another major report on higher education in Maryland, this one prepared by the Rosenberg Commission, recommended merging UMES and Salisbury State."[13] The Donaldson Report was the third pronouncement concerning merger. Because of the nature of the proposal, supporters of UMES who bitterly opposed closure were disarmed. Many more, however, realized the proposal was masking a more sinister plan to completely annihilate UMES and its mission.

Dr. Hytche and his administrators saw the proposal for what it was. "Hytche and his school fought back. 'They have tried to make us a number of things,' Hytche told the media and his political allies in Annapolis. 'They have had every idea under the sun—from turning this place into a chicken farm or a prison. But this place will be, I vow, what it has always been, a place of

(Figure 6.6)
Attorney John W. T. Webb,
member of the Board of Regents
and chair of the infamous
Webb Task Force

educational opportunity for the youth of the Eastern Shore and the state of Maryland.'"[14]

Fortunately, someone on the Appropriations Committee contended that the recommendation for merger should be given more thought before the vote. As a result, the State decided not to act on the analyst's report that year. Though the decision not to act was less than desirable at the time, it turned out that it may have been the best thing that ever happened to UMES. Dr. Sheldon Knorr, executive director of the State Board for Higher Education (SBHE), which is now the Maryland Higher Education Commission (MHEC), had the responsibility of appointing a blue-ribbon task force to look into the feasibility of UMES being closed or the two institutions (UMES and SSU) merging. The person appointed as chair of that committee was a well-known attorney by the name of John W. T. Webb, affectionately known as Jack.

The Webb Task Force became a prestigious group. They held hearings open to the public to get the community's response to this imminent issue. They heard some eighty to ninety verbal testimonies and received about twice as many written testimonies, which were not read in open meetings. The assertion of the chancellor and his Advisory Council remained to be that UMES had never really been given a chance because it was never properly structured, never properly funded, and never given a focused mission. The message came across loud and clear to the Webb Task Force whose members, all from Maryland, consisted of:

Mr. John W. T. Webb, Chairman,
Salisbury (a highly visible, local attorney)

Dr. Richard I. McKinney, Vice-Chairman, Baltimore
(retired professor of philosophy at Morgan State University)

Ms. Bertha Adkins, Oxford (former, employee of U.S. Secretary of Health, Education, and Welfare)

Mr. William Chaffinch, Easton (local well-to-do businessman)

Dr. Kermit Cottman, Princess Anne (first Black assistant superintendent of schools in Somerset County)

Mr. Edward Gallagher, III, Ocean City (a local well-to-do businessman)

Dr. DeWayne Whittington, Marion (high school principal and well-known Somerset County educator)

Dr. Joseph Durham, SBHE staff

Mr. Fred Spigler, SBHE staff

During testimony, the attacks on UMES came from without as well as from within the campus community. One white professor from the campus spewed out accusations of racism, while another defended the campus against the accusations. Along the same vein, a professor talked about the type of students the university had. "He said they weren't worthy to be at UMES, that he didn't know how they got out of high school, and that UMES was admitting anybody who applied. He said there were no UMES students capable of handling college work, and that the university ought to be kicked off the map."[15] This statement was a vicious attack, one that caused all spectators to wonder about the well-being of the campus. They were very difficult days for the university and its leader. Said Hytche, "I had nights I couldn't sleep, worrying about what was going to happen next. The thing that bothered me more than anything else was that nobody knew anything about the institution. They would just refer to a single, minor incident they heard about and generalize it to the entire campus without getting the facts. Fortunately in this case, theirs weren't the only testimonies the task force had to hear. I had my say, also."[16]

On Tuesday, August 3, 1977, Dr. William P. Hytche responded to the

the Webb Task Force. His historical plea is a summary of the struggle:

Mr. Webb, members of the Task Force of the State Board for Higher Education, Ladies, and Gentlemen:

As Chancellor of the University of Maryland Eastern Shore, I appreciate this opportunity to appear before you, although I regret the circumstances which brought this Task Force into being. For ninety-one years, this institution known variously as the University of Maryland Eastern Shore, as Maryland State College, as Princess Anne College, as Princess Anne Academy, and as the Delaware Conference Academy, has had a precarious existence indeed. On every occasion when the state of Maryland has altered its course of direction in higher education, as in 1890, 1947, and 1971, this campus has had to re-justify its worthiness and right to exist. We suspected another challenge would be hurled when the Rosenberg Commission gave so much attention to so small a part of higher education in Maryland.

The subsequent turn of events have long since confirmed our suspicions, and the present situation seems more threatening than usual. The creation of this Task Force falls neatly into a series of forecasts and recommendations, which we have read in reports made by the Maryland Council for Higher Education dating back to 1968 in its Master Plan for Higher Education in Maryland. These recommendations were reinforced whenever the occasion permitted. Rumors of merger, of change in governance, and of closing the University of Maryland Eastern Shore have kept this campus off balance.

At the same time, University officials are asked at least on an annual basis to explain why enrollments have not grown and why long-term plans are slow in taking form. The potentially disastrous impact on enrollment of the recent legislative analyst's recommendation to close UMES remains to be assessed. One day spent in the field of recruitment is worth more than thirty days in the halls of Annapolis when trying to understand how an institution can be so hurt. No other public college in Maryland has been asked to persevere under similar man-made adverse conditions.

I know the risks we run in raising questions about a course of political action, which appears reasonable and rational and even popular in some quarters. And I know that even though UMES enrolls slightly less than three percent of the total University of Maryland student population, the entire University may be jeopardized for taking a position it regards as both educationally and ethically sound. These potential consequences present me with a difficult choice just as it has other University officials. But the dignity of my position as the principal officer of an institution with ninety-one years of dedication to a humanitarian mission, usually under duress, dictates the inevitable choice. I willingly choose ranks with John T. Williams and Waldo Kiah, asking once again that fairness, equity, and justice prevail.

My approach, however, is not simply one to plead a defense of the UMES case. Rather, I am content simply to let the record speak for itself and to offer suggestions about the scope and direction of your inquiry. We believe that a complete, systematic, objective study on your part will support our position.

I am sure Mr. Webb, a distinguished and successful attorney, would not enter a courtroom on a complex case without engaging in a long period of intensive research and discovery. He would insist upon a firm grasp of the chronology of events. I commend this careful, deliberate approach as standard operating procedure for this Task Force.

I present my suggestions in four major categories.
1) Program duplication entered into by Salisbury State College;
2) The status of cooperation between the University of Maryland Eastern Shore and Salisbury State College;
3) Facilities; and
4) Costs.

Item 1. <u>Program duplication entered into by Salisbury State College.</u>

The record will show that in hurtful competition, Salisbury State has duplicated programs which had been offered at the University of Maryland Eastern Shore. On July 13, 1977, you received from your staff a report on academic programs offered at UMES and at Salisbury State. Presumably, the one-page report presents all of the programs there are on the two campuses.

Unfortunately, the data provided falls short of completeness. It falls short of being useful. Only one program bears a date – the January 1977 Leisure Studies entry – and dates are important when considering duplication. We simply cannot understand why this crucial matter was given such cursory treatment. You would have been better informed if you simply read the current college catalogs.

Art, music, physical education, and business administration were for some time the most promising programs UMES had with respect to attracting "other race" students and to building enrollment. And they were low in cost when compared with agriculture, home economics, and industrial education. They were our avenues to reducing overall per student costs. If your staff report had been complete, it would indicate when Salisbury State duplicated these UMES programs.

Is it by intention, or by error that music is not cited as a program of study at Salisbury State? The files of the State Board for Higher Education will show that in March 1974 the University identified and inquired about this duplication. We were aware of this intrusion into music and its consequences, and we assumed it escaped review under the "catchall" term of liberal studies. Art developed at Salisbury State in the same manner with the same results.

It is my suggestion that you use one of the newest Salisbury State programs, Social Work, to ascertain how a given program emerges at Salisbury State. In 1972, the catalog announces a collateral field in social welfare for majors in sociology. By 1976,

195

this collateral offering was transformed into a program with professional accreditation. How does this occur in a State which required all public institutions to clear its programs through what was then the Maryland Council for Higher Education (MCHE)? How can a program be professionally accredited and still not be a program? You will note that the list of programs given to you on July 13 makes no mention of social work.

Physical education and business are particularly sensitive matters. Physical education held promise for growth on the UMES campus until we experienced the inequity of a one million dollar "bare bones" gymnasium on the UMES campus and a 5.1 million dollar physical activity facility at Salisbury State. Under these circumstances, we can only anticipate that recruiting students for this program at UMES will be extremely difficult at best. Yet five years from now we will be asked to explain our enrollment trend at UMES in the area of physical education when the support facilities, constructed by the same State, are so vastly different. Then there is the program in business administration, the principle link between a college and the business/industrial community. And again, the program has been duplicated at SSC.

The overall effect of the duplication at SSC has been to divide an already limited pool of students, the majority of whom might otherwise have been enrolled at UMES. It has obviously had a very negative effect on enrollment growth at the Eastern Shore campus while producing a very positive effect on enrollment at SSC. With the decline in enrollment at UMES has come an increase in per student costs and decreased opportunity for state funds to develop new programs and facilities since enrollment is perceived to be the primary criterion for funding. On the other hand, increased enrollment at Salisbury State College has resulted in lower per student costs and increased leverage for obtaining state funds. It is this set of dynamics that has brought us to the point where Salisbury State College has grown to capacity while UMES continues to be underutilized from the standpoint of space and personnel.

Item 2. <u>*The status of cooperation between these two public, Eastern Shore institutions.*</u>

It is my contention that cooperation cannot be left to the initiatives of the institutions as long as there is an imbalance in the capabilities of the institutions to obtain funding and other resources. Such an imbalance provides no incentive for the more privileged institution to cooperate and casts the lesser institution into a compromising and inferior bargaining position. The result is, at best, unilateral efforts on behalf of the lesser institution and, at worst, an adversarial relationship between institutions even with the best of personalities heading the two institutions. This has historically been the case in the UMES-SSC situation. Review the record relating to the efforts made by President Williams and President Devilbiss in 1967 to share faculty appointments, to have students from Salisbury State and UMES in the same classes, and to make joint faculty appointments.

What brought these progressive plans to a screeching halt? You should be careful not to regard 1967 as beyond the "statute of limitations" since that was precisely the year of the MCHE development of a master plan, which expressed a special concern for Maryland State College. Of more recent vintage is the program in medical technology, a plan made under the aegis of the then Maryland Council for Higher Education and confirmed in writing on April 23, 1974. One basic, required course in biochemistry was to be offered exclusively at UMES. This firm agreement was unilaterally scuttled by Salisbury State sending a message that had implications far beyond the significance of a single course.

The Board of Regents of the University of Maryland has seen to it that academic resources shall not be duplicated needlessly on the UMES campus. Elementary teacher-education is an example of their follow-through in saying that the certification courses will not be offered at UMES. All of this is to explain how UMES has taken the initiative, made the concessions, and then still has to bear the burden for lack of cooperation.

Item 3. *Facilities.*

Reference to the "bare bones" gymnasium at UMES and the physical activities facility at Salisbury State has highlighted our concern over how a facility has a long range influence on a program and enrollment. To be sure, UMES has several high quality buildings of which it is justly proud. These include the library, the Ella Fitzgerald Center for the Performing Arts, the Center for Student Development, Carver Hall, a science building, and the recently renovated Wilson Hall. Renovation can bring two additional buildings up to an acceptable level of quality. Other academic and academic support buildings are liabilities. Entering obsolete facilities into any computation of square feet per student is using arithmetic to mislead. Maintenance costs increase with the age of a structure, even when buildings are well built. We suffer in a dual way with our surplus square footage in obsolete buildings, which are costly to maintain.

Our acreage is a definite asset, providing as it does for a vastly greater building program along with the appurtenances, which are a part of a college campus.

New programs proposed for the UMES campus have been spelled out in detail in a long-range curriculum plan. These include two programs which are unique to the area and to the state, namely, hotel/motel management and construction technology. Each program will need a new facility. One of the two, construction technology, requires a building with relatively sophisticated equipment.

The Catch 22 relates to present enrollment and projected enrollment. Here we feel the full impact of the MCHE's early master plan and its continued recommendation of ominous change for UMES. It is extremely difficult to obtain a favorable hearing with any State agency for new buildings on a college campus against the background of rumors of closing, of merger, of redirection and declining enrollment, especially when the present square footage record is not correctly discounted for obsolete plant.

Place this facility concern of UMES within the context of

an almost completely new plant for elementary and secondary schools throughout the twenty-three counties of Maryland. Place it within the context of the sometimes elaborate facilities built for the community colleges of Maryland. What magic are we expected to perform in attracting students to programs with inferior facilities?

The University of Maryland Eastern Shore campus has the potential for up-to-date, functional facilities in a setting with intrinsic beauty. Only after development of that potential, should our accountability in terms of enrollment begin.

Item 4. *Costs.*

Per student costs are high on the UMES campus. We acknowledge that the University of Maryland, through the Board of Regents and administrative officers, have distributed the University's operating funds in a manner which has favored UMES.

We ask the Task Force to look behind the scenes and become acquainted with the facts, which are obscured by gross figures. Some attention needs to be given to differences in programs, for example. Within the land-grant tradition, UMES is committed to agriculture, home economics, and the mechanical arts. All of these programs involve hands-on instruction from the freshman year onward. Low overall enrollments only aggravate the high cost ratio.

Historically, UMES has given special attention to a percentage of students who enter college with academic deficits. Programs of remediation have an immediate high cost, but the social and economic benefits are very substantial. It should be understood, however, that over 80% of the support for our remedial program comes from funds which we are able to obtain for ourselves.

A greatly exaggerated and misleading figure sometimes cited for UMES and expressed on an FTE (full time equivalent) basis includes dormitories, dining halls, and federally sponsored projects including student loan funds.

199

In your review of costs, please compare like matters. State-funded activities would appear to be a good starting point. When this refinement is made, the UMES figure compares favorably with three institutions within the System of State Colleges and Universities where enrollments are considerably larger.

Costs for every campus fall under eight major headings (activities) of which instruction is one. Normally the major instruction cost per student will be $1,522. This amount is slightly less than Bowie with 2,100 students, according to the figures available to us and $300 more per student than at Salisbury with an FTE of 3,264.

The next highest cost at UMES is the physical plant operation. Some of the reasons for this high cost have been previously cited.

An expanded enrollment at UMES of an additional 500 students could be accommodated within presently budgeted sums with the exception of the instruction cost item and a modest increase of no more than 20 percent in student service costs. Under these conditions, our per student cost would fall safely within the range of public sector costs in Maryland. If we could also assume more diversified and lower-cost academic programs within the mix of programs, per student costs would be further reduced.

Essentially, the cost factor is a way of summarizing concerns over cooperation, programs, and facilities which translate into enrollments.

We can no longer continue under a situation where the odds are clearly against us, and we feel that it can only be remedied by action at the state level. At the very least, state policies and plans must be developed that will provide for: (1) the curtailment of unnecessary program duplication between institutions of higher learning; (2) some realignment of duplicated programs in those areas where there is little, if any, capital investment in specialized facilities; (3) the development of new and unique programs at UMES; and (4) a clarification of the mission and role of UMES in terms of its status as a university campus and in relation to SSC as a state college. These kinds of policies will provide the framework in which the University of Maryland Eastern Shore can be developed into a highly attractive University branch with uniqueness in research, public service, and academic programming at the undergraduate and graduate levels.

Despite the adverse impact of duplication on enrollment, UMES has moved aggressively since 1970 toward the goal of making UMES a respectable University. Increased emphases have been given to research and public service through federal funds deriving from UMES' designation as an 1890 land-grant institution. Likewise, efforts have been made to broaden and expand the curriculum in accordance with unmet needs on the Eastern Shore. While we may not have moved as fast as we would have liked in these areas, we feel confident that continued thrusts toward the creation of a viable university in this region can most effectively and expeditiously be facilitated with UMES remaining an integral part of the University of Maryland System. Nowhere else in Maryland's public higher education is there amassed the unique set of characteristics and support necessary to the task of developing the Eastern Shore campus.

Within the University, there is a great commonality of interests in terms of the land-grant mission and the basic functions of instruction, research, and public service. There is available within the System an abundance of administrative, scholarly, and organizational support so necessary to the development of high quality undergraduate and graduate programs on the Shore. Then, too, the University has three research facilities on the Eastern Shore, which could very well be used to support graduate instruction and further enhance the research component of UMES. As a University branch, the Eastern Shore campus retains its 1890 land-grant designation without any question of continued federal funds. I would like to emphasize that these are very real benefits and services rather than conjecture and speculations of what might be.

Beyond the merits of University affiliation, there is another very important dimension of the UMES-SSC question that relates to the issue of desegregation. The State has committed itself to desegregating public institutions. The courts and the federal government have also demonstrated intentions to reinforce that commitment through the ruling in the case of Adams vs. Califano and by the guidelines published recently by the Department of Health, Education, and Welfare. It suggests that if there is to be a merger, it must have the effect of preserving and enhancing UMES as an institution. The same criteria would apply to any change in structure and governance. This concept of desegregation clearly underscores my position that UMES should be developed as an attractive university for the region, and, at the same time, would accommodate the position of the Board of Regents to incorporate Salisbury State College into the University of Maryland System.

In closing, I think the Task Force hearings, though sometimes boring and tiring, have been for the most part very valuable – maybe not so much in studying alternatives as in hearing testimony which dispelled much of the misunderstanding about UMES and provided knowledge of the real issues to be addressed in your study of higher education on the Eastern Shore. There has certainly been some risk of alienating fellow professions in this process with whom we must continue to maintain a level of communication and interaction. But I think you will concede that a clear understanding of this very complex issue could only be attained through the candid evaluations of those concerned. This has been my guiding principle in this presentation.

The presentation by Dr. Hytche was both informative and effective. In a strategic move that would serve to buoy up UMES, Dr. B. Herbert Brown, Chairman of the Board of Regents, and President Elkins made the recommendation that instead of UMES merging into Salisbury State College, Salisbury State College should merge with UMES. Their recommendation successfully sabotaged the original recommendation. "People listened, and the politicians wanting UMES to merge with SSU got quiet. This was a positive turning point for UMES."[17] Dr. Brown was a strong advocate for UMES.

The opposition was so fierce. Two members of the Webb Task Force wrote their report far in advance of the deadline and before all of the testimonies were submitted. When UMES was involved, there was no middle ground.

Basically, people felt what they felt regardless of the facts. Jack Webb, however, put a stop to the report because it did not represent the feelings of all concerned—namely, the people who submitted their testimonies and the other members of the task force.

"The principal recommendation of the Webb Task Force was that this campus should not be closed or merged with SSU because the two campuses had two distinct missions; and if the State would properly fund this campus, there would be no difficulty at all in bringing students to UMES. It's evident now that the people on the Webb Task Force had properly researched the matter."[18]

Therefore, in an effort to enhance the program and to help UMES gain a sure footing, the Webb Task Force recommended the transfer of all agricultural programs from the University of Maryland College Park to the University of Maryland Eastern Shore. "Everyone knew that wasn't going to happen because of politics and the money the flagship campus was getting to operate its agricultural program. But the recommendation served its purpose, and UMES no longer was under threat of merger or closure. That was the kind of strong advocacy that this task force used in order to get UMES on track. This was the beginning of UMES going a little bit higher as far as development and moving in the right direction."[19]

The next blue-ribbon task force was commissioned by Dr. Elkins to propose the direction in which Dr. Hytche and his administrators needed to go to implement new programs at UMES and to look at what programs could be transferred from what colleges in the University of Maryland System. Dr. Albin Kuhn, executive assistant to Dr. Elkins and later to Dr. Toll, was the chairman of that committee. Additionally, Dr. Hytche served on that committee that was comprised of representatives from the five university campuses in the University system. After much time and consideration, "the committee submitted its proposal to Dr. Elkins, hoping that he would approve it and pass it on to the Board of Regents and from there to SBHE. Instead, Elkins took the proposal but didn't act on it because he was retiring."[20] This was a temporary yet disappointing setback, because the administration at UMES was ready to move on. Nevertheless, without their knowledge or even their consent, a new era was being ushered in for UMES. It began when Dr. Elkins' replacement, Dr. John Toll, took office on July 1, 1978.

The Prospectus

Dr. John Toll had a new attitude about UMES and the responsibility of the University System to UMES. He voiced sentiments about the University that had never been shared before, not by someone at the top. He had plans for the campus from the beginning of his tenure. He wanted "the world to know that institutions such as these [UMES] don't have to be less nurtured or less funded."[21] He also said that the key was that it would not take a lot of money to enhance UMES. "It's a small institution; I don't think it will ever be like College Park, but I think it can be respectable. Twenty-five to thirty-five hundred students will make it a very nice place because it's located in a good area."[22]

(Figure 6.7)
Dr. John S. Toll,
speaker at the 1992 University
of Maryland Eastern Shore
Honors Convocation

Dr. Toll was known for his hard work and ability to pull the best out of every person and every situation. He felt that "the University System had a diamond in the rough in UMES."[23] At the time Dr. Toll was interviewed, Dr. Hytche knew that "he was the savior for the University of Maryland System – a kind and humble man who had vision."[24] That vision, along with the vision of Hytche, changed the forecast given by the hecklers and the doubters. Shortly after the decision of the Webb Task Force to abandon all thoughts of merger, the proposal from the blue-ribbon task force for a document outlining a direction for UMES; and finally, the appointment of Dr. John Toll, a document called *The Prospectus* was developed to lay out a path for UMES to follow towards academic success.

A summary of the goals and aim of the UMES *Prospectus* follows:

1. The University will establish a work force of highly competent people drawn from throughout the University to work with the president of the University and the chancellor of the UMES campus in carrying out the changes, which are identified as necessary or desirable.

2.   The objective of the University is to make the UMES campus the focal point of the University's activities on the Eastern Shore.

3.   The University will continue to involve UMES as a partner within a system, sharing both human and physical resources, and engaging the campus in cooperative planning for the optimal use of available resources.

4.   The instructional resources at UMES will be expanded to allow various new and interrelated "majors." It is assumed the SBHE will approve the program plans, which are covered in this paper.

5.   Facilities will be brought up to a competitive level of quality, and the cost of their maintenance will be related to the functions they serve.

6.   Cost estimates are offered in response to the State Board for Higher Education's requirement that the cost per student at UMES become consistent with the per student costs at other Maryland four-year public institutions.

7.   The research efforts at UMES will be coordinated with research efforts at other units of the University and supportive services will be provided.

8.   Sustained cooperative effort between the University of Maryland Eastern Shore and Salisbury State College is important to the educational welfare of Eastern Shore residents. The plan being offered by the University assumes the responsibility for this cooperation will be shared equitably by the two campuses.

9.   We share in common an awareness of the historical, legal, political, demographic, and economic circumstances, which have made educational planning difficult at UMES. The academic programming presented in this paper is addressed to regional needs and in some instances to Statewide needs. With adequate support, the objectives can be accomplished.

Most importantly, contained in the language of the *Prospectus* was a request for the approval of eight new undergraduate programs, one stand-alone graduate program, and one joint graduate program that would begin at UMES in the fall of 1978. The undergraduate programs were: construction management technology, hotel and restaurant management, environmental science, poultry technology and management, elementary/special education, computer science/data processing, engineering technology, and physical therapy. The stand-alone master's degree program was in guidance and counseling, and the joint program in agriculture and extension education was with the University of Maryland College Park (UMCP). All of the programs were approved by the State Board for Higher Education (SBHE) along with an approval for UMES to become a participant in the University-wide marine-estuarine-environmental sciences doctoral program. UMES is the only institution of higher education in Maryland that offers construction management technology, hotel and restaurant management, and engineering technology. The approval of the *Prospectus* along with the new programs was a first for the campus, but this transition was not accomplished without bitter opposition and complaint from some members of SBHE, who had failed to acknowledge UMES as an institution of higher learning at all. Indeed, there were even members on that board who did not care about the well-being of the campus. "They, along with other politicians in the state of Maryland, thought that this school had no reason to exist."[25]

One writer, Dr. Ruth H. Young, explained that period with the following words, "For UMES, long a survivor of unclear and conflicting mandates, the implications of the *Prospectus* could have been overwhelming and inspirational at the same time."[26] In actuality, the process was both draining and wonderful for Dr. Hytche, but some of his faculty and staff members could not imagine that UMES would be able to withstand such strong currents of change. In addition, the media took every cheap shot they could. A *Baltimore Sun* reporter by the name of Peter Jay was always looking for something negative to report about the campus. He did not seem to care about the truth of a matter; instead, he simply circulated malicious gossip. It was a stressful period for the campus. Hytche was, as usual, determined to see the plan to fruition. For the new graduate program, however, he needed more faculty members and he needed students.

In spite of the obstacles, the Hytche administration went about advertising the new graduate program that was approved; and by September 1978, twenty-six students had enrolled in the program with Dr. Toll very much a part of the whole process. He was particularly involved in making faculty members available to teach in the new programs, even if they had to travel to UMES from College Park. Said Hytche, "Johnny Toll, without any concern about the cost, flew faculty members to UMES twice a week to help us get started while I began getting a little strength from my faculty. At about this stage, my faculty began to say, 'Look, we've got something here. Let's go.'"[27] Things began to greatly improve for UMES. The course was set, and Hytche along with his faculty and staff took up the baton and continued forward. Dr. Toll was forceful in his support and dedication to UMES, and it made a difference in high places.

Consequently, UMES became known statewide and nationwide for its success in many programs, particularly in hotel and restaurant management, construction management technology, and physical therapy. Additionally, "Dr. Hytche soon became a familiar figure in the corridors of political power in Annapolis; and, capitalizing on the strong support of President John Toll and the University Board of Regents, the new chancellor was able to win appropriations to upgrade the instructional and research components of the university."[28]

Many of the problems that plagued the University for so many years were eliminated under the leadership of Dr. Toll at the University of Maryland System and Dr. Hytche at the University of Maryland Eastern Shore. For the first time, the University was completely autonomous; because in his wisdom, Toll insisted that any problem that originated on the campus would be handled on the campus, and the programs on campus were managed on campus. The house was no longer divided; indeed the University would stand.

By 1980, two years after the *Prospectus*, the Hytche administration had successfully led the University into a new direction. Indeed, the new programs had been implemented and brought an influx of new and varied students, faculty, and staff. "In addition, the [System] President authorized the use of University funds to build new dormitories. At the same time, he sought outside help. He was fortunate in securing a Ford Foundation grant to strengthen UMES and to help it become the equal member of the University system that was foreseen in the *Prospectus*."[29] "The Josiah Macy Foundation provided a grant essentially for the development of the honors program in medicine at UMES."[30] That particular program was established so that the UMES faculty could work in conjunction with the faculty from the University of Maryland at Baltimore (UMAB) to facilitate easy articulation for students who successfully completed their undergraduate programs at UMES. Under the direction of a joint committee they would be admitted into one of the professional schools at UMAB.

Opportunities for preprofessional studies were established in the fields of medicine, dentistry, pharmacy, law, social work, and nursing with both schools involved in the selection of students, the development of the curriculum, and the evaluation process of the students in their undergraduate phase. "In the fall of 1979, thirty-one students enrolled in the honors program . . . in the fall of 1980, twenty-eight students enrolled."[31] Along with the normal stresses and demands that excellence brings, UMES stayed under the watchful and somewhat doubtful eye of the originators of the program. UMES had to be able to provide the facilities, the equipment, and the instruction demanded by the path to professional fulfillment each honors student would take. The honors program brought out the best of UMES. It has consistently met the demands characteristic of such an undertaking.

Not long after the inception of the honors program in 1979, the honors committee added physical therapy to the undergraduate program offerings at UMES. A four-year program was developed, and the first students were enrolled in 1982. Subsequently, a graduate program was established in the fall of 1991. In addition, funding was acquired to build a facility for the construction management technology program. Its first students were accepted in 1979. Also, the first students for the poultry technology and management program were accepted in 1979. No doubt, implementing ten new programs (eight undergraduate and two graduate) in two years, along with the business of running a university, was a remarkable feat. In 1989, a new constituent was added to the honors program at UMES. The Virginia-Maryland Regional College of Veterinary Medicine formed a partnership with UMES following the same types of guidelines as the previous UMES-UMAB program. Since that time, twenty-five or more new programs, undergraduate to doctoral, have been added to the program offerings at UMES.

1890 Land-Grant Progression

The 1890 land-grant universities, under the leadership of Dr. R.D. Morrison, thought to influence the revision of the 1977 Farm Bill to ensure greater access to federal funding for the 1890 land-grant universities, including UMES. This decision resulted in a major increase in resources and the emergence of increased involvement of UMES in statewide research and extension programs. Soon after that, Hytche became the chair of 1890 Presidents and Chancellors; and thus, UMES emerged as a major player in the 1890 land-grant community as well as in the total national land-grant association. Hytche, in his new capacity, decided to place more emphasis on the Food and Agriculture Program.

In the state of Maryland, agriculture had become a focal point for defining the uniqueness of UMES, being one of the two land-grant universities designated by the State and ratified by the federal government. It was then that Hytche hired Dr. Mortimer Neufville as head of the UMES Agriculture Program. Neufville also assumed the position of Associate Director of the Maryland Agricultural Experiment Station. Dr. Frank Bentz, then vice president for agricultural affairs at the University of Maryland System, facilitated much of the statewide collaboration in agricultural research and extension between the University of Maryland College Park (UMCP), and UMES. He was very instrumental in working with Dr. Hytche to attract Neufville and others to expand the agricultural activities on UMES's campus. It was quite evident that attitudes were changing in Maryland. It was during this era that UMCP saw its first black chief executive officer.

Athletics

In the midst of the many beginnings, in 1980 UMES saw the end of the football program — a program that at one time had been the life of the school. By 1978, the athletic department had a deficit of over $300,000 that was due to financing a football program without the support it once had from sponsors and fans. Because of the deficit, coaches at UMES were unable to offer the types of scholarships that attracted first-rate athletes. Consequently, UMES enjoyed fewer wins with the passing of each game. Every effort was made to save the program, but UMES had the job to do alone. The community had stopped attending the games shortly before 1978. Also, fundraising efforts were made at one meeting after another to no avail. The deficit could not be decreased without the suspension of football on the campus of UMES until such time that the athletic program could support such a venture. Therefore, football was suspended in 1980, and all efforts were placed on academia.

The Moos Report

In the midst of all of the transitions, the Moos Report was published in 1981. The first draft of the Moos Report recommended the closure of UMES. Ironically its author, Dr. Malcolm Moos, had not been to the campus but instead had compiled his information from the biased reports of crafty, deliberate enemies of UMES such as Dr. George Callcott. Dr. Hytche, through the intercession of Dr. Toll, was able to intervene on behalf of UMES by first visiting Dr. Moos at his home in Minnesota and then by inviting him to the campus. Ultimately the final report was not as bad, though it was not a full endorsement of UMES; in fact, it mimicked the sentiments of many of the reports that preceded it. The Moos Report cited all of the accomplishments that UMES was excited about but, in essence, stated that they were not enough.

In his report, Dr. Moos stated that "the efforts of the Regents, President Toll, and Chancellor Hytche have been Herculean, their commitment fierce."[32] Although his words were poetic and even flattering, they contained such an air of condescension. The central theme of the report is found in the following words: "Because of its heartbreaking history and despite the extraordinary achievements of the past few years, however, UMES has not obtained the level of scholarship and research characteristics of other university campuses."[33] His recommendation was: "The facts of life in the long story of UMES are simple: a failure to support a meaningful mission for an important region of the Free State of Maryland. Unless this is forthcoming, and muscularly so, after a transition period this institution should continue its already discernable progress toward confederation with the State College at Salisbury."[34]

In addition, the report contained the bold prediction that the enrollment at UMES would most likely remain under 2000. Once again there was the hurtful cry for merger. In spite of this, the progress continued so that UMES remained focused and determined to do what the "experts" said it could not do. As expected of any institution of higher education, one must recognize opportunities for positive change and grasp them. Hytche and his University seized many such opportunities.

1981 Farm Bill

In the National Agricultural Research, Extension, and Teaching Policy Act of 1981, The Farm Bill, the Congress of the United States authorized grants to upgrade research facilities in the food and agricultural science areas on the campuses of the 1890 land-grant institutions. In subsequent Farm Bills, the Congress authorized grants to upgrade extension and teaching facilities in the same areas. The major purpose of the "Facilities Grant Program" was the acquisition and improvement of food and agricultural science facilities and equipment, including libraries, so that the eligible institutions could participate fully in the production of human capital and conduct basic and applied research.

The University of Maryland Eastern Shore was one of the eligible institutions that received facility grants funds. These funds, more than $10 million during the life of the program, allowed UMES to construct larger facilities and to obtain state-of-the-art equipment. It presented an opportunity for positive change and UMES grasped it. The federal funds were leveraged to obtain state and private funds and the following upgrades eventually occurred on the campus:

- Construction of the Richard A. Henson Center (1993) – offices, meeting rooms, demonstration kitchen, down link satellite capabilities, commercial teaching kitchen, bakery, beverage training lab, taste lab, handicapped teaching kitchen, twenty-five hotel rooms, classrooms, fabric testing lab, historical costume collection, two display cases, computer labs, drafting room, etc.
- Remodeled Early Childhood Center
- Remodeled farm machinery building, and
- A food-science facility currently in the planning phase.

Utilizing these facilities and equipment have allowed UMES to respond better to critical issues and to the needs of its students and others in the local community and beyond. Additionally, the facilities grants program has helped UMES to compete more effectively in responding to requests from USDA and other federal agencies from the private sector and from the State. Thus UMES became a better partner in the federal/state/private partnership relative to meeting the needs of agriculture specifically and society in general as well as in carrying out its land-grant mandate.

UMES/SSC Collaborative Program

In 1982, Hytche saw an opportunity to devise a cooperative program between UMES and SSC. The issue was that UMES could not get approval to implement programs that were offered by SSC, although the reverse could be accomplished. Two joint programs — elementary education and medical technology – were offered, and UMES students regularly attended Salisbury State to participate in those classes. The programs left a lot to be desired, however, because students frequently complained about being ignored while in classes at SSC. In Hytche's words, "UMES has been on the rough side of the mountain, and that side was the effort to develop the UMES/SSC cooperative program." In fact, Dr. J.T. Williams first attempted to secure joint faculty appointments between Maryland State College and Salisbury State College in the 1967-68 school year. Then, in July 1973, Dr. Buffkins submitted a detailed proposal to Dr. Norman C. Crawford, then president of Salisbury State College (SSC), outlining an organized and pointed approach to developing a structured cooperative program. Evently it was the wrong time for such a step.

Dr. Thomas Bellevance, the next president of SSC, and Dr. Hytche were finally able to work out the particulars for a cooperative program, and their proposal was approved in 1983 — first by their respective boards and then by the State Board for Higher Education. A program of such caliber was perhaps unique to any institution in the State and maybe even in the country. In addition to its educational benefits, the plan established that each of the two universities could not duplicate the other's programs. At the time, UMES had a strong program in sociology while SSU had an excellent program in social work. Each administrator, Hytche and Bellevance, desired to afford each other the benefit of offering their perspective students the opportunity to obtain a degree in both majors. As a result of the completed collaborative agreement, students at each of the universities have the opportunity to earn a dual degree by enrolling in either one of the programs. Each university maintained programs in business administration, accounting, mathematics, English, history, and social science while the marine science program, for example, was approved for UMES exclusively. Accordingly all allied health programs, except those that were already in place at SSU, were approved for UMES.

In the semester that followed the approval of the collaborative plan, each university purchased a bus in order to accommodate the added need for transportation. Students began to be transported between the universities every hour on the hour. The staff fully supported what the administrators had put in place. It was the first time such a unique program was given an opportunity to grow and at the same time to save the State funds. With new programs at UMES and a formal cooperative agreement in place, enrollment continued to increase and the morale of the faculty, staff, and students was greatly boosted.

(Figure 6.8)
Dr. Richard A. Henson, President of Henson Airlines and Philanthropist, presents to Dr. Hytche a check in the amount of two million dollars to endow the Richard A. Henson Scholars Program.

Physical Plant

Although Dr. Hytche experienced much success with reference to his program initiatives, the physical plant was falling apart. Dr. Richard A. Henson, an Eastern Shore tycoon and philanthropist, had the means; and Dr. Hytche had the foresight to ask him to make a financial gift to the University. In January 1987, Dr. Henson made a gift of two million dollars to the University — a gift that generated more than twenty-six million dollars in endowment funds. At the time, his was the largest gift ever made to a historically black university by an individual. Additionally, Dr. Henson made a call to the governor's office to request that appropriations be made to improve the appearance of the campus, and it was done. Said Hytche, "I recall Dr. Henson telling the governor that the appearance of the campus did not match the caliber of faculty and students he had met here, and he wanted to improve the campus' appearance."[35] Thus, buildings on campus were renovated, and new ones were built. Most importantly, the campus was adorned with sidewalks and lights from one end to the other. Dr. Henson's concern for the campus of the University of Maryland Eastern Shore started a positive domino effect and his gift commenced the Richard A. Henson Scholars Program.

The Higher Education Bill of 1988

In October 1985, Governor Harry Hughes appointed the Hoblitzell Commission to study the condition of higher education in Maryland. More specifically, "this study was to recognize economic and demographic conditions influencing the system as well as interests and needs of the citizens for higher education."[36] The chairman of the Commission, Alan P. Hoblitzell, submitted the commission's recommendations to Governor Schaefer, Hughes' successor, in January 1987. This commission recommended a complete restructuring of the governance of higher education. Dr. John Toll led the effort by creating the "Toll Plan." Eventually, a bill was created and submitted to the Senate and

(Figure 6.81)
State and federal supporters of UMES. Left to right: the Honorable Roy Dyson, the Honorable Governor Harry R. Hughes, President William P. Hytche, The Honorable Senator Paul Sarbanes, and The Honorable Comptroller Louis Goldstein in front of the President's home. (1988)

214

(Figure 6.82)
Senator Barbara Mikulski, an avid supporter of UMES, receives a gift from President William P. Hytche.

the House during the 1988 legislative session. The bill that was finally passed contained some of the "Toll Plan" as well as some of the Hoblitzell Commission's plan. As a result, a new state agency was formed that replaced the State Board for Higher Education. This new agency, the Maryland Higher Education Commission (MHEC), was given more power than its predecessor, governing questionable, deficient areas in the public system of higher education. MHEC had authority over such areas as admission standards, personnel, academic programs, funding, and accountability plans for public campuses.

In addition to establishing the new MHEC, the Higher Education Bill of 1988 brought all Maryland state colleges and universities, except Morgan State University and St. Mary's College, under the authority of the University of Maryland Board of Regents. At first, Dr. Hytche was concerned that UMES could not continue to receive the support it had obtained from the Board of Regents under the leadership of Dr. Toll. It did not seem feasible with so many institutions under the same umbrella. Dr. Toll, however, strongly supported the bill; and Dr. Hytche trusted Dr. Toll. Another component of the bill changed the title of the university's CEOs from chancellor to "president," while the title of the head of the system was changed from president to "chancellor."

Meanwhile Hytche, with Dr. Edward V. Ellis, vice president for academic affairs, instituted a major academic reorganization at the University. Three schools were established — each under the leadership of an academic dean to whom a number of departments reported. The schools were the School of Agricultural and Natural Sciences, the School of Arts and Professions, and the School of Business and Technology. A graduate school was later established with the vice president of academic affairs acting as its dean. The schools, with additional state resources, began to place more emphasis on student recruitment and excellence in academic instruction and research. Several outstanding labs were established, many with national recognition.

When a downturn in the economy of the State created financial problems for all of higher education, all educational institutions suffered a recision of funding. As a result, UMES was asked to seek ways to reduce spending. Under Hytche's leadership, the campus adapted several strategies, including increasing class size, increasing teacher load, and restructuring administration. The schools remained in operation; however, the dean's positions were suspended as a cost-saving measure, and department chairs reported to an associate vice president for academic affairs. Later, the economy began to boom, and additional investments were made in UMES. Although the University's deans were reinstituted, some realignment of departments took place.

Global Links

At a time when internationalization of the curriculum was at the forefront and center of most curriculum revitalization committees across the nation, UMES did not assert itself as a part of the global community beyond attracting a few international students. The Title XII legislation, which was to become the cornerstone for the globalization of some 1890 universities, had just been implemented. While UMES had very little motivation to become a global competitor in research, education, or outreach prior to 1980, with the Title XII legislation providing the avenue, the faculty responded with a proposal to the Agency for International Development. The guidelines required collaboration with an 1862 counterpart who had considerable experience in international work and who could serve in a mentoring role in facilitating a smooth transition for the 1890 university into international work. UMES chose the University of Illinois Urbana-Campaign (UIUC) as its partner.

The partnership was both effective and successful, and Dr. Hytche went on to be instrumental in establishing many international links on behalf of the University of Maryland Eastern Shore. The resulting international partnerships and linkages drastically enhanced UMES's capacity and competitiveness in the international arena. Several projects were developed.

UMES worked with UIUC to assist Zambia with developing its Agricultural Research and Extension Programs in agronomic crops. Specifically, the government of Zambia and the ministry of agriculture and water development sought to improve the production of maze, soybeans, and sunflowers. The project was a great success story for all who participated. Dr. Hytche was able to visit Zambia in 1983 as part of an administrative team of the United States Agency for International Development (USAID). In 1985 and 1986, he returned to personally assess the benefits gained by Zambia from the linkage.

Based on the success of the project in Zambia, the UMES faculty developed an unsolicited proposal to do legume work on the continent of Africa. The project proposal was an ambitious one, but USAID first rejected the concept, doubting UMES's capacity and once again emphasizing UMES's struggle for recognition in spite of its successes. Dr. Hytche had to exert his lobbying talents. After much debate and collaboration with Drs. Neufville, Acquah, and Wutoh, the project proposal was rewritten and entitled, "Roots and Tuber Crop Research Project" (ROTREP). "After considerable debate with the African bureau and several meetings with the Cameroon USAID mission, the University received approximately $8 million to conduct a root and tuber crops program in Cameroon."[37]

(Figure 6.9)
President Hytche enjoys a conversation with Vice Chancellor (President) of Ain Shams University in Egypt

In 1986, Dr. Hytche traveled to Cameroon "to sign the protocol agreement to implement the project."[38] The project lasted from 1986 to 1994. Three trips were made to the country. During one of the trips, Dr. Hytche participated in the dedication of a $2 million biotechnology lab, which was designed for tissue culture work. The work would enable Cameroon researchers to propagate effectively yams, coco yams, sweet potatoes, and cassava and to provide adequate planting materials for farmers as they expanded their production of these crops. The

(Figure 6.10)
President Hytche being greeted by officials
upon arriving in China (Mainland)

laboratory was a "state-of-the-art facility with modern equipment, and a building designed specifically for the research being done."[39] It was the first of its kind in that region. Much of the success was attributed to the USAID mission director, Mr. Jay Johnson, who provided immeasurable leadership to all USAID activities in Cameroon at the time.

By 1988, UMES faculty had "begun to pursue with greater interest overseas fellowships, Fulbright awards, and student summer internships while from overseas Ph.D. and master's degree seeking students were enrolling at the University of Maryland Eastern Shore."[40] Through a program called *The Channel System*, which was a product of the University of Maryland College Park, UMES was able to accept graduate students from Egypt who wished to complete graduate work at American universities. "The University Linkage Program became a reality for UMES in 1991 when Dr. Hytche traveled to Egypt to sign a collaborative agreement with the Supreme Council of Egyptian Universities. Linkages were made specifically with Cairo University, Ain Shams University, and Suez Canal University."[41] Additionally, exchanges were made between UMES and the Egyptian Universities to include dignitaries, college presidents, professors, faculty, and students. After the

(Figure 6.11)
President Hytche joins in signing a Joint Memorandum of Understanding between Egerton Univ., Kari and UMES in Kenya

218

initial trip in 1991, subsequent trips were made to the country in 1993 and 1996. "The talents of UMES were fully recognized and applied on this vastly populated continent that recognized that UMES could contribute to their food and agricultural development and to the education of their people."[42]

In 1991, the University received funding for a two-year research project. The administration agreed to pursue environmental and marine activities in Namibia. "UMES also provided administrative advice for the government regarding its school of agriculture programs."[43] The Namibian President had a considerable amount of dialogue with UMES President Hytche in an attempt to map out clear plans that would link Namibian businesses with U.S. investors. In 1995, Dr. Hytche returned to deliver the commencement address at the University of Namibia. While in the region, he was able to stop in Zimbabwe to provide consultation to the vice-chancellor of Africa University. "UMES assisted in the development of their agribusiness program with the expectation that, through USAID funding, a major initiative could be pursued."[44]

In addition, Dr. Hytche visited South Africa in 1995, as a senior associate to the American Council on Education. While there he visited with Transkei Technikon, now Eastern Cape Technikon, which was in the process of changing from a technical school to a full-fledged university. Dr. Hytche offered the facilities of UMES as training sites for Transkei leadership. Several leaders have taken advantage of the opportunity to train on the UMES campus

(Figure 6.12)
Dr. Hytche with Drs. William "Bill" Cosby and Richard Bernstein

in intensive training seminars.

In 1995, through the National Association for Equal Opportunity in Education (NAFEO), UMES was able to secure linkages with Chinese universities. At that time, Chinese universities suffered from the same developmental challenges the 1890 land-grant universities faced in the fifties and sixties. Also during that year, a linkage agreement was signed with Egerton University in Kenya for UMES to support educational training, research, and economic development in Kenya.

These visits inspired the creation of the international flag mall on the UMES campus. The mall was built in 1994 and showcases the flags of the countries of origin of its many foreign students. Twenty flags are flown for a period of six weeks. After six weeks, another rotation of flags are flown so that country's flag for each foreign student is flown at least two six-week periods in a year.

Metropolitan United Methodist Church

At one time, the Metropolitan United Methodist Church was still a major part of campus life. In fact, the bond between the church and the school has not been severed since its commencement in 1886. Throughout his tenure, Dr. Hytche always talked freely about his personal life, his aspirations, his unerring belief in God, his vision of what UMES could become, and his affiliation with Metropolitan United Methodist Church. When he retired from his university presidency, he openly promised that he would devote significant time and energy to addressing some of the needs of Metropolitan; and he did just that in small, meaningful steps. First, he became chairman of the trustees of Metropolitan and provided the leadership and direction needed to pave a small parking lot adjacent to the church. Next, the trustees led the way in getting two purchases of land near the church for a very modest price, and a new van with Metropolitan detailing and insignia, which was enthusiastically welcomed by the church.

Just as Dr. Hytche demonstrated his open heart for UMES and for Metropolitan, he also cherished the strong, historical relationship between the two institutions and visibly supported the nourishment of their common developmental and current roots. For it was the Peninsula Delaware Conference, later merged with the Salisbury Conference, that gave birth to UMES. In 1989, when the annual conference convened at UMES, President

Hytche opened the session by setting the tone for what it meant to have the conference on the campus when he said, "Welcome home." He has kept the memory of the close relationship between UMES and the Methodist church alive and has securely taken the words of the church with him wherever he goes.

Hytche's Retirement

Dr. William P. Hytche retired in January 1997 as President of UMES after serving twenty one and one-half years and bringing closure to the many and various battles of his predecessors. His retirement from UMES marked the end of a progressive era. Several events that brought out large community support and recognition marked a triumphant march into retirement with full satisfaction that UMES was now planted on a solid foundation and no longer threatened with extinction.

Despite his retirement, in 1998 Dr. Hytche took another trip to Nigeria to observe a national election, the first free election after military rule. He co-chaired a delegation of black college presidents from the United States, who participated as observers under the auspices of Americans for Democracy in Africa. In addition, Dr. Hytche has since maintained a position of leadership on numerous commissions, committees, and boards.

"Could They Have Known?"

Many years have passed since those early days when the first students had to refurbish the campus before they could start classes. The founders, the pioneers who set the plans in motion for the education of the black man over one hundred years ago have all been long gone.

Could these descendants of African heritage, former slaves. . . have known or even imagined that their little school, which opened in an old colonial building called Olney with one teacher and nine students, would become a university with over 65 major buildings, over 600 acres of land, over 200 teachers and approximately 3200 students? Could they have known?

Could those former slaves have imagined that students would eventually come from every county in the state of Maryland, 35 of the nations' states, D.C., Puerto Rico, the Virgin Islands and approximately 50 international countries? Could they have known?

Could these former slaves have imagined that the student body would one day be seventy-three percent Black, seventeen percent White, seven percent International and three percent other ethnic minorities? Could they have known? Could these visionaries have imagined that a mathematician from Oklahoma by the name of John Taylor Williams (1947) some 61 years after its founding would become president at a time when there were 5 buildings, 113 full-time students, 21 full-time employees (including 11 faculty), and a budget of $187,114, and lead the little academy for 23 years through a period of political and racial unrest until 1970? Could they have known?

Could these visionaries of African decent have imagined that a mathematician from Oklahoma by the name of William P. Hytche, almost 74 years after its founding would come to the campus in 1960, become president in 1975, lead the campus through some of its most turbulent history, expand the Physical Plant, oversee the development of some 20 new programs (two through the Ph.D.), see the number of employees grow to over 700, see the budget grow to approximately $45,000,000, and the enrollment reach 3000? Could they have known?

Could these visionaries, former slaves, have imagined that a mathematician from Louisiana, by the name of Dolores R. Spikes, in 1997 would become the first female president with an emphasis on strategic planning and garnering a fair share of legislative fiscal support? Could they have known that she would promote equity, work to create a student-centered environment and proclaim that "Nothing can be more paramount than our realizing and acting accordingly that the proper education of students must take highest priority?" Could they have known that she would pledge to strengthen the academic and operational processes to ensure that the University becomes and remains a dynamic community of academic excellence, prepared to play a vital role in tomorrow's society?

Could they have known that through Dr. Spikes and the development of a comprehensive information technology infrastructure, the University will seek pre-eminence in using technologies across the curriculum, in other university operations, and in providing distance learning across the region and around the world? Could they have known that she would affirm public service as an integral part of the University's mission by committing to improve the condition of human life through service and publications by extending its knowledge-based services and resources to address regional, national and international needs? Could they have known?

Could these sons and daughters of kings and queens from the continent of Africa - former slaves who worshiped from the balcony of St. Andrews Episcopal Church, founders of three churches, founders of the first school for black children in Somerset County, and founders of the new Delaware Conference Academy - have imagined that descendents of slaves and the descendants of slave owners would one day, after the fear subsided, lift their voices in unison to sing:

> *To Thee dear Alma Mater,*
> *We raise our grateful song.*
> *For through thy noble teachings*
> *Thou has made thy children strong;*
> *And thousands still shall praise thee,*
> *All earth shall hear their swell,*
> *And bind our hearts yet closer,*
> *To thee we love so well. . . .*

Could the former slaves have known? Could these visionaries have imagined?[45]

Dr. William Percy Hytche turned over the helm to the very capable Dr. Dolores Margaret Richard Spikes in 1997.

ENDNOTES

CHAPTER 6

[1] Laws, 1949, ch. 282. This action was taken by the Assembly several months after a conference of Negro land-grant college presidents resolved to oppose regionalism even if legal action was found to be necessary, Afro-American, October 30, 1948.

[2] University of Maryland Eastern Shore (UMES). Centennial Commemorative Magazine, pg. 9, September 1986. – Special Collection.

[3] Task Force "Report to the Maryland Council for Higher Education" pg i-2.

[4] Ibid. pg. iv-10.

[5] Special Collections, University of Maryland Eastern Shore.

[6] John R. Wennersten, Maryland's Eastern Shore: A Journey in Time and Place. p. 169.

[7] Dr. William P. Hytche, Step by Step to the Top: The Saga of a President of a Historically Black University. pp 152-153.

[8] John R. Wennersten, p.170.

[9] Dr. George H. Callcott, "The Maryland Education Commissions," pg. 1-2.

[10] Dr. George H. Callcott, pg. 1-2.

[11] "Maryland Statewide Plan for Postsecondary Education", Adopted by The State Board for Higher Education, July 6, 1978.

[12] Department of Legislative Services, Presentation to the Task Force to Study the Governance, Coordination, and Funding of the University System of Maryland. Pg. 10.

[13] Ruth H. Young, Campus in Transition: University of Maryland Eastern Shore. Pg 3.

[14] John R. Wennersten, pg. 170.

[15] Dr. William P. Hytche, p. 165-166.

[16] Dr. William P. Hytche, pg. 166.

[17] Dr. William P. Hytche, pg. 167.

[18] Dr. William P. Hytche, pg. 168.

[19] Dr. William P. Hytche, pg. 168.

[20] Dr. William P. Hytche, pg. 169.

[21] Dr. William P. Hytche, pg. 170.

[22] Dr. William P. Hytche, pg. 170.

[23] Dr. William P. Hytche, pg. 171.

[24] Dr. William P. Hytche, pg. 171.

[25] Dr. William P. Hytche, pg. 174.

[26] Ruth H. Young, pg. 7.

[27] Dr. William P. Hytche, pg 176.

[28]   John R. Wennersten, pg. 170.

[29]   Ruth H. Young, pg. 9.

[30]   Ruth H. Young, pg. 9.

[31]   Ruth H. Young, pg. 10.

[32]   Malcolm Moos. The Post Land-Grant University: The University Report. Pg. 178.

[33]   Ibid.

[34]   Ibid. pg 181.

[35]   Dr. William P. Hytche, pg. 208.

[36]   "Higher Education: An Investment in Excellence" Report of the Governor's Commission on Excellence in Higher Education. Pg. iii.

[37]   Dr. William P. Hytche, pg. 250.

[38]   Dr. William P. Hytche, pg. 250.

[39]   Dr. William P. Hytche, pg. 250.

[40]   Dr. William P. Hytche, pg. 252.

[41]   Dr. William P. Hytche, pg. 253.

[42]   Dr. William P. Hytche, pg. 254.

[43]   Dr. William P. Hytche, pg 257.

[44]   Dr. William P. Hytche, pg. 258.

[45]   Dr. Herman Franklin, 113th Founder's Day Convocation, "When Fears Subside" September 14, 1999.

EPILOGUE

A CANDID INTERVIEW
WITH THE PRESIDENT

(Figure 7.1)
Dr. Dolores Margaret Richard Spikes,
President of the University of Maryland Eastern Shore
(1997 - 2001)

Dolores Margaret Richard Spikes

     Dolores Margaret Richard Spikes became the first appointed female president of the University of Maryland Eastern Shore on January 13, 1997. She came to the University from the Southern University and A & M College System where she served as president from 1988 to 1996. She was educated in the parochial and public schools of Baton Rouge, Louisiana, and continued her education, receiving a Bachelor of Science degree in liberal arts with a major in mathematics from Southern University in Baton Rouge. Subsequently, she received a Master of Science degree in mathematics from the University of Illinois Urbana Champaign. In December 1971, she earned a Ph.D. in mathematics from Louisiana State University.

Dr. Spikes came to UMES with numerous awards, honors and memberships as well as a tremendous amount of experience. She has not missed a step in continuing to uphold the integrity of a university that has fought long and hard for its place in higher education. She is continuing the fight by expanding the scope of a triumphant University that had a humble beginning and a turbulent existence.

Dr. Spikes' flare and vision shines forth in this very candid, up close, and personal interview that was conducted a few months prior to her resignation.

Interviewer: What was your motivation for coming to the University of Maryland Eastern Shore?
Dr. Spikes: *I am here because of the man called Bill Hytche, who I had known for a number of years through our work with the 1890s land-grant institutions. Southern University, my previous place of employment, was an 1890 school. So he and I were meeting together and working together.   I always liked what he said and his demeanor with people. There was an 1890 meeting here at UMES about two or three years before I came as president. At that time, of course, I had no notion that I would be back in this capacity. I admired the campus, though, and what Dr. Hytche had done to bring it from where it was.*

Also, I knew of Dr. William Kirwin, president of the University of Maryland College Park, who had an immense commitment to diversity – to enrolling more women and African Americans. He has since left that university. As a result, College Park has lost a wonderful man, and I am sure he is carrying on that tradition at Ohio State University. In addition, I did not know him personally but I knew of Dr. Donald Langenberg, chancellor of the University System of Maryland (previously the University of Maryland System), and of his reputation academically and administratively. I also knew Delegate Howard "Pete" Rawlings of the Maryland House of Delegates, because we had worked on a number of national committees and commissions together. Pete, I always thought, was a very challenging man who did not buy into anything easily. He asked hard, hard questions; but that is fair, because if you gave him the right answers, the correct answers, he would listen. If necessary, he would even change his mind. I thought that was good. So, I figured I was coming to a system that was ahead of the one that I was involved in

227

collectively in the state of Louisiana. Frankly though, I must tell you now that I am not so sure that is true.

Still, it was a matter of individuals that enticed me to come to UMES. At Southern, I had no intention whatsoever of staying beyond eight or nine years as president. Unlike Dr. Hytche, I am one that believes that presidents ought not to stay longer than ten years. So, I am not a long-term president. For some people who have what it takes, there is no reason for them not to stay; but still, I felt I had found a good jumping-off point. I had just signed an agreement with the U.S. Department of Justice for the Southern University System that brought in millions of dollars for new programs and millions of dollars for new facilities. Just about every facility that is being constructed on that campus right now is because of my signature on that agreement, which I helped to negotiate and bring to closure. To help oversee the development of these programs and the building facilities, I would have had to stay there another ten years. As I said, it was just not my thing to stick around that long. I had some person tell me, "But your name should be on these buildings because you are the cause of them being there." Well, that does not matter to me. What does matter is that the buildings are there for the students and the faculty. It is immaterial as to whose name is on them as long as they are there. In fact, I have not been back to see any of the buildings, because I did not want to seem to be interfering in any way. I suppose that when I leave here, I will go by just to take a look and marvel at what I know will be, or should be anyway, tremendous progress. I certainly left them the paper, endorsed by the court, with the resources to go as high as they dared to go. It was a wonderful opportunity and a wonderful state.

When I was getting to the point of finishing up at Southern, I had made the mistake of telling Dr. Hytche that I thought I would be leaving there in another year or so. I had not told anybody else; because once before when I had tried to leave, the board members convinced me to stay. Dr. Hytche called back and he said, "Well, if you are planning on leaving anyway, why not leave a little early and come to UMES." Before I knew it, almost everybody in Maryland was calling me. So, we split the difference. I said, "Look, give me six months to clear up here and then I will come down." That is why I started in January rather than at the beginning of the fiscal year.

228

Epilogue — Dr. Dolores R. Spikes

Interviewer: Dr. Spikes, of which of your personal accomplishments are you most proud?

Dr. Spikes: *I suppose that whenever I am asked that question, I always say I will leave it to the next generation to answer. I can only say this; I fully recognize that I was one of the first women to hold a Ph.D. in mathematics. Throughout most of my life, I have had opportunities to work in what many call some of the most prestigious universities. I have also had the privilege to work in business and industry, and perhaps by this time would have been at least a president or vice-president and making tons of money.*

All of those doors have been open to me, and I have been invited to enter. I chose this life of service to my people primarily because when I was coming up, there was not a single Ph.D. on the faculty of Southern University, Baton Rouge in mathematics - not one. There were a couple of faculty members who were off studying for the degree; but in general, there were not many black Ph.D.'s around period though there were some very talented people there.

My best legacy would be not in a building with my name on it, not in my having made hundreds of thousands or a million bucks or so, but my best legacy would be in nurturing young minds to become the Ph.D.'s that were not there during my tenure. My best legacy would be in inspiring students to be there for others who, in turn, would nurture others so that it would go on and on and on. Perhaps no one would ever know whence it started or who started it, but just that it was started and that it worked. Sometimes I kind of smile to myself when I think about that, because nobody is going to remember that a Dolores Spikes passed through and actually nurtured and encouraged young people to seek doctorate degrees. Nobody is going to remember that Dolores Spikes encouraged young people to obtain their doctoral degree and go back to their institutions to teach while some go other places, too.

We must let it be known that African-Americans can do anything that they want to do. Nobody is going to remember my contributions. That is alright as long as the job gets done, and it is getting done. I like that thought. But, I will leave it to others to decide whatever my legacy was or is.

Interviewer: Anyone who has become intimately acquainted with the struggles of the University of Maryland Eastern Shore and with the previous heads of the University can see that certain kinds of struggles have been prevalent throughout the whole history. For example, Dr. William P. Hytche, the tenth head of the school, had some of the same struggles as Principal Benjamin O. Bird, the first head of the school. Would you say that these types of struggles are unique to Maryland, to the Eastern Shore, or are they simply unique to Historically Black Colleges and Universities?

Dr. Spikes: *The struggle is something that is unique to HBCU's, I believe, and perhaps to some of the tribal colleges even. But if I had to give you my own personal theory about why this is so, I think that one of the worst legacies of legalized segregation, and before then of slavery, was what I call institutional racism and the view that any thing, person, or institution that is black is inferior. That, I believe, in a nutshell is the reason for the ongoing struggles that black institutions have to endure, and I am able to give you examples that go beyond the individual black person to black institutions.*

We had a brilliant young lady in mathematics and computer science here at the University who is white. She is from Maryland and wanted to attend graduate school in Maryland, so she went to visit both the University of Maryland College Park and Johns Hopkins University. Unfortunately, she got the impression that neither of them were particularly interested in her as a graduate student. On the other hand, she had been to other graduate schools who really just fawned over her and made her feel that she was wanted. She was made to feel unwanted here in Maryland only when they learned that she was from the University of Maryland Eastern Shore.

Well, she also got a fellowship to Rensselaer Polytechnic Institute in New York. She wanted to study applied math and computer science; and I suggested to her that in my opinion, Rensselaer is a reputable institution that is better than either of College Park or Johns Hopkins in those areas of study. That is where she is attending and doing quite well.

Another student, a white young man, found himself in somewhat the same situation. While attending school here, he maintained close to an "A" average. He took the law school admissions test and made a 142, which is not particularly high. If a black student would take it, however, 142 would really be a respectable score; because as you know, many Blacks just do not do well on these standardized tests. I have a nephew, for example, who took that test and he may have scored a little higher than that, but went on to be accepted into Tulane's law school where he did extremely well and then went on to New York University, the best law school in the nation in tax law. There he earned a masters degree and is now making six figures in salary in a prominent Houston law firm. My point is that people make judgements about other people based on the legacies of slavery and the legalized separation of the races. The young man that I first talked to you about, the UMES student, was a very aggressive young man. He had found a way to get internships with congressmen, with local legislators, with anybody from which he believed he could learn. He was interested in politics – not partisan politics, but the art and science of politics. In fact, he did not care whether a person was republican, democrat, or independent if he figured he could learn something from that person. So, he volunteered to serve and got himself internships in their offices. I do not think that at first he was really thinking about law school as much as about another career. Therefore, he probably did not give much attention to studying for the LSAT as many students do and was surprised when he was turned down by the two schools in the State that offer law degrees. He was, however, accepted by a law school in New York and is doing absolutely great and will one day come back to this State and make the people who did not give him a chance ashamed of themselves.

Additionally, we are supposed to have a relationship between UMES' honors program and the University of Maryland at Baltimore, but I am told it has not worked for years. Based on our collaborative agreement, our students are supposed to be almost automatically accepted if they keep up their grade point averages here. Yet we have become so test-reliant in some institutions, because we want to be in Newsweek's top ten or somebody else's top ten. One of the factors of being in that top ten, though, is that institutions must exclude rather than include students, and the easiest way to do that is to require an SAT score of twelve or thirteen hundred. Now I find that interesting, because you are not going to tell me that all of these football and basketball players who are at these schools and who are mostly African American have SAT scores of twelve or thirteen hundred. I mean, it just does not coincide with the statistical facts that they would. And the other thing, I am amazed when I look at the cheerleaders and the bands of these institutions where these black young men are hustling and making money and fame. How many black cheerleaders or band members do you see? These institutions will only accept what is in their self-interest; and thus, the institutional racism that has us in this perpetual mode. The unfortunate thing is the earlier black presidents could not speak out and say the things I am saying. If they did, they knew that their institutions would not get one red cent, and they themselves would not last long. Well even now, we may be penalized by not getting all of the things we want; but the difference is when it comes to people like me, if they say they do not want me, they do not bother me. I have prepared myself to earn a living in almost any fashion that is legal, so it does not bother me. I have never been afraid of being fired by saying what is the truth, and I still am not.

To summarize my response to your question, it is not something peculiar to the Eastern Shore. It is the legacy, I believe, not only of persons from institutions that are black and of slavery but also of legalized separation, which in itself fostered the belief that anything black was inferior to anything white. It persists to this day. Anybody who denies it has to have his or her eyes completely closed. Just turn to the Internet, and you will find sites that monitor the hate groups that have popped up like crazy all over this country in the last decade or so.

Interviewer: How would you characterize the state of Maryland when it comes to institutional racism?
Dr. Spikes: *This state is no different when it comes to institutional racism. It has that same history, except in Maryland it is greater in some parts than in others. I am told that the Eastern Shore had the longest and the hardest legacy; but it really was the entire state of Maryland, which was a border state, that embraced slavery and segregation. Now, one of the good things about the so-called Border States is that slaves, like Frederick Douglass, could escape more easily to the North and do some good things. Thus, the Underground Railroad worked because of the proximity of Baltimore, Maryland to the northern states where slaves could escape more easily than they could from the deep South, where they had to cross through other southern states where they were more likely to be caught and lynched or beaten. But, still the scars are there.*

Accordingly, it is a marvel to understand what the presidents of this University had to go through.

Interviewer: What, in your opinion, is the demeanor of the legislators in the year 2001 concerning UMES?

Dr. Spikes: *I want to tell you that when I came here, there were legislators who told me about all they had done for the University of Maryland Eastern Shore. I could not help but reply, "We really thank you for the advances, but they were merely a down-payment on a debt long overdue because we still have so many needs." They looked so surprised. I really believe that they believed they had done all that they were supposed to do. We took pictures that we carried to the Regents to show faculty members in closet offices and classrooms overflowing. We showed students in the physical therapy program, which is one of our very best programs, having to work on cadavers in the hallways of the basement of Kiah Hall. We showed offices in some of our buildings where wires were lying loose and professors had to step over them. We showed the conditions over in Banneker Hall in which I was ashamed to ask faculty members even to stay, where their offices have ceilings that are sinking and the quality of air is bad. It was not until we showed them those pictures that a few people started paying attention.*

I started begging from the moment I came here to have the planning for a new classroom building moved up and started. We finally did get the planning money after two years. If nothing else goes wrong, we will have the groundbreaking for that building this fall. Perhaps in another two years (2003), we will have a classroom building. For the students here, it will be the first classroom building in about forty years. The Richard A. Henson Center, built in 1993, offers some classroom space but is a specialized building. Meanwhile, the enrollment here has tripled over the last ten to twelve years. I feel that it is going to take another enrollment spurt like that, and it is going to happen, before anyone decides they will put another needed classroom building at UMES. Nobody is going to listen to us now about planning for that classroom building in five years. In their minds, they have given us enough and too much already.

I have to tell you, I think we have done quite well in the last two or three years since I have been here in capital projects, but those projects

233

were projects that were long overdue. We are not finished yet with the program. Whoever succeeds me must have the tenacity to keep it going. We can stop only when, I suppose, people are convinced that they have not ever done right by this institution.

Interviewer: What has the land-grant mission meant to UMES?
Dr. Spikes: *The problems of the Congress in establishing the 1890 institutions was that the southern senators did not want black land-grant institutions integrated with 1862 land-grant institutions. So they gave us our own set of institutions, and these are the so-called 1890 land-grant institutions, whose missions are the same as the 1862 land-grant institutions. The promise of that mission being fulfilled, however, is still waiting. We do not, obviously, have the same resources that University of Maryland College Park (an 1862 land-grant institution) have as a land-grant institution, and yet we have held to the historic notion of the land-grant mission – that we are not an institution of the elite, but one that will grow man/woman power for these United States to help in the growth of the economy.*

When the land-grant mission was formulated, there was a large agrarian economy. Now the economy is shifting to accommodate the information age, but the essence of the mission is still there. We have opted to hold on to our historical mission and to the mission of the Land-grant University. We do not aspire to be another College Park; but we do aspire to have a sense of identity that is above and beyond the usual comprehensive university, because that is what we were meant to be. Consequently, we must have certain programs here in their entirety. For example, we are supposed to have an engineering program here, not a three-way debacle, which is not working, like we have with Salisbury University and College Park. I will tell anybody it is not working and go as far as to say it will not work. Not because we do not want it to work, but because we serve a clientele that requires different deliveries of instruction and a different support structure. Accordingly, I define a curriculum not only in terms of content but in terms also of the method of delivery of instruction. They are two different things. We have adapted different methods, therefore, because of the needs of our students. It is different at College Park, for example, where the instructor lectures and forgets about it because they are admitting students who have SAT scores of 1300 and above. If anything, sometimes the professor becomes a hindrance to the students' learning so that if they get out of the way, the students will do okay anyway.

Interviewer: Dr. Spikes, in light of the your deep insight into the struggles of this institution, both past and present, what do you see as your role in the on-going development of the University?
Dr. Spikes: *Well, we have some obligations, too. Our obligation is to not just sit back and ask for resources that have been denied us but to make the best use of what we have and to be responsible in the uses of these resources. I have a responsibility to promote amongst our students, our faculty, and amongst us as administrators that we should have higher expectations than we have been having, but that does not mean that we set the bar up so high and tell people to jump over it. We have got to help them by giving them the resources they need to jump over it. Then, they will be able to do what is required. I know that because we have always, in times of difficulties and adversity, been able to surmount obstacles when we have had help. Slaves were able to escape slavery with the help of Harriet Tubman and the Underground Railroad. They were able to overcome that adversity given the will and the tools to do it. So given the tools and the will, we can overcome apathy, we can overcome the lack of higher expectations, and we can overcome the mind-boggling brainwashing that has been put upon our students in their young years, especially if they are not as good as everybody else.*

We hear constantly about the number of black young men in prisons. There are too many. We build too many prisons, but we never hear about those outside of the prisons who are making it though they struggle. Somehow, people paint us all in the same picture. And is not it strange now that it is easier to get legislators to give money to build prisons than it is to get them to give for the betterment of our institutions of higher education. Now, I have to say honestly that the past few years I have been here, it does seem that the Governor has put education at the forefront. In addition, the legislative assembly has been kind enough to respect and to want to do something, too. But there has always been a reluctance to give more and too much to the black institutions. That has not changed, but we have gotten a little bit more here lately. All in all,

UMES has not done too badly though there is still much to be done.

Interviewer: What are your observations and projections concerning the physical plant?
Dr. Spikes: *I have talked to Whites and Blacks about what this campus used to be. They described the appearance of the campus in terms that were less than flattering, shall we say, until finally Dr. Hytche got the attention of some of the local people like Attorney Tony Bruce of Princess Anne, Maryland. There was also a chancellor named John Toll and a few others, some legislators, who said that they were going to do something in the name of higher education for UMES. It is not by accident that this University has succeeded, and it was not out of the goodness of some of the hearts of these people, except for locals like Tony and others. There was, however, the fact that the Office of Civil Rights was bearing down on the State. They said that something had to be done about the state of affairs. Consequently, when this campus was transformed into the beautiful place that it is now, that is when the enrollment started climbing.*

Today, we have three little buildings on this campus that were built by students in our construction program back in the 1950s. One of them is Banneker Hall, one is an extension to the science building where we do labs and use some of the space for storage, and the other is where engineering aviation sciences are taught. The fact that they are still standing is a wonderful tribute to that program, but they were not meant to last this long and to be classroom facilities. Nevertheless, they are here and we can not tear them down because we have nowhere for those faculty, staff, and students to go.

Also, an aviation sciences and engineering building is not to be built until the year 2010, ten years from now. Well, the program is still growing. We did manage in part through the Office of Civil Rights agreement to have it moved up to 2004, but there is still a line in the language which bothers me. It says, "subject to the availability of funds." That bothers me, because there was little or no discussion when Dr. Mote went before the finance committee of the Board of Regents to say that he needed sixty million dollars for a life sciences building. The following statement was his justification: "You will not find any school in the top ten without a good life sciences program." The reply of course was,

236

Epilogue — Dr. Dolores R. Spikes

"Well, Dr. Mote, you have got to have this building!"

Subsequently, I went to the governor and asked for a million dollars for some temporary buildings. I was told, "Well you know, I really do not like to build temporary buildings because it is a waste of money. You have already got the classroom building approved." I replied, "But Governor, that classroom building (at that time) will not be ready until another four or five years, and I need space now. I do want to remind you that last year you gave UB seven million dollars for a temporary building, and before that you gave Towson four million dollars for a temporary building. So, there is some precedence for temporary buildings in this State." He smiled and finally gave us the million dollars for the temporary buildings.

Those are the hurdles we have to get over, so whoever sits in this seat when I leave must continue to be the "Lion of Judah." They must not be afraid and will have to advance in a dignified but yet factual way and not back away from the needs of this University. That is going to be important. In fact, the most important job of the Board of Regents remains to be the selection of its presidents. The most important part of the job for the constituents of this University will be to see that the Board of Regents selects the right person for this position. We will see how it comes out whenever that time comes.

Interviewer: Is there any part of the history of the University of Maryland Eastern Shore, whether it is negative or positive, that motivates you in your day-to-day administration?
Dr. Spikes: *Yes. I did not know this before I came here, but I learned from the students that there is a negative perception of UMES out there. They have told me the unsavory description of what some people say the initials U. M. E. S. stand for. They have told me some other things also, and I became determined that that would not be the enduring image of UMES. I am determined that this will be an institution that is truly one of exceptional academic standards, but we do not have to set SAT scores of fourteen, thirteen, or even twelve hundred as a requirement for enrollment to accomplish it. If we do, we are going to exclude most black people in the state of Maryland, and we do not want to exclude potentially good students. If we are to inspire change, we have to educate;*

and the figures say that Blacks in Maryland have a better chance of earning a four-year degree if they go to a four-year college. It is as simple as that.

There are some who say Blacks ought to start in community colleges. Well the track records there are not too good, and it is there for all to see. We are working, therefore, very hard on specific collaborations with some community colleges. I am actually going to put a person in Dr. Eucharia Nnadi's office, the office of the vice president of academic affairs, whose responsibility will be to connect with the community colleges that we have agreements with, checkup on the persons in those community colleges to be sure that they transfer, and to make sure all of their needs are met and things of that sort. So, we do believe we can have some impact on helping community college students to help themselves by earning a four-year degree. We would hope the community colleges would do the same kind of thing for their students.

Interviewer: While the struggles to keep the doors of the University remained in the forefront for many years, one day a different breed of student as well as educator began to come through the doors. What are your observations and your goals concerning the students and educators at UMES?

Dr. Spikes: *We want to hold our students to a higher level of accountability. You have got students here who are extremely bright and talented. Sometimes I marvel at the talents that many of our students have. Regrettably, too many of them waste that talent. One of the reasons we wanted to designate the more recent dorm as an honors dorm was that we wanted to, first of all, provide an excellent live-in study facility for those who are truly serious about their studies. We want to point out that academic excellence really is a priority of ours; and our new dorm, which is currently in construction, is a symbol of that. I always say that our students must learn more outside of the classroom and we have to help them to do that. We have to teach them the social graces and we can start with how they live on the campus.*

Sometimes students ask me why they do not see me walking on the yard a bit more. I tell them that I do not have the time to just walk idly. I may be going somewhere, and I will visit with them. If I have

238

some time in the evenings or on the weekend, I may walk about. But just to hang out all day, I can not do that and they can not either - - not with the graduation and retention rates that we have. When they are not in class, students ought to be in a small study group, in the library, or in a laboratory. We try to encourage them to do that.

Concerning our educators, we also try to encourage our faculty to be more nurturing, the way faculty used to be. We still have some who are still around like that, but I am afraid there are some who are coming in who are not as committed to our original mission as others are. It is not their fault, because they have just never known of the mission. Those of us who do know of the mission, however, must take them under our wings and nurture them to make them better teachers and better supporters of UMES.

Interviewer: What are some of your future aspirations for UMES in general?
Dr. Spikes: *We have no money to do a lot of things that we think would make this university better. We just do not have it. We have to do the best with what we have, but academics have to come first. For example, we need a medical services facility that offers more than Band-Aids. We obviously cannot (and do not wish to) compete with hospitals and doctors' offices; but as it stands, we have an infirmary where we can only administer minor physical health services to students. We then refer them somewhere else for major healthcare services. With the medical facility, we need a built-in counseling center with a full-time psychologist on board to help students who may have difficulty adjusting and who have some emotional problems as well. Many of our students come here with those kinds of problems from home or from the neighborhoods in which they grew up. Unfortunately, the State does not fund us for things of that kind. I have someone already looking, first of all, to plan what we want; and then, we are going to have to go out and see if we can get some private money to help support it. That may be four or five years down the road, but we have to start sometime. So, we might as well start now and hope that in four or five years we can have it in place.*

Interviewer: Many major universities have faculty members living on campus. At one time many of the buildings, like the police department and the infirmary, served as faculty housing and it seems the arrangement resulted in more of a family-like atmosphere. Do you foresee faculty living on this campus again? Do you give credence to the benefit it would have for the campus?

Dr. Spikes: *I certainly do give credence to the benefit it would have, but I do not foresee it. It is simply that we have a hard time getting housing for students, let alone faculty. But, what we did do was to ask Mr. Marvin Jones, director of Residence Life, if in each of the dorms he would put a room aside for faculty members to come to visit in the evenings or even on weekends with students and just talk and interact with them. He did that, but he found that there were few takers. Because we will have trouble finding spaces to put all of our kids in the fall, we have ended up using the space to house students. I have asked Residence Life to talk with Dr. Nnadi about a mentoring program and to give it another chance. Maybe she, the deans, and the chairs can have faculty discussions and come up with something that will get it to work a little better.*

Interviewer: What are your projections for the future of the University of Maryland Eastern Shore in terms of enrollment?

Dr. Spikes: *There was a study commissioned in 1980 by the University of Maryland System. In that study, they thought that UMES was so bad that they had to give us a special chapter. In their published report, they said that we would never have more than two thousand students and would need five thousand students to successfully operate. Well guess what, there are lots of small liberal arts colleges doing very fine — some with only six or seven hundred students. We have grown beyond, in twenty years, the two thousands students that they projected we might eventually get. It feels good to sort of say, "In your face!" to those people who made those projections. Still there is an immense opportunity to grow.*

My admissions people are telling me that if the model we are using works as it did last year, we are going to have a banner year for new students. So the students will be here, but what are we going to do with them in terms of classroom space and in terms of living space? We are now making contingency plans should they come so that we hopefully do

240

are that we will be okay if we can get the classroom building up in a record two-years time and we are not delayed as with most buildings built on this campus. For example, we should have had this new honors dorm finished for this year. The builders may not be finished, however, and that will be a big disappointment to us. In two years, when we either built or purchased the general classroom building, the honors dorm, and Hawk's Landing just outside of the campus, I think we will then (within the next four or five years) be able to accommodate at least five thousand students on this campus. They are there - there for the taking and the asking, and they want to come to college. Half of the job of getting them here is getting them on this campus. Once we get them on campus, we have got them; because we have a wonderful campus with a lot of amenities. Our new student services center is a huge inducement to anybody. We have the William P. Hytche Athletic Center, and it is a huge inducement to students to come. Most importantly, however, they should come for the value of the academic programs. For that reason, we want to insure that all of our programs are at the top of their games. We look forward to students coming to study here because of the programs, the quality of teaching, and the support that we can give to them.

Interviewer: **To sum up, you have been very instrumental in every area in terms of the campus. Of which one of your successes here are you most proud?**
Dr. Spikes: *Well, I hope it is one that is intangible - that people have been inspired to do their best and to raise their level of expectations. Although, I have to say that the acquisition of more capital buildings has to be up there, too, because we need them so badly.*

All indicators show that this leader, who is endowed with tested ability, relentless courage, sound judgement, keen perception, vision, and a profound faith in humanity, performed her duties with unswerving integrity and fearless determination. Her many attributes won for her a welcomed administrative changeover, a strong working relationship with her predecessor, and a host of friends and supporters.

It is our sincere hope and prayer that Dr. Spikes may be blessed with health, strength, and increased opportunities for even greater achievement, somewhere along the line, in the noble work of this University.

APPENDIX A

BIBLIOGRAPHY

1. GENERAL

Beard, Augustus F., A Crusade of Brotherhood, A History of the American Missionary Association, New York: The Pilgrim Press, 1909.

Beard, Charles A., The Rise of American Civilization, New York: Macmillan, 1931.

Bowers, Claud G., The Tragic Era, Cambridge: Houghton Mifflin, 1929.

Bond, Horace Mann, Education of the Negro in the American Social Order, New York: Prentice-Hall, 1934.

Bragg, George F., History of the Afro-American Group of the Episcopal Church, Baltimore: Church Advocate Press, 1922.

Brawley, Benjamin G., Doctor Dillard of the Jeannes Fund, New York: Fleming H. Revell, 1930.

Brawley, Benjamin G., A Social History of the American Negro, New York: Macmillan, 1921.

Conrad, Earl, Harriet Tubman, Washington: The Associated Publishers, 1943.

Cubberly, Ellwood P., Public Education in the United States, Boston, 1919.

Derbigny, Irving A., General Education in the Negro College, Stanford University Press, 1947.

Detweiler, Frederick G., The Negro Press in the United States, Chicago: The University of Chicago Press, 1922.

Deiffendorfer, Ralph E. (ed.), The World Service of the Methodist Episcopal Church, Chicago, 1923.

Douglas, Aubrey A., The American School System, New York: Rhinehart, 1940.

Douglass, Frederick, Life and Times of Frederick Douglass, Chicago: J.S. Goodman, 1882.

Drinker, Frederick E., Booker T. Washington, The Master Mind of Slavery, Philadelphia: National Publishing Co., 1915.

DuBois, W.E.B., Black Reconstruction, New York: Harcourt, 1935.

DuBois, W.E.B., The Negro Common School, Atlanta: Atlanta University Press, 1901.

Appendix A — Bibliography

Fleming, Walter L., The Sequel of Appomattox, New Haven: Yale University Press, 1921.

Eels, Walter C., Surveys of American Higher Education, New York: Carnegie Foundation, 1937.

Embree, Edwin R., Review of the Julius Rosenwald Fund to June 30, 1928, Chicago, 1928.

Franklin, John Hope, From Slavery to Freedom, New York, Knopf, 1947.

Frazier, E. Franklin, The Negro Family in the United States, Chicago: The University of Chicago Press, 1939.

Gaines, Francis P., The Southern Plantation: A Study in the Development and Accuracy of a Tradition, New York: Columbia University Press, 1935.

Gallagher, Buell G., American Caste and the Negro College, New York: Columbia University Press, 1938.

Gosnell, Harold F., Negro Politicians, Chicago: the University of Chicago Press, 1935.

Guzman, Jessie P., The Negro Year Book, Tuskegee: Tuskegee Institute, 1947.

Hawk, Emory, Economic History of the South, New York: Prentice-Hall, 1934.

Howard, O.O., Autobiography, New York: Baker and Taylor, 1907.

Jack, Robert L., History of the National Association for the Advancement of Colored People, Boston: Meador Publishing Co., 1943.

Johnson, Charles S., The Negro College Graduate, Chapel Hill: The University of North Carolina Press, 1938.

Johnson, Julia E., Federal Aid for Education, New York: H.W. Wilson, 1941.

Kerlin, Robert T., The Voice of the Negro, New York: E.P. Dutton, 1920.

LaFarge, John, The Race Question and the Negro, New York: Longmans, 1943.

Lewison, Paul, Race, Class, and Party, New York: Oxford University Press, 1932.

Locke, Alain (ed.), The New Negro, New York: Boni, 1925.

Logan, Rayford W. (ed.), What the Negro Wants, Chapel Hill: The University of North Carolina Press, 1944.

McCuiston, Fred, Graduate Instruction for Negroes in the United States, Nashville: George Peabody College, 1939.

McKinney, Richard I., Religion in Higher Education among Negroes, New Haven: Yale University Press, 1945.

Manguson, Charles S., The Legal Status of the Negro, Chapel Hill: The University of North Carolina Press, 1940.

Mitchell, Broadus, The Industrial Revolution in the South, Baltimore: John University Press, 1930.

Myrdal, Gunnar, An American Dilemma, New York: Harper and Brothers, 1944.

Nottingham, Elizabeth K., <u>Methodism and the Frontier</u>, New York: Columbia University Press, 1941.

Nowlin, William F., <u>The Negro in National Politics</u>, Boston: Stratford, 1931.

Penn, I.G. (ed.), <u>The United Negro: His Problems and His Progress</u>, Atlanta: Luther Publishing Co., 1902.

Phillips, Ulrich B., <u>American Negro Slavery</u>, New York: D. Appleton and Co., 1918.

Phillips, Ulrich B., <u>Life and Labor in the Old South</u>, Boston: Little, Brown and Co., 1930.

Redclay, Edward E., <u>County Training Schools and Public Secondary Education for Negroes in the South</u>, Washington: Monumental Printing Co., 1935.

Talbot, Edith A., <u>Samuel Chapman Armstrong: A Biographical Study</u>, New York: Doubleday, 1901.

Thompson, Holland, <u>The New South</u>, New Haven: Yale University Press, 1919.

True, Alfred C., <u>The History of Agricultural Education in the United States</u>, Washington: U.S. Government Printing Office, 1929.

Vance, Rupert B., <u>Human Geography of the South</u>, Chapel Hill: The University of North Carolina Press, 1935.

Washington, Booker T., <u>An Autobiography</u>, Napierville, Illinois: J.L. Nichols, 1901.

Washington, Booker T., <u>The Future of the American Negro</u>, Boston: Small, Maynard and Co., 1902.

Washington, Booker T., <u>Up From Slavery: An Autobiography</u>, New York: Doubleday, 1901.

Washington, Booker T., <u>Working with the Hands</u>, New York: Doubleday, 1904.

Wilkerson, Doxey A., <u>Special Problems of Negro Education</u>, Washington: U.S. Government Printing Office, 1939.

Williams, W.T.B., <u>Report on Negro Universities in the South</u>, New Orleans: Tulane University Press, 1913.

Woodson, Carter G., <u>The History of the Negro Church</u>, Washington: Associated Publishers, 1921.

Woodson, Carter G., <u>The Rural Negro</u>, Washington: Associated Publishers, 1930.

2. SPECIFIC

Adams, Myron W., <u>A History of Atlanta University</u>, Atlanta: Atlanta University Press, 1930.

Appendix A — Bibliography

Alderman, Edwin., J.L.M. Curry, A Biography, New York: Macmillan, 1911.

American Association of Educators of Colored Youth, Journal of Proceedings, 1891, Winston-Salem, North Carolina: 1892.

American Guide Series, Maryland: A Guide to the Old Line State, New York: Oxford University Press, 1940.

Armstrong, Samuel Chapman, Twenty-Two Years? Work of Hampton Institute, Hampton: Normal School Press, 1893.

Baltimore Association for the Moral and Educational Improvement of the Colored Race, Annual Report 1865, Baltimore: 1865.

Bede, Brother (Michael F. Rouse), A Study of the Development of Negro Education Under Catholic Auspices in Maryland and the District of Columbia, Baltimore: Johns Hopkins University Press, 1935.

Blackwell, Jefferson D., The Organization and Supervision of Vocational Education in Maryland County High Schools, Baltimore: The Twentieth Century Printing   Co., 1929.

Boyd, Leroy S., Maryland Agricultural College, Washington: Beresford, 1912.

Brackett, Jeffrey R., The Negro in Maryland: A Study of the Institution of Slavery, Baltimore: Johns Hopkins University Press, 1889.

Bragg, George F., Men of Maryland, Baltimore: Church Advocate Press, 1925.

Brawley, Benjamin G., Early Effort for Industrial Education, Charlottesville, Virginia (?):   1923.

Byrd, Harry C., "The University of Maryland and Higher Education of Negroes," College Park: Mimeographed statement before the Legislative Council on July 16, 1947.

Citizens Committee on Higher Education, "Some Facts about the Higher Education of Colored People in Maryland," Baltimore: Mimeographed pamphlet, 1948.

City Wide Congress of Baltimore, Report of Committee on Maryland Agricultural College, May 16, 1914, Baltimore, 1914.

Clark, Charles B. (ed.), The Eastern Shore of Maryland and Virginia, New York: Lewis Historical Publishing Co., 1950.

Clark, Felton C., The Control of State-Supported Teacher-Training Programs for Negroes, New York: Columbia University Press, 1934.

Clark, William, Geography of Maryland, Baltimore: Johns Hopkins University Press, 1918.

Conference of the Presidents of Negro Land-Grant Colleges, Proceedings of the Annual Conference, 1948.

Cordell, Eugene F., University of Maryland, 1807-1907, New York: Lewis Publishing Co., 1907.

Appendix A — Bibliography

Craven, Avery O., Soil Exhaustion as a Factor in the Agricultural History of Virginia and Maryland, Chicago: University of Chicago Press, 1926.

Delaware Association for the Moral and Educational Improvement of the Colored People, Report, Wilmington: 1868.

Davis, Jackson, County Training Schools, Hampton: 1918.

Davis, John W., Land-Grant Colleges for Negroes. West Virginia State College Bulletin, Institute: 1934.

Davis, John W., Problems in Collegiate Education of Negroes, West Virginia State College Bulletin, Institute: 1937.

Dunlap, Mollie E. (ed.), Institutions of Higher Learning among Negroes in the United States, Negro College Quarterly, Wilberforce University, 1947.

Forman, Henry C., Early Manor and Plantation Houses of Maryland, Easton, Maryland: Published by the author, 1934.

Gilman, Daniel C., The Launching of a University, New York: Dodd-Mead, 1906.

Haygood, Lewis M., The Colored Man in the Methodist Episcopal Church, Cincinnati: Cranston and Stowe, 1890.

Hemmeter, John C., The Centennial Celebration of the Founding of the University of Maryland, Baltimore: Williams and Wilkins, 1908.

Hill, David S., Federal Relations to Education, Washington: American Council on Education, 1931.

Holmes, D.O.W., Evolution of the Negro College, New York: Columbia University Press, 1934.

Ingraham, Prentiss, Land of Legendary Lore, Easton, Maryland: Gazette Publishing Co., 1898.

James, Edward J., The Origin of the Land-Grant Act of 1862, Urbana: University of Illinois Press, 1910.

Kent, Frank R., The Story of Maryland Politics, 1867-1910, Baltimore: Thomas and Evans, 1911.

Knight, Edgar W., The Academy Movement in the South, Chapel Hill: The University of North Carolina Press, 1919.

Knight, Edgar W., The Influence of Reconstruction on Education in the South, New York: Columbia Press, 1913.

Knight, Edgar W., Public Education in the South, Boston: Ginn and Co., 1922.

Lantz, Emily E., The Spirit of Maryland, Baltimore: Waverly Press, 1929.

Leavell, Ullin W., Philanthropy in Negro Education, Nashville: George Peabody College, 1930.

McCormick, Leo J., Church-State Relationships in Education in Maryland, Washington: Catholic University of America Press, 1942.

Appendix A — Bibliography

McGuinn, Henry J., The Courts and the Changing Status of Negroes in Maryland, Richmond: 1940.

Maryland, Its Resources, Industries and Institutions, Baltimore: 1893.

Monhan, Thomas P., "The University of Maryland, A Challenge to Democracy," Washington: Mimeographed booklet, 1943.

Mumford, Frederick B., The Land-Grant College Movement, Columbia: University of Missouri Press, 1940.

National Association of Colored Agricultural and Mechanical Colleges and Schools for Secondary and Higher Education, Annual Report, 1904, Hampton: 1906.

Pierce, Paul S., The Freedmen?s Bureau, Iowa City: University of Iowa Press, 1904.

Puryear, Bennet, The Public School in its Relations to the Negro, Richmond: Clemmett and Jones, 1877.

Reid, Ira De A., The Negro Community of Baltimore, Baltimore: The Baltimore Urban League, 1934.

Rust, Richard S., Educational Work in the South, Cincinnati: 1882.

Rust, Richard S., The Freedmen's Aid Society and the Methodist Episcopal Church, New York: 1880.

Rust, Richard S., The Freedmen's Aid and Southern Education Society and Its Work, Baltimore, 1898.

Steiner, Bernard C., The History of University Education in Maryland, Baltimore: Johns Hopkins University Press, 1891.

Stevens, Abel, Supplementary History of American Methodism, New York: Eaton and Mains, 1899.

Stowell, Jay S., Methodist Adventures in Negro Education, New York: Methodist Book Concern, 1922.

Thomas, Isaac L., Methodism and the Negro, New York: Eaton and Mains, 1910.

Torrence, Clayton, Old Somerset on the Eastern Shore of Maryland, Richmond: Whittet and Shepperson, 1935.

Truitt, Charles J., Historic Salisbury Maryland, Garden City, New York: Country Life Press, 1932.

Whitney, Annie W., Folklore from Maryland, New York: American Folklore Society, 1925.

Woods, A.F., The University of Maryland—What it is Doing, College Park. U of Maryland: 1922.

Wright, Arthur D., The Negro Rural School Fund, 1907-1933, Washington: Anna T. Jeanes Foundation, 1933.

Wright, James M., The Free Negro in Maryland, 1634-1860, New York
    Longmans, 1921.

3. OFFICIAL PUBLICATIONS OF MARYLAND

A. Miscellaneous

Annual Report of the Superintendent of Public Instruction (1865-1930)
A Proposed Program of Education for Maryland (1944)
Elementary School Supervision in the Counties of Maryland (1917)
Journal of Proceedings of the House of Delegates
Journal of Proceedings of the Senate
Laws of Maryland (1866-1949)
Progress in Education in Maryland (1938)
Supervision of Colored Schools in Maryland (1919)
State Papers and Addresses of Governor Albert C. Ritchie
State Papers and Addresses of Governor Herbert O'Connor

B. Reports of Commissions

Commission on Higher Education (1931)
Commission on Higher Education (1947)
Commission on Higher Education of Negroes (1937)
Commission on Industrial Education (1910)
Commission to Examine into the Relation of Maryland to the Maryland
    Agricultural College (1914)
Commission on Scholarships for Negroes (1939)
Commission on State Aid to Colleges (1924)
Educational Survey Commission (1927)
School Survey Commission (1941)

4. METHODIST EPISCOPAL CHURCH

Annual Report of the Freedmen's Aid Society
Minutes of the General Conference
Minutes of the Baltimore Conference
Minutes of the Delaware Conference
Minutes of the Washington Conference
Minutes of the Wilmington Conference

5. NEWSPAPERS AND MAGAZINES

Baltimore Afro-American
Baltimore American
Baltimore Sun
Baltimore Evening Sun
Christian Education (Cincinnati)
Marylander and Herald (Princess Anne)
Salisbury Times (Salisbury)
Wicomico News (Salisbury)

6. SCHOOL PUBLICATIONS

Annual Report of the University of Maryland
Catalogue of Princess Anne Academy
Catalogue of Princess Anne College
Maryland State College Bulletin
Morgan College Bulletin
Yearbook of Morgan College

7. PUBLICATIONS OF THE U.S. OFFICE OF EDUCATION

Accredited Higher Institutions, Ella B. Ratcliffe, 1934.
Accredited Secondary Schools in the United States, Margaret J.S. Carr, 1934
Agricultural and Mechanical Colleges, 1900.
A Background Study of Negro College Students, Ambrose Caliver, 1933.
Bulletins of the Bureau of Education 1906-1927, Edith Wright and Mary S.
        Phillips, 1928.
College of Agriculture and Mechanic Arts, R.H. Alvey, 1893.
The College Bred Negro, W.E.B. DuBois, 1903.
Digest of Legislation Providing Subsidies for Education, W.W. Keesecker, 1930
Educational Boards and Foundations - 1922-1924, Henry R. Evans, 1926.
Education of the Colored Race, 1898.
Education of the Colored Race, 1901.
Education of Negroes: A Five Year Bibliography, Ambrose Caliver, 1937.
Education of Negro Teachers, Ambrose Caliver, 1933.
The Educational Movement in the South, Wyckliffe Rose, 1905.
Federal Legislation and Administration Pertaining to Land, L.E. Blauch, 1924

Final Establishment of the American Common School System in West Virginia, Maryland, Virginia and Delaware 1863-1900, Amory D. Mayor, 1905.

The Future of the Colored Race, 1900.

Hampton Normal and Agricultural Institute, Walton C. John, 1923.

History of Education in Maryland, Bernard C. Steiner, 1894.

Index to the Reports of the Commissioner of Education - 1867-1907, 1909.

J.L.M. Curry and His Services to Education in the South, 1905.

Land-Grant College Education - 1910-1920, Walton C. John, 1924.

The Land-Grant Act of 1862 and the Land-Grant Colleges, Benjamin F. Andrews, 1918.

The Land-Grant Colleges in Relation to National Development 1910-1920, E.D. Ball. List of Publications, 1910.

National Survey of Higher Education of Negroes, 1943 (4 vols.)

Negro Education, A Study of the Private and Higher Schools for Colored People in the United States, Thomas Jesse Jones, 1916.

Philanthropy in the History of American Higher Education, Jesse B. Sears, 1922.

Public and Private High Schools, 1912.

Statistics of Land-Grant Colleges, Walter J. Greenleaf, 1926.

Statistics of the Education of the Negro Race, David T. Blose, 1928.

Schools for Negroes, 1902.

Schools for Negroes, 1912.

Statistics of Private High Schools and Academies, Frank M. Phillips, 1925.

Semi-Annual Report on Schools for Freedmen, John W. Alvord, 1866-1870.

Survey of Negro Colleges and Universities, Arthur J. Klein, 1928.

Statistics of Land-Grant Colleges and Universities, 1947.

Statistics of Universities, College, and Technical Schools, 1911.

The Work of Certain Northern Churches in the Education of Freedmen, 1861-1900, Amory D. Mayo, 1903.

8. MANUSCRIPTS AND UNPUBLISHED THESES

A. Manuscripts

National Archives: Records of the Department of Interior
                         Records of the Freedmen?s Bureau
                         Records of the Census
Somerset County: Land office Records

Appendix A — Bibliography

	Registry of Wills
U.S. Office of Education:	Mails and Files (Maryland)
Morgan College:	Minutes of the Trustees
Princess Anne Academy:	Student Account Ledgers (1912-1924)

B. Unpublished Theses

Casey, Mary A., "Rise of the Free School System in Maryland," M.A., Teachers College, Columbia University, 1909.

Davids, Robert B., "A Comparative Study of White and Negro Education in Maryland," Ph.D., Johns Hopkins University, 1936.

Ebaugh, Mary O., "The Beginnings of Higher Education in Maryland," Ph.D., Johns Hopkins University, 1932.

French, John E., "The Separation and Reunion of the Methodist Church," M.A., University of Delaware, 1940.

Hartle, Rexford, "The Teacher in Maryland," M.A., University of Maryland, 1932.

Marion, Claud C., "A Qualitative and Quantitative Study of the Effectiveness of Instructional Programs in Technical Agriculture in Negro Land-Grant College," Ph.D., Cornell University, 1948.

Morrison, Vera E., "State Aid to Higher Education in Maryland," M.A., University of Maryland, 1931.

Talbert, Charles A., "The Methodist Episcopal Church and the Negro during the Reconstruction Period 1865-1885,? M.A., Northwestern University, 1932.

Warngy, Frank O., "Education of the Freedmen by Philadelphia and Baltimore Quakers During the Civil War and Reconstruction," M.A., Johns Hopkins University, 1947.

9. PERIODICALS

"Admission of Negroes to State Universities and College," School and Society, Vol. 42, p. 284.

"Admission of a Negro Student to the University of Missouri," School and Society, Vol. 43, p. 765.

Alexander, Will W., "Our Conflicting Racial Policies," Harpers, January, 1945.

Blauch, L.E., "The First Uniform School System of Maryland, 1865-1868," Maryland Historical Magazine, Vol. 26, pp. 205-227.

Appendix A — Bibliography

Bunch, Ralph J., "The Negro in the Political Life of the United States," Journal of Negro Education, July 1941.

"Case of Donald G. Murray," School and Society, Vol. 43, p. 152.

Clement, Rufus E., "Legal Provisions for Graduate and Professional Instruction in States Operating Separate School Systems," Journal of Negro Education, April 1939.

The Courts and the Negro Separate School, Journal of Negro Education, July 1935.

Cohn, Doris Maslin, "The Haynie Letters," Maryland Historical Magazine, June 1941.

Frazier, E. Franklin, "Graduate Education in Negro Colleges and Universities," Journal of Negro Education, July 1933.

Frazier, E. Franklin, "The American Negor?s New Leaders," Current History, April 1928.

Jackson, Luther P., "The Origin of Hampton Institute," Journal of Negro History, April 1925.

Johnson, George M., "The Present Legal Status of the Negro Separate School," Journal of Negro Education, July 1947.

Johnson, Guy B., "Negro Racial Movements and Leadership in the United States," American Journal of Sociology, Vol. 43, pp. 57-71.

Lane, David A., Jr., "The Junior College Movement Among Negroes," Journal of Negro Education, July 1933.

Locke, Alain, "The Negro: ?New? or ?Newer,'" Opportunity, January 1939.

Peters, Iva L., "A Social Interpretation: Maryland," Social Forces, March 1936.

Ransom, Leon A., "Education and the Law," Journal of Negro Education, January 1944.

APPENDIX B

IMPORTANT DATES

1795   Ezekiel Haynie, a physician, purchases 114 acres in Somerset County, Maryland from Josiah Hobbs. This property was eventually acquired by the school.

1798   Haynie builds "Olney," a colonial home that later became the first building on the campus.

1800   Washington Academy moves into a brick structure near Jones Creek, south of Princess Anne in Somerset County. This building, abandoned after the Civil War, was considered as a site for the school.

1806   Maryland Agricultural College is founded.

1812   University of Maryland (Baltimore) is incorporated by Chapter 159 of the General Assembly.

1848   John A.B. Wilson, a founder of the school, is born in Milton, Delaware (Sept. 14).

        Oregon opened as a free territory.

1849   United States Department of Interior is created (March 3).

1852   Levi Scott and Edward R. Ames, founders of the Centenary Biblical Institute (Morgan College), become bishops in the Methodist Episcopal Church.

        Uncle Tom's Cabin is published.

1855   Benjamin O. Bird, first principal of the school, is born near Harper's Ferry, Virginia (Aug. 14).

1856   Maryland Agricultural College receives annual appropriation of $6,000 from the State.

        Joseph R. Waters, a founder of the school, is born at Fairmount, Maryland (May 8).

        Conflict in Kansas over slavery; John Brown attacks in Kansas.

1859   Portia Bird, the second principal, is born in Clarke County, Virginia, (Feb. 10).

        John Brown makes raid at Harpers Ferry, Virginia.

1861   Pezavia O'Connell, the third principal of the school, is born in Natchez, Mississippi (Mar. 2).
        Civil War.
1862   The U.S. Department of Agriculture is established (Mar. 15).
        The first Morrill Act is passed (July 2).
        The Emancipation Proclamation is issued (Sept. 22).
1865   Maryland creates a State Board of Education.
        The Federal government makes provision for the establishment of the Freedmen's Bureau (Mar. 3).
        Lee surrenders to Grant at Appomattox, Virginia (April 9).
        Lincoln is fatally shot in Washington, DC (April 15).
1866   Trustees of the Maryland Agricultural College gives the State an interest in exchange for an appropriation of $45,000.
        The Freedmen's Aid Society of the Methodist Episcopal Church is established.
        Registration of "loyal" unionists is questioned in Maryland.
1867   U.S. Department of Education is created (Mar. 1).
        "Radicals" in Congress pass first Reconstruction Act.
        Ku Klux Klan organization is in progress.
        The Peabody Fund is established.
        Atlanta University if founded.
        Maryland's Constitution provides for a system of free public schools.
        Wicomico County is formed from Somerset.
        The Centenary Biblical Institute is chartered in Baltimore (Nov. 27).
1868   Andrew Johnson is impeached and tried.
        Fourth Reconstruction Act is passed.
        The Fourteenth Amendment is passed.
        Hampton Institute is founded.
1869   Grant is inaugurated (Mar. 4).
        James U. Dennis deeds "Olney" and 16 acres to Buelah Hirst (Nov. 8).
1870   The Fifteenth Amendment is ratified (Mar. 30).
        Congress passes an anti-Klan act (May 31).
        The U.S. Department of Justice is created (Junes 22).
        Buelah Hirst deeds "Olney" and 16 acres to Aaron D. Woodruff, a physician (Dec. 9).
1871   The first Negro land-grant college is founded at Alcorn, Mississippi.
1872   Anne Arundel County election cases involve civil and political rights of Negroes (May).

The Centenary Biblical Institute is formally opened at 44 Saratoga Street in Baltimore (Oct. 9).

Horace Greeley, "Liberal" Republican, campaigns in Baltimore (Oct. 10).

1873 First catalogue of Centenary Biblical Institute is published.

A wealthy merchant endows Johns Hopkins University.

1874 James U. Dennis deeds more of old Haynie property to Louis W. Morris, a physician of Princess Anne.

Maryland makes the first appropriation for support of the "Colored Normal School."

1876 Bell's telephone is patented (Mar. 17).

Johns Hopkins University is opened in Baltimore.

The National election of Hayes is disputed.

1877 The Centenary Biblical Institute graduates its first class (3).

Baltimore and Ohio Railroad strike occurs in Baltimore.

Benjamin O. Bird enrolls at the Centenary Biblical Institute.

1879 Joseph R. Waters is admitted to the Delaware Conference. John F. Goucher purchases land at Fulton and Edmondson in Baltimore and donates $5,000 for a new home of the Centenary Biblical Institute.

1880 Cornerstone is laid for new home of Centenary Biblical Institute at Fulton and Edmondson in Baltimore (June 16).

Aaron D. Woodruff, living in Philadelphia, appoints Richard C. Dale of Princess Anne as executor (Sept. 24).

1881 The Freedmen's Aid Society gives the Centenary Biblical Institute nearly $6,000 for real estate.

Garfield dies as a result of assassin's shot fired July 2 (Sept. 19).

1882 The John F. Slater Fund is established.

Enoch Pratt, a wealthy merchant, donates money for a "free" library in Baltimore.

Bishop Levi Scott, one of the founders of the Centenary Biblical Institute, dies.

1884 Land for Metropolitan Methodist Episcopal Church (former site of county jail and slave auction block) is purchased in Princess Anne through Joseph R. Waters and the trustees.

First manual training high school for whites is established in Baltimore. George Alfred Townsend, a former Civil War correspondent, writes Entailed Hat, a historical novel with its plot laid about "Teackle Mansion" of Princess Anne.

1885   Joseph R. Waters and A.R. Shockley are appointed by the Delaware Conference as visitors to the Centenary Biblical Institute.

Waters is appointed as minister to Princess Anne.

1886   Maryland adds $25,000 to the usual $100,000 for the public support of Negro education.

Waters is reappointed to Princess Anne.

A committee of the Delaware Conference gives up consideration of Princess Anne as a site for a "Female College."

Labor riots occur in Chicago's Haymarket. (May 3).

John A.B. Wilson purchases "Olney" and 16 acres from Richard C. Dale for $2,000 (June 12).

The above deed is delivered at Somerset County Courthouse (Aug. 18).

Wilson deeds "Olney" and 16 acres to the Centenary Biblical Institute of Baltimore (Aug. 24).

School opens in "Olney" with nine students (Sept. 13).

Cornerstone is laid for the Metropolitan Church (Sept. 19).

The American Federation of Labor is organized (Dec.).

1887   The Hatch Act (for support of agricultural experimental stations) is passed by Congress.

The school in "Olney," called the Delaware Conference Academy, has its first "commencement" (June 3).

1888   A severe blizzard strikes Maryland; commerce is delayed in Baltimore.

A fire destroys a great deal of Pocomoke, Maryland.

Elihu E. Jackson, a Democrat of Salisbury, becomes governor of Maryland.

Baltimore courts decide that Negroes can practice law in the State.

Women's College of Baltimore is established. (In 1910 it was named in honor of its great benefactor, John F. Goucher).

The name of the Freedmen's Aid Society of the Methodist Episcopal Church is changed.

Pezavia O'Connell marries Marie Jane Johnson in Raleigh, N.C. (Oct. 24).

Negro teachers of Baltimore filed suit for equal salaries.

1889   Harry Clifton Byrd, later president of the University of Maryland, is born in Crisfield, Somerset County.

The Bank of Somerset is established in Princess Anne.

Johns Hopkins University Hospital is opened.

Oklahoma Territory is opened for settlement (April 22).

1890   The school acquires 103 acres of the old Haynie property from Clara E. Morris of Princess Anne. (Jan. 3).

The name of the Centenary Biblical Institute is legally changed to Morgan College by Chapter 326 of the Laws of the Assembly (April 3).

The Maryland State Teachers Association (white) is incorporated by the Assembly (April 3).

Idaho and Wyoming are admitted to the Union (July 3, 10).

The Second Morrill Act is passed (Aug. 30).

The Maryland Agricultural College and Morgan College sign a contract making the Delaware Conference the "Eastern Branch of the Maryland Agricultural College" in order for the State to receive Federal land-grant funds. (Dec. 31)

1891   The U.S. Assistant Secretary of Interior (in absence of the Secretary) certifies Maryland to receive Federal land-grant funds after having seen the contract of Dec. 31.

The American Association of Educators of Colored Youth meets at Hampton Institute (Dec. 29-31).

Total enrollment at Princess Anne for 1891 was 85 students of whom 54 were male, ages 8 to 33.

1892   The Virginia Collegiate and Industrial Institute, a branch of Morgan College, is organized at Lynchburg, Virginia.

The first girls dormitory, given by the Dexter Smith family of Massachusetts, is dedicated in Princess Anne.

Richard C. Dale releases the mortgage on "Olney" (Feb. 4).

The People's Party (Populist) is organized in St. Louis, Missouri (Feb. 22).

Maryland accepts the provisions of Morrill Act of 1890 (March 15).

A labor strike is held in the Carnegie steel plant in Homestead, Pa. (June 30).

1893   "Coxey's Army" marches on Washington, DC.

Johns Hopkins University opens its medical school (March 7).

One hundred and one students, of whom fifty-five were male, enrolled at Princess Anne Academy.

1895   Jacob C. Dunn, one of the first three teachers at the school, is admitted to the Delaware Conference.

1896   Maryland appropriates $2,500 to build an "industrial arts" building in Princess Anne (April 2).

Publication of the bulletin of the Bureau of Education is authorized (May 28).

1897   Benjamin O. Bird dies in Princess Anne (April 25).

Work begins on the "industrial arts" building (May 11).

Portia Bird assumes the duties of principal of Princess Anne Academy.

1898   The battleship "Maine" is blown up in Havana's harbor; the Spanish American War begins (Feb.).

American troops embark for Cuba (June).

1899   Severe blizzard; below zero temperatures recorded on the Eastern Shore (Feb. 12-13).

Portia Bird dies in Princess Anne (Nov. 25).

1900   Pezavia O'Connell becomes the third principal of the school.

Charter of Morgan College is amended by Chapter 357 of the Laws of the Assembly (April 7).

1901   McKinley dies from assassin's shot (Sept. 14).

1902   Maryland passes the first Workingmen's Compensation Law in the United States.

Frank Trigg, at the age of 52, becomes the fourth principal of the school (July).

John Oakley Spencer becomes president of Morgan College and its branches.

1903   The General Education Board is established.

Wheelwrighting and blacksmithing course begun at Academy – a novelty on the Eastern Shore (Jan 4).

Wilbur and Orville Wright fly at Kitty Hawk, N.C., (Dec. 17).

1904   Fire causes more than 100 million dollars damage in downtown Baltimore (Feb. 7-8).

First four-year graduating class.

1907   Land-grant colleges are designated as depositories of public documents (Mar. 1).

Nelson Amendment is passed increasing land-grant appropriations (Mar. 4).

University of Maryland has its centennial celebration (May 30-June 2).

Campaign by John Oakley Spencer – "A Prayer a Day, A Penny A Week" to raise $20,000 to build a domestic science building for the Academy.

1908   State Board of Agriculture is created in Maryland with trustees of Maryland Agricultural College as ex officio members.

Commissioner of Education says that Nelson funds for Princess Anne cannot be used in Negro public schools of Maryland (Oct. 14).

William H. Taft wins the national presidential election.

1909 The Morgan College Bulletin, printed at Princess Anne, is entered as second-class mail at the post office (Jan. 11).

U.S. Bureau of Education says that Morrill funds for the school cannot be spent otherwise (June 23).

1910 Kendrick C. Babcock and Arthur C. Monohan, specialists in the Bureau of Education, make survey of land-grant institutions (July-Nov.).

Thomas Henry Kiah becomes the fifth principal of the school at the age of 38.

Commission on Industrial Education, appointed in 1908, reports to the General Assembly.

Trigg leaves Academy with high praise for a successful eight-year tenure.

1911 The U.S. Attorney General assures the Secretary of Interior of the Secretary's power to certify each institution receiving land-grant funds (Feb. 11).

The Maryland Normal and Industrial school is opened at Bowie, Maryland (Sept.).

The Secretary of Interior rules that no Morrill funds may be used for fuel, equipment or furniture (Nov. 2).

1912 The U.S. Commissioner of Education advises that the school in Princess be placed under the control of its own board of trustees (Feb. 2).

Woodrow Wilson is elected President of the United States (Nov. 5).

The Rosenwald Foundation is established.

1913 The U.S. Department of Labor is created (Mar. 4).

1914 Maryland takes over interests in the Maryland Agricultural College with consent of private stockholders (Mar. 20).

Organized and intensive lobbying is carried on at Annapolis for more state aid for the Maryland Agricultural College.

John Oakley Spencer, president of Morgan College, tours Europe (July).

The school's second summer session ends (Aug. 7).

World War I begins in Europe (Aug.).

The Academy receives its first appropriation of $500 for maintenance from the Assembly.

1915 The "Lusitania" sinks; 1,100 lives lost (May 7).

A girls dormitory, adjacent to Eliza Smith Hall, is completed at a cost of

$8,000.

Jacob C. Dunn dies at Orange, N.J.

Fire destroys the plant of Princess Anne's Marylander and Herald; printing continued by the school.

1916   Maryland provides for a white supervisor of Negro schools.

The Maryland Agricultural College receives a new charter and becomes the Maryland State College of Agriculture.

The U.S. Bureau of Education publishes Thomas Jesse Jones' study of Negro education.

Villa raids Columbus, New Mexico.

The school acquires a part of the old Broughton homestead.

John Dewey publishes Democracy and Education.

Abraham Flexner of the General Education Board conducts a study of public education in Maryland.

1917   The United States declares war on Germany (April 6); Camp Meade becomes a training center.

Morgan College purchases 42 acres at Hillen and Arlington on the outskirts of Baltimore (June 1).

The school has its first student strike (about food).

Morgan?s branch in Lynchburg is destroyed by fire (Dec. 10).

1918   Appropriations to the Maryland State College of Agriculture and its "Eastern Branch" are itemized for the first time by Chapter 206.

Morgan College (Baltimore) receives its first grant from the State amounting to $1,000.

Wilson issues his "fourteen points."

The National Association for the Advancement of Colored People protests ordinances restricting the residence of Negroes in Baltimore.

Harry Clifton Byrd becomes vice president of the Maryland State College of Agriculture.

Mary Kiah, wife of the principal, dies (Oct. 7).

World War I ends with signing of Armistice at Compiegne in France (Nov. 11).

1919   Prohibition is made legal by the Volstead Act (Oct. 28).

An influenza epidemic hits the Eastern Shore (Jan.).

"Olney" is gutted by fire (April 19).

Maryland opens its ferry across the Chesapeake Bay (May).

Morgan College and the Maryland State College of Agriculture sign an agreement relative to the control of the school.

Enrollment at MSC reaches 180.*
1920   Maryland makes legal provisions for Negro high schools.
The Maryland State College of Agriculture and the University of Maryland are combined by Chapter 480 of the Assembly (April 9).
The Nineteenth Amendment providing for woman suffrage is legalized (Aug. 28).
1920   A conference on Negro education, initiated by the Bureau of Education, is held in the Senate Chamber, Atlanta, Georgia (Nov. 19-20).
1921   A small memorial bridge is built across the Manokin River at Princess Anne commemorating the white and Negro dead of World War I.
A dining hall costing $30,000 is built on the campus.
Warren G. Harding is inaugurated as the 28th president of the United States (Mar. 4).
The General Education Board makes a report on education to Governor Albert C. Ritchie after which the governor appoints a commission to investigate state aid to colleges (Oct. 4).
1923   The opening of King Tut's grave at Luxor, Egypt is highly publicized (Jan. 3).
The American Mercury of H.L. Mencken of Baltimore makes its appearance and attacks prohibition.
The Conference of Negro Land-Grant Colleges is organized at Tuskegee, Alabama.
1924   A Maryland commission on higher education reports that the University of Maryland should not be made a   "great university." The school in Princess Anne is not recognized as offering "higher education" (Jan. 5).
A joint resolution by Maryland's Assembly authorizes the governor to appoint a commission to investigate the "welfare of the colored people." It was one of the nation's first "Interracial" commissions. Prominent citizens planned to help the University of Maryland obtain more state aid (Jan. 13).
Prominent citizens plan to prevent the invasion of Negroes into traditional white residential areas of Baltimore (Jan. 18).
Governor Ritchie questions the wisdom of making large investments at College Park (Mar. 18).
The old boys dormitory burns at Princess Anne.
Enrollment drops to 120.
The Assembly allots $40,000 to replace the building (Chapter 280).

(April)

The Morgan College Bulletin is entered as second-class matter at the Post Office in Baltimore, indicating that this publication is no longer printed at Princess Anne (Dec. 26).

A conference on Negro education at Hampton Institute is attended by the U.S. Commissioner of Education and representatives of all Negro land-grant institutions.

1925   The State is deeded about one-half acre on the campus on which to erect a proposed "mechanic arts" building (June 29).

Nineteen twenty-five edition of Morgan College Bulletin reports enrollment of seventy students at Princess Anne Academy.

This building is completed at a cost of about $35,000.

The school opens as a "junior college" with an enrollment of four students.

1926   Eldon Galway Marksman, later the physician for the school, passes the State Board of Medical Examiners (Dec. 14).

1927   The Interracial Commission recommends the equalization of teacher salaries and more state aid for Morgan College.

Lindberg flies the Atlantic Ocean (May).1928

Arthur J. Klein's study of Negro land-grant institutions is published.

The University of Maryland, formerly the Maryland State College of Agriculture, and Morgan College agree that a fair price for the sale of the school to the State is $100,000.

The University of Maryland took over the sole management of the Academy.

1929   A commission on higher education is appointed by Chapter 26 of the Assembly.

The U.S. Commissioner of Education changes the name of his department to the Office of Education (Oct.).

The stock market "crashes" marking the beginning of the Great Depression. (Oct)

1930   Pezavia O'Connell, third principal of the school, dies in Baltimore, Maryland (Nov. 26).

Enrollment at the Academy drops to 96.

1931   The Regents of the University of Maryland are authorized to acquire a site for a hospital in Baltimore and to sell land to the United States Bureau of Mines.

The case of Ewell Lee involves the question of a fair trail for Negroes on the Eastern Shore.

Enrollment drops to forty-four.

1931   Washington College in Chestertown observes the 150th anniversary of its founding (June 11).

Princess Anne Academy prints its first catalog.

1933   Franklin D. Roosevelt begins the first of his four terms (Mar. 4).

The Assembly provides for scholarships for Negroes who cannot take courses "offered in the said Princess Anne Academy" (April 21).

An extraordinary session of the Assembly considers the problem of liquor and law enforcement (Nov.).

The University of Maryland is authorized to accept donations, including those from the Government of the United States.

George Armwood publicly lynched in Princess Anne.

1935   Donald Gaines Murray applies to enter the Law School of the University of Maryland (Jan. 24).

Baltimore courts order that Murray be admitted.

The Assembly creates a commission on higher education of Negroes (April 1).

The Assembly authorizes the State to purchase the school in Princess Anne for the use of the University of Maryland (April 25).

A probe of student unrest at the University of Maryland is ordered in regard to the administration of the University (April 23).

Criticism of officials of the University appears in the Baltimore press and the Diamondback, a student publication.

Princess Anne Academy becomes Princess Anne College "a few years after 1932." It was an unofficial change.

The Bankhead-Jones Act increases Federal land-grant appropriations (June 29).

Harry Clifton Byrd becomes acting president of the University of Maryland (July).

Congress passes the Social Security Act (Aug. 14).

Murray enters the Law School of the University (Sept. 25).

The Federal government gives nearly 9.2 million dollars for relief in Maryland (Oct. 8).

Soper Commission on the Higher Education of Negroes in Maryland appointed by the Assembly.

Maryland Legislature appropriates $30,000 for scholarships for out-of-state education for Blacks.

1936   Byrd becomes president of the University (Feb. 22).

Robert A. Grigsby becomes head of school.

Morgan College formally deeds the Academy to the State for the use of the University of Maryland (March 14).

Students at Princess Anne strike for social privileges.

Dwight Olive Wendell Holmes becomes the first Negro president of Morgan College following the death of John Oakley Spencer.

An extraordinary session of the Assembly passes an unemployment compensation law (Dec.).

Thomas Henry Kiah dies in Salisbury, Maryland (Dec. 30).

1937   The first student dance is held on the campus of Princess Anne.

Maryland passes its first income tax law.

Voting machines are introduced in Baltimore.

Teacher's dwelling destroyed by fire.

Soper Commission reports. Assembly appoints special commission to study scholarships for Negroes.

Robert A. Grigsby becomes head of Princess Anne College with an official title of acting dean.

John Oakley Spencer dies.

1938   The transfer of Morgan College to the State is approved by Morgan's Trustees (Sept. 28).

The United State Supreme Court decides in favor of Lloyd Lionel Gaines in regard to his education within the State of Missouri (Dec. 12).

1939   A report is made by the commission on scholarships for Negroes (Feb. 21).

This commission, created in 1937, is placed under the control of Morgan College.

The Assembly sets up a commission with powers to make Morgan a State institution (May 3).

Morgan College is officially transferred to the State (Nov. 20).

The United States Office of Education, formerly an agency of the Department of Interior, is placed under the control of the Federal Security Administration.

Nazis and Soviets sign Pact that set World War II into motion (Aug 23).

1940   Three WPA buildings are dedicated at the school in Princess Anne.

Crystal Bird Fauset dedicates one of them to the memory of her father as Bird Hall. (April 19).

1941   The old "mechanic arts" building burns: five persons perish. The

Assembly votes $100,000 for the school (March 31).

The Japanese attack Pearl Harbor (Dec. 7).

1942   The Eastern Shore has its tercentenary celebration (Aug.).

The United States Office of Education publishes a study of the higher education of Negroes.

A third women's dormitory is built and dedicated as John Murphy Hall.

1944   Enrollment at Academy decreases to fifty as a result of the draft.

1945   The Public Works Commission of Maryland asks for post-war plans for institutions of higher learning.

An atomic bomb is dropped on Hiroshima, Japan.

World War II ends (Sept. 2).

Marbury Commission appointed to do comprehensive study of higher education in the State.

1947   Marbury Commission reports.

Robert A. Grigsby retires.

Dr. John Taylor Williams becomes seventh head of the school with the official title of president.

Princess Anne College becomes Maryland State College, Division of the University of Maryland at Princess Anne.

Thomas O'Neill of the Baltimore Sun published article entitled, "Branch at Princess Anne Rated Worst Land-Grant College in U.S." (Nov 19).

1948   Miss Amelia Merchant named as first Miss Maryland State.

1949   A half dozen suits filed for Negroes to enter various professional schools of the University of Maryland.

Baltimore Sun headline, "No Students Ever Flunked This School." (Feb 27).

1950   Charles Hamilton Houston, Negro graduate of Harvard Law School, legal counselor for Donald Gaines Murray, and champion for Negro rights dies (April 22).

Somerset Dining Hall erected on campus by the State.

State appropriations rose from $116,367 to $429,768.

Princess Anne allotted $3,450,000 for building program.

Maryland State College admitted to Eastern Collegiate Athletic Conference(ECAC).

Student Council initiated "Good Will Tours."

One wing of second floor of a boys dormitory partially destroyed by fire.

1951   Student Council initiated exchange programs with Salisbury State College and Washington College of Chestertown.

First homecoming parade.

1954   Maryland State College admitted to Central Intercollegiate Athletic Conference (CIAA).

First Lady Eleanor Roosevelt delivers commencement address.

1959   Delcon Hall destroyed by controlled fire (Feb. 1)

Dr. Martin Luther King, Jr. delivers commencement address.

1961   Vietnam War.

1963   Princess Anne Biracial Committee published desegregation agreement.

1964   Student protests begin as students seek service from restaurants that reneged on desegregation agreement (Feb 20).

Dick Gregory speaks to student protesters (Feb 28).

1966   Dr. Williams takes issue with unfair and inadequate state appropriations beginning major conflicts that would lead to his forces retirement.

1967   Dr. Williams attempts joint faculty appointments between Maryland State College and Salisbury State College.

1968   MSC student, Miss Saundra Williams, named the first Miss Black America.

Mr. Jackie Robinson delivers commencement address.

1970   Student demonstrations on campus in protest of poor conditions lead to multiple arrests (April 7).

Williams announces his retirement in midst of controversy (May 26).

Williams retires (Aug 1).

Maryland State College becomes University of Maryland Eastern Shore.

Dr. Howard Emery Wright appointed as Acting Chancellor during search for Chancellor.

1971   Dr. Williams dies at Peninsula General Hospital.

Dr. Archie Buffkins named chancellor of UMES after national search (June 1).

1973   Dr. Archie Buffkins submits proposal to develop cooperative program between UMES and Salisbury State College.

1974   Cox Commission report concerning the enhancement of the role and image of the predominantly black public colleges in the State submitted to Maryland Council for Higher Education (Aug. 9).

1975   Dr. William P. Hytche appointed Acting Chancellor (July).

Leonard H. Rosenberg Foundation Commission appointed to explore cooperation between different sectors of education and better utilization of educational resources.

Rosenberg Commission recommends merging UMES with Salisbury State.

1976   Maryland Commission for Higher Education becomes State Board for Higher Education.

Dr. William P. Hytche appointed chancellor of UMES.

1977   The Donaldson Report is presented during the legislative session.

Dr. Hytche testifies at hearing held by Webb Task Force, which was commission to study the feasibility of UMES merging with Salisbury State (Aug 3).

1890 land-grant institutions influence revision of the Farm Bill to insure greater access to federal funding.

1978   Dr. John Toll takes office as chancellor of the University System.

UMES Prospectus approved along with eight new undergraduate programs, one stand-alone graduate program, and one joint graduate program (Fall).

Twenty-six students enrolled in graduate program (Sept).

1979   Josiah Macy Foundation gives grant for UMES to begin Honors Program in conjunction with the University of Maryland at Baltimore.

Honors Program begins with the enrollment of thirty-one students.

1980   Football suspended at UMES.

First students enrolled for Construction Management Technology Program, one of the eight approved in 1978.

1981   Moos Report published in 1981.

1982   First students enrolled for Poultry Technology and Management Program, one of the eight approved in 1978.

First students enrolled in the Physical Therapy Program, which was added to the curriculum shortly after the inception of the Honors Program (Fall).

1983   Collaborative agreement between UMES and SSU approved.

Dr. Hytche visits Zambia as part of an administrative team of USAID. International linkages begin.

1984   Governor Hughes appoints Hoblitzell Commission to study condition of higher education in Maryland.

1986   Dr. Hytche visits Cameroon to sign agreement to begin a root and tuber crops program.

1987   Dr. Richard Henson makes two-million-dollar gift to UMES.

1988   Higher Education Bill of 1988 brought all state colleges and universities, except Morgan State University and St. Mary's College, under the control of the University of Maryland Board of Regents.

1989   New constituent, Virginia-Maryland Regional College of Veterinary Medicine, is added to the Honors Program.

1991   Dr. Hytche travels to Egypt to sign collaborative agreement with Supreme Council of Egyptian Universities.

Dr. Hytche visits Namibia as a consultant to Namibian president to map out plans to link Namibian businesses with U.S. investors.

1993   Richard A. Henson Center constructed.

Physical Therapy graduate program established.

1994   International Flag Mall built on UMES campus.

1995   UMES, through NAFEO, secures linkages with Chinese universities.

Dr. Hytche delivers commencement address at the University of Namibia.

Dr. Hytche visits South Africa as senior associate to the American Council on Education.

1997   Dr. Hytche retires.

Dr. Dolores R. Spikes takes the helm as the first appointed female president of the University of Maryland Eastern Shore.

1998   Dr. Hytche travels to Nigeria to observe the first free election after military rule.

APPENDIX C

LEGAL DOCUMENTS

U.S. STATUTES

Morrill Act of 1862
Morrill Act of 1890
Nelson Amendment of 1907

LAWS OF THE GENERAL ASSEMBLY OF MARYLAND

Assent to Morrill Act of 1890 (1892)
First State grant to the Academy (1896)
Scholarships for Negroes (1933)
Assent to Regional Education (1949)

SOMERSET COUNTY

Deed from Wilson to the Centenary Biblical Institute
Deed from Morgan College to the University of Maryland

CONTRACTS RELATIVE TO CONTROL

Control of 1890
Contract of 1919

Act of July 2, 1862 (First Morrill Act)
[Providing for the Endowment, Support and Maintenance of Colleges of Agriculture and Mechanic Arts]

[An ACT Donating public lands to the several States and Territories which may provide colleges for the benefit of agriculture and the mechanic arts]

Be it enacted by the Senate and House of Representatives of the United States of America, in Congress assembled, That there be granted to the several States, for the purposes hereinafter mentioned, an amount of public land, to be apportioned to each State a quantity equal to thirty thousand acres for each

Senator and Representative in Congress to which the States are respectively entitled by the apportionment under the census of 1860: Provided, That no mineral lands shall be selected or purchased under the provisions of this act.

LAWS OF THE GENERAL ASSEMBLY, 1892, CHAPTER 125
Assent to Morrill Act of 1890

SEC.1. Be it enacted by the General Assembly of Maryland, That the Act of Congress approved August thirtieth, eighteen hundred and ninety, entitled "An act to apply a portion of the proceeds of the public lands for the more complete endowment and support of the colleges for the benefit of agriculture and the mechanic arts under the provisions of an act of Congress approved July second, eighteen hundred and sixty-two," be an is hereby assented to and accepted in behalf of the State of Maryland, subject to all the purposes and conditions of said grant.

SEC. 2. Be it enacted, That the Maryland Agricultural College, to which the benefits of said act of Congress apply in this State, be and is hereby authorized and directed to make suitable provisions for complying with all the requirements of said act.

SEC. 3 And be it enacted, That this act shall take effect from the date of its passage.

Approved March 15, 1892.

LAWS OF THE GENERAL ASSEMBLY, 1896, CHAPTER 261
First State grant to the Academy

AN ACT to appropriate a certain sum of money to aid Morgan College, a body corporate, duly incorporated for the education of the colored people, under the General Laws of Maryland, and an amendatory Act of the General Assembly of Maryland, passed at the January session of 1890, to be used for the erection at Princess Anne in Somerset County, Maryland, of an additional building, to increase the facilities for the industrial education of the colored people of Maryland, as carried on by said college at Princess Anne.

SECTION 1. And be it further enacted by the General Assembly of Maryland. That the sum of twenty-five hundred dollars be and the same is hereby appropriated to aid Morgan College in the erection of an additional building to provide better facilities for industrial education of the colored people at Princess Anne, in Somerset County, Maryland.

SECTION 2. Be it further enacted, That the Treasurer of the State be and is hereby authorized and directed upon warrant of the Comptroller of the Treasury, to pay the said sum of twenty-five hundred dollars to the order of the treasurer of said Morgan College, out of any moneys not otherwise appropriated.

SECTION 3. And be it enacted. That his act shall take effect from the date of its passage.

Approved April 2, 1896.

LAWS OF THE GENERAL ASSEMBLY, 1933, CHAPTER 234
Scholarships for Negroes

AN ACT to add a new Section to Article 77 of the Code of Public Geneal Laws of Maryland (Edition of 1924), entitled "Public Education," under a new subtitle to be known as "Negro Education under the Morrill Act," said new section to be known as Section 214A, and to follow immediately after Section 214 of said Article; to provide for a division of certain appropriations for education received by the University of Maryland from the Federal government; and to authorize partial scholarships for exceptionally worth negro students.

WHEREAS, The University of Maryland has for many years conducted for Negro students of the State of Maryland at the Princess Anne, Maryland, educational work required for them under the Federal Morrill Act of 1862; and

WHEREAS, The Academy at Princess Anne, Maryland, educational work required for them under the Federal Morrill Act of 1862; and

WHEREAS, The General Assembly of Maryland has never authorized an apportionment of funds received from the Federal Government under this Act, as required by Federal regulation in those States where education for colored students is given in separate instituions.

APPENDIX D

Negro Schools in Maryland, 1866

Total number of schools for Negroes 73
Baltimore 22
Counties (19) 51

Pupils registered 7,300
Baltimore 2,500
Counties 4,800

Average attendance 5,645
Number of teachers 78
Number of school months 9

<u>Total expense of schools</u> (including books and furniture) $52,515.14

Average cost of each school 719.38
Average salary of teachers (per year) 364.46
Average cost per pupil per month .... .80

Contributions
Citizens of Baltimore 7,179.47
City Council of Baltimore 5,964.35
Associations in other states 15,701.55
"Friends" in England and Ireland 3,848.58
        (Not be confused with Quakers)
Negroes of Maryland 9,831.19
Loan 10,000.00

Commencement Speakers
Since 1948

YEAR	SPEAKER
1948	Dr. Horace Mann Bond, President, Lincoln University, Lincoln, PA
1949	Dr. Vernon Johns, Pastor, First Baptist Church, Montgomery, AL
1950	Mr. Julius A. Thomas, Director, Depart. of Industrial Relations, Natural Urban League, New York, NY
1951	Honorable William H. Hastie, U.S. Circuit Judge, Philadelphia, PA
1952	Honorable Francis E. Rivers, Justice, City Court of the City of New York, NY
1953	Reverend Archibald J. Casey, Jr., Alderman, Third Ward, City Council of Chicago, IL
1954	Mrs. Franklin Delano Roosevelt, "The First Lady of the World," New York, NY
1955	The Honorable Theodore R. McKeldin, Governor of Maryland, Annapolis, MD
1956	The Honorable Adam Clayton Powell, Representative in Congress, Twenty-Second New York District; Pastor, Abyssinian Baptist Church, New York, NY
1957	Attorney Thurgood Marshall, Director-Counsel, NAACP Legal Defense and Education Fund, Inc. New York, NY
1958	The Right Reverend Frank Madison Reid, Presiding Bishop of the Second Episcopal District, The African Methodist Episcopal Church, Washington, DC
1959	Dr. Martin Luther King, Jr., Member, Dexter Avenue Baptist Church, Montgomery, AL
1960	Attorney Charles W. Anderson, Jr., Member, U.S. Delegation to the United Nations, Louisville, KY
1961	Dr. Horace Mann Bond, Professor Education, Atlanta University, Atlanta, GA
1962	Mr. Andrew T. Hatcher, Associate Press Secretary,

The White House, Washington, DC

1963	The Honorable Wayne Lyman Morse, U.S. Senator, State of Oregon, Washington, DC
1964	Bishop John Wesley Lord, Resident, Washington (DC) Area, The Methodist Church, Washington, DC
1965	Dr. Whitney M. Young, Jr., Executive Director, The National Urban League, New York, NY
1966	Dr. Furman L. Templeton, Executive Director, Baltimore Urban League, Baltimore, MD
1967	Dr. John Taylor Williams, President, Maryland State College, Princess Anne, MD
1968	Jackie R. Robinson, First Black Major League Baseball Player
1969	Julius A. Thomas, Industrial Relations Counselor, New York City
1970	The Honorable Verda Freeman Welcome, State Senator, 4th District
1971	The Honorable Parren J. Mitchell, U.S. House of Representatives
1972	Dr. King Virgil Cheek, Jr. President, Morgan State College
1973	Dr. Barbara M. Watson, Administrator, Bureau of Security & Consular Affairs, Department of State
1974	Nikki Giovanni, Contemporary Author, Poet & Critic
1975	Dr. James Edward Cheek, President, Howard University
1976	Dr. Samuel D. Proctor, Professor of Education, Rutgers University
1977	Dr. Frederick S. Humphries, President, Tennessee State University
1978	The Honorable Andrew Young, U.S. Ambassador to the United Nations
1979	Dr. Joan S. Wallace, Assistant Secretary, U.S.D.A.
1980	Judge Juanita Kidd Stout, Judge, Court of Common Pleas, Philadelphia, PA
1981	Mr. Homer E. Dowdy, Senior Vice President, C.S. Mott Foundation
1982	Mr. James C. Hart, Jr., Assistant City Attorney, Omaha, NE

Appendix E — Commencement Speakers

1983   Mr. James A. Joseph, President, Council of Foundations

1984   Dr. Cynthia Shepard Perry, Chief, Education & Human Resources Division, Bureau of Africa, Agency for International Development

1985   The Honorable William H. Gray III, Congressman (House of Representatives), Pennsylvania's 2nd Congressional District

1986   Dr. John Slaughter, Chancellor, University of Maryland, College Park, MD

1987   Dr. Benjamin F. Payton, President, Tuskegee University, Tuskegee Institute, AL

1988   The Honorable Roy Dyson, U.S. House of Rep.

1989   Dr. Henry Ponder, President, Fisk University, Nashville, TN

1990   Judge Clifton J. Gordy, Jr., Judge, Circuit Court, Baltimore, MD

1991   Dr. Clayton Yeutter, Chairman, Secretary, U.S. Department of Agriculture

1992   Dr. Carolynn Reid-Wallace, Assistant Secretary of Education for Postsecondary Education, U.S. Department of Education

1993   The Honorable Paul S. Sarbanes, United States Senator from Maryland

1994   Dr. Earl S. Richardson, President, Morgan State University, Baltimore, MD

1995   Dr. Yvonne B. Freeman, Associate Administrator, Office of Equal Opportunity Programs, National Aeronautics and Space Administration

1996   Dr. William P. Hytche, President, University of Maryland Eastern Shore, Princess Anne, Maryland

1997   Dr. Henry Ponder, CEO and President, Nat. Assoc. of Equal Opportunity in Higher Education (NAFEO)

1998   Dr. William H. Cosby, Jr., Educator, Philantropist, and Entertainer

1999   Mr. Glen Turman, Actor, Director, Producer

2000   Dr. Thomas N. Todd, Attorney–at-Law, Chicago, IL

2001   Ms. Patricia Russell-McCloud, Professional Orator and Author

APPENDIX F

University of Maryland Eastern Shore
National Alumni Association Presidents

President	Years Served
Edward Wilkins*	1955-1957
Roma Jones	1957-1962
Ernest Lee*	1962-1964
Harold Rush	1964-1975
Lawrence Cundiff	1975-1979
Theodore Adams	1979-1983
Valerie Watts	1983-1987
Willie Baker	1987-1991
Cecil Short	1991-1995
Richard Jones	1995-1997
Eleanor Turner	1997-1999
Charles D. Gregg	1999-2001

APPENDIX G

"Mr. & Miss UMES"

Amelia Merchant
Miss Maryland State
1948-1949

Kathleen Taylor
Miss Maryland State
1949-1950

Mary Smither
Miss Maryland State
1950-1951

Yvonne Jones
Miss Maryland State
1951-1952

Constance Eldean Hill
Miss Maryland State
1952-1953

Marjorie Frazier
Miss Maryland State
1953-1954

Appendix G — Mr & Miss UMES

Colinthia Burton
Miss Maryland State
1954-1955

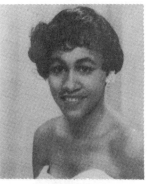

Shirley Adams
Miss Maryland State
1955-1956

Martha McGee
Miss Maryland State
1956-1957

Delores Harley
Miss Maryland State
1957-1958

Emma Smith
Miss Maryland State
1958-1959

Andrades Alexander
Miss Maryland State
1959-1960

Lois Kelly
Miss Maryland State
1960-1961

Ivy Jean Carter
Miss Maryland State
1961-1962

Carolyn Thompson
Miss Maryland State
1962-1963

Appendix G — Mr & Miss UMES

Louida Fletcher
Miss Maryland State
1963-1964

Theresa Cheeks
Miss Maryland State
1964-1965

Vashti Saunders
Miss Maryland State
1965-1966

Zuella Gayle
Miss Maryland State
1966-1967

Brenda Barnes
Miss Maryland State
1967-1968

Jacqueline Matthews
Miss Maryland State
1968-1969

Diane Hampton
Miss Maryland State
1969-1970

Wanda Stewart
Miss UMES
1970-1971

Delores Cook
Miss UMES
1971-1972

Appendix G — Mr & Miss UMES

Hattie Jones
Miss UMES
1972-1973

Carolyn Anderson
Miss UMES
1973-1974

Chantell Haskins
Miss UMES
1974-1975

Garcia Egerton
Miss UMES
1975-1976

Gloria Maye
Miss UMES
1976-1977

Carol Perkins
Miss UMES
1977-1978

Donna Walton
Miss UMES
1978-1979

Sharon Elliott
Miss UMES
1979-1980

Catherine Hall
Miss UMES
1980-1981

Appendix G — Mr & Miss UMES

Vickie Hairston
Miss UMES
1981-1982

Greta Elliott
Miss UMES
1982-1983

Sandra Smith
Miss UMES
1983-1984

Portia Dennis
Miss UMES
1984-1985

Veronica Briscoe
Miss UMES
1985-1986

Freda Harris
Miss UMES
1986-1987

Monica Thomas
Miss UMES
1987-1988

Renee' Goodison
Miss UMES
1989

Theresa Jones
Miss UMES
1990

Appendix G — Mr & Miss UMES

Jacqueline Mims
Miss UMES
1991

Rhonda Terry
Miss UMES
1992

Tyra Harding
Miss UMES
1993

Thomasina McCoy
Miss UMES
1994-1995

Malkia Singleton
Miss UMES
1995

Kristil Henderson
Miss UMES
1996

Frank "Malik" Collins
Mr. UMES
1996

Margo Thomas
Miss UMES
1997

Michael Johnson
Mr. UMES
1997

Appendix G — Mr & Miss UMES

Michelle Jefferson
Miss UMES
1998

Jeffrey Carpenter
Mr. UMES
1998

Shawnetta Barnett
Miss UMES
1999

Elden Hawkes
Mr. UMES
1999

J'Naudia Hunter
Miss UMES
2000

Amchet
Mr. UMES
2000

JaMarr Jones
Mr. UMES
2001

January Washington
Miss UMES
2001

APPENDIX H

"UMES Football Professionals"

MACK ALSTON
Washington Redskins

BILL BELK
San Francisco 49ers

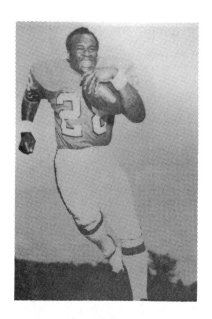

WILLIE BELTON
Atlanta Falcons

EMERSON BOOZER
New York Jets

ROGER BROWN
Los Angeles Rams

MARSHALL CROPPER
Pittsburgh Steelers

MOSES DENSON
Washington Redskins

JIM DUNCAN
Baltimore Colts
(deceased)

CURTIS GENTRY
Chicago Bears

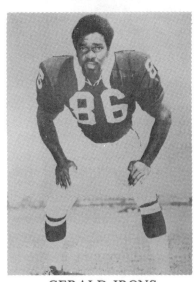

GERALD IRONS
Oakland Raiders

ROY KIRKSEY
New York Jets

ART LASSITER
Buffalo Bills

JOHN SAMPLES
New York Jets

ART SHELL
Oakland Raiders

CHARLES STUKES
Los Angeles Rams

BOB TAYLOR
New York Giants

BILL THOMPSON
Denver Broncos

WAYNE WHYE
Chicago Fire

List of Abbreviations

CAC	Chancellor's Advisory Council
CIAA	Central Intercollegiate Athletic Conference
CEO	Chief Executive Officer
ECAC	Eastern Collegiate Athletic Conference
FTE	Full-time Equivalent
HBCU	Historically Black Colleges and Universities
MCHE	Maryland Council for Higher Education
MHEC	Maryland Higher Education Commission
MSC	Maryland State College
NAACP	National Association for the Advancement of Colored People
NAFEO	National Association for Equal Opportunity in Higher Education
NAIA	National Athletic Intercollegiate Association
NASULGC	National Association of State Universities and Land-Grant Colleges
PAC	President's Advisory Council; formerly CAC
ROTREP	Roots and Tuber Crop Research Project
SBHE	State Board for Higher Education
SSC	Salisbury State College
SSU	Salisbury State University; formerly SSC
UB	University of Baltimore
UIUC	University of Illinois at Urbana Champaign
UMCP	University of Maryland at College Park
UMES	University of Maryland Eastern Shore; formerly Maryland State College
USAID	United States Agency for International Development
USDA	U.S. Department of Agriculture
WPA	Works Progress Administration

APPENDIX J

"UMES Concert Choir"

The Maryland State College Choir has evolved into the University of Maryland Eastern Shore Concert Choir and performs all forms of choral literature during the year. The choir has performed at universities; academies; public, private, and parochial schools; and churches of various denominations. In the states, their travels have taken them to Virginia, Delaware, Maryland, Florida, and New York, including a performance at the United Nations "Zeus Area". Internationally, they have toured Trinidad, West Indies; and, in May, 2001, the choir traveled to London, England.

The 30-member ensemble represents six states and the District of Columbia, students of all classifications (freshman-senior), and eight academic majors. The UMES Concert Choir is under the direction of Shelia McDonald Harleston.

APPENDIX K

About the Author

Dr. William P. Hytche was born in Porter, Oklahoma, and educated in the public schools of Fort Gibson and Tullahassee, Oklahoma. He received his Bachelor of Science degree from Langston University and his Master of Science and Doctor of Education degrees from Oklahoma State University. He has also studied at Oklahoma University, Oberlin College (Ohio), the University of Wisconsin at Madison, and the University of Heidelberg (Germany).

He came to the University of Maryland Eastern Shore, then known as Maryland State College, in 1960 after having taught in the public schools of Ponca City, Oklahoma, and Oklahoma State University. After coming to UMES, he served as an instructor of mathematics, Chairman of the Department of Mathematics, Dean of Student Affairs, and Chairman of the Division of Liberal Studies. He was appointed Acting Chancellor of the University of Maryland Eastern Shore in July 1975 and was given a permanent appointment in June 1976. In 1988, after the Higher Education Bill passed, his title was changed to president while the title of the system's leader was changed to chancellor.

Dr. Hytche was appointed by President Bush and served on the President's Board of Advisors on Historically Black Colleges and Universities. He was also appointed by the U.S. Secretary of Agriculture as co-chair of the USDA/1890 Task Force. In addition, he provided leadership for the 1890 Universities when he was Chair of the Council of 1890 Presidents/Chancellors from 1985-1990. Dr. Hytche also holds, or has held, memberships in numerous organizations, among which are National Association for Equal Opportunity in Higher Education (immediate past secretary of the board), National Aquarium Advisory Board, Agribusiness Promotion Council, Department of Energy's Historically Black Colleges and Universities' Task Group, Federal Aviation Administration/Airway Science Task Force, Peninsula Regional Medical Center Board of Trustees, Del-Mar-Va Advisory Council, Alpha Phi Alpha Fraternity, Phi Sigma Society, Phi Delta Kappa, and Phi Kappa Phi.

Additionally, Dr. Hytche is the recipient of numerous honors and awards. These awards include listings in the Personalities of the South, Outstanding

Educators of America, Who□s Who in the World, Who's Who in America, Who's Who in the East, Who□'s Who in American Education, Who's Who Among Black Americans, Academy of Arts and Sciences Fellow (Oklahoma State University, 1978); and he was selected as the recipient of The Thurgood Marshall Educational Achievement Award for 1992 (sponsored by Johnson Publishing Company, Inc.). He was also honored by induction into the Oklahoma State University Alumni Association Hall of Fame in January 1993. In 1994 Dr. Hytche received the George Washington Carver Public Service Hall of Fame Award from Tuskegee University. Fisk University (Tennessee), Washington College (Maryland), University of Maryland Eastern Shore, and Tuskegee University all bestowed upon him honorary doctorate degrees.

Dr. Hytche's published articles include □Information Technology and the 1890 Land-Grant Colleges and Universities," *Journal of Agricultural & Food Information,* 1993; chapter in book, *A Century of Service, Land-Grant Colleges and Universities, 1890-1990,* 1992; article entitled, □Historically Black Institutions Forge Linkages with African Nations□ in *Educational Record,* Spring 1990; and *1989 Justin Smith Morrill Memorial Lecture, A National Resource; National Challenge, The 1890 Land-Grant Colleges and Universities,* 1989. His most recent publication came off the press on September 14, 1999. His book is entitled *Step By Step To The Top* and subtitled *The Saga of a President of a Historically Black University.*

Dr. Hytche has traveled extensively throughout Africa and Asia. In 1998, he led a delegation of ten college presidents who observed the voting process in a national election in Nigeria. The trip was sponsored by an organization known as Americans for Democracy in Africa. Also, Dr. Hytche served as a Senior Associate for the American Council for Higher Education.

Dr. Hytche and his wife, the former Deloris Juanita Cole, have three children: Pamelia, Jaqueta, and William Jr., and four grandchildren, William III, J'Naudia, Jamison, and Devlin.

INDEX

Index

Index

Index

Index

303

Index

Index

305